the White Stripes

and The Sound of Mutant Blues

Everett True

the White Stripes **and The Sound of Mutant Blues**

Cover & Book designed by Andrew Clare

ISBN: 0.7119.9836.1
Order No: OP49456

Exclusive Distributors
Music Sales Limited,
8/9 Frith Street,
London W1D 3JB, UK.

Music Sales Corporation,
257 Park Avenue South,
New York, NY 10010, USA.

Macmillan Distribution Services,
53 Park West Drive,
Derrimut, Vic 3030,
Australia.

To the Music Trade only:
Music Sales Limited,
8/9 Frith Street,
London W1D 3JB, UK.

Cover image courtesy of Los AnTimes / Retna Ltd. USA

Printed in Spain

A catalogue record for this book is available from the British Library.

Visit Omnibus Press on the web at www.omnibuspress.com

CAST OF CHARACTERS

All of the following consented to talk to either Ben Blackwell or myself for this book.
Many thanks for their time and—in many cases—considerable hospitality.

Amy Abbott (bartender, The Gold Dollar)
Greg Baise (promoter, The Magic Stick)
Eddie Baranek (singer, The Sights)
Julie Benjamin (Slumber Party, The Fondas)
Ben Blackwell (drummer, The Dirtbombs, Cass Records)
Marcie Bolen (guitarist, The Von Bondies)
Aliccia Berg Bollig (Slumber Party)
Bob Bert (*BB Gun*, ex-Pussy Galore, ex-Sonic Youth)
Bruce Brand (drummer, Thee Headcoats, Holly Golightly)
Dave Buick (bassist, ex-The Go, Italy Records, co-owner Young Soul Rebels)
Wendy Case (singer, The Paybacks)
Stevie Chick (music critic, *Loose Lips Sink Ships/Kerrang!*)
Mick Collins (The Dirtbombs, ex-The Gories)
Marco Delicato (Rocket 455)
Jim Diamond (The Dirtbombs, ex-Bantam Rooster, Ghetto Recorders)
Jessica Espeleta (ex-Love As Laughter)
Dion Fischer (guitarist, ex-The Go, Godzuki, co-owner Young Soul Rebels)
Gretchen Gonzales (Slumber Party)
Deanne Iovan (The Come-Ons)
Simon Keeler (Cargo Records, UK)
Dan Kroha (Demolition Doll Rods, ex-The Gories)
Chris Handyside (drummer, ex-The Dirtbombs, ex-The Hentchmen)
Rich Hansen (promoter, The Lager House)
Johnny Hentch (The Hentchmen)
Surge Joebot (The Wildbunch, ex-Electric Six)
John Krautner (bassist, The Go)
Jeff Meier (Rocket 455, ex-Detroit Cobras)
Mary Mihelakos (music editor, *The Beat*)
Dan Miller (Blanche, ex-Two Star Tabernacle, ex-Goober And The Peas)
Bruce Milne (In-Fidelity Records)
Rachel Nagy (singer, The Detroit Cobras)
Steve Nawara (The Wildbunch, ex-Electric Six, The Detroit Cobras)
Pat Pantano (The Dirtbombs, The Come-Ons)
Tom Jackson Potter (Bantam Rooster, Detroit City Council, ex-The Dirtbombs)
Mary Restrepo (guitarist, The Detroit Cobras)
Rock And Roll Indian (The Wildbunch, ex-Electric Six)
Leigh Sabo (Slumber Party)
Steve Shaw (ex-The Detroit Cobras, The Fondas)
Ko Shih (Ko And The Knockouts, The Dirtbombs)
Matthew Smith (Outrageous Cherry, producer)
Jason Stollsteimer (singer, The Von Bondies)
Carrie Smith (bassist, The Von Bondies)
Ben Swank (Soledad Brothers)
David Swanson (singer, Whirlwind Heat)
Dick Valentine (singer, Electric Six)
Johnny Walker (Soledad Brothers)
Liam Watson (Toe-Rag Studios)
Jack White (The White Stripes)
Meg White (The White Stripes)
Neil Yee (promoter, The Gold Dollar)

Thanks to Andrew Male, Keith Cameron, Stevie Chick, Steve Gullick, Jennifer Maerz, Nita at Goldstar, 'Ma' Blackwell; my interns Melissa, Bella and Richard ("The first eight minutes of this tape is really muffled, it sounds like the tape recorder is in a jacket pocket. Most of the conversation is fairly irrelevant, about going out with Jack White and Renée Z and getting written about"); all the people whose floors I kipped on in Detroit—Julie, Dave, Dion, Ben, Maureen, Wendy, Meg and Ko; my designer Andrew Clare; and my wonderful, loving and patient wife Charlotte Thackray

Major thanks to Ben Blackwell for his invaluable, unflagging assistance. This book would've been next to impossible without him.

Dedicated to Steve Gullick, Joey Ramone and Meg White

everett_true@hotmail.com

Intro/The Big Three Killed My Baby

"I cannot get enough of watching live music. It's what keeps me going. I cannot get over the fact how you can make so many different types of music with the same instruments. I am blown away by the magic of music every time"
—Mary Restrepo, guitarist with The Detroit Cobras

Left: Jack and Meg
(Chris Floyd/Camera Press)

"The underside of a chimp's scrotum is decorated with a thin white stripe"
—sticker on the cash register in Young Soul Rebels Records And Tapes, Detroit, Michigan

"Ladies and gentlemen... my father!"
—Dirtbombs drummer (and Jack White's nephew) Ben Blackwell to audience at The Blind Pig, Ann Arbor MI, after having just simulated sex rolling around the stage with this book's author, 9 January 2004

This is how I come to it.

Rock'n'roll creates communities—cynical and manipulated in the case of corporate punk bands such as Good Charlotte and Blink 182: smaller yet more inclusive when it comes to disenfranchised individuals attempting to reinvest the music of their parents with a spark of energy with no thought for how much money might end up on the taxman's table. Individual cities across America are some of the last places these communities can spring up unbidden—mainly because of the distances involved. Why play music? It's goddamn fun, it keeps you off the streets and it allows underage musicians to drink in bars unhampered by The Man. If no one pays attention to what you do beyond a few choice friends, do you continue to do it anyway? Would Kylie Minogue or Dave Matthews exist in a vacuum?

In the late Eighties, in the Pacific Northwest of America, a handful of musicians hung out together, grew their hair and started searching through the same second-hand record bins: the isolation of Seattle allowed its artists time to develop, away from the media glare of trendier places like New York. (This was before the Microsoft and Amazon boom.) The resulting music gave a tired art form fresh life through its participants' need for community. Sub Pop records took the music business by surprise: no one in control thought anyone cared anymore. The fact that music fans evidently did was something that needed to be dealt with, and packaged, fast. Hence grunge catwalk chic, and the manufactured bands that followed in the wake of Nirvana's success—Stone Temple Pilots, Offspring *et al.*

Although it's hard to imagine now, Seattle was once a deeply unfashionable music city—even though it had a strong lineage of Sixties garage bands to draw upon (The Sonics, Jimi

Above: Residents watch as fire consumes a building on Detroit's West Side during racial riots. July 28, 1967, Detroit, Michigan, USA (Bettman/Corbis)

Hendrix). Yet good music is always around, for those willing to search. All that ever changes is the focus. Any number of great Northwest bands got overlooked during the grunge circus: The Wipers, The U-Men, Some Velvet Sidewalk… If you look hard enough, every town or city has great music going on: some are more exposed than others.

Take Detroit, for example. No one wanted to come near the place: its reputation gained during the race riots of '67 saw to that. Yet Detroit was once called the Paris of the United States: during the Forties, the best jazz musicians would play in town, attracted by the money generated by the arms manufacturers. It was the first city to have freeways. The first four-cylinder, single-block, car engine was invented here. During the Arsenal Of Democracy in World War II, planes were being turned out at a rate of two an hour, tanks five a minute at the General Motors plant up on the 15 Mile. After the war finished, the work started to dry up. By the late Fifties, people were beginning to leave. The riots were the end spasm. Everyone who hadn't left by '67 was gone by 1970. The final insult came when the automobile industry moved out during the Eighties; since then, matters have gone from bad to worse. The latest attempt by the city government to attract money has been the building of several mega-casinos downtown: not exactly a long-term solution.

As Jack White told *Guardian* writer Keith Cameron in April 2003: "The city has never come back from the riots. It's grey and desolate, a very un-modern American city. A lot of people in the richer suburbs will say, 'I've never been below 10 Mile Road'. I used to work various jobs, and people'd go, 'Where do you live?' 'Oh, I live in south-west Detroit, the Mexican neighbourhood', and they'd be like, 'You live down there?! Are you insane?!' I'm like, 'Well, I've lived there my whole life'. The animosity between the city and the suburbs is huge. It's like two different worlds.

"The city still looks as it did 30 years ago," Meg White agreed. "Basically there is no downtown. There's nobody on the streets. Downtown Detroit has more vacant buildings over 10 storeys than any city in the world."

If there's a new surge in music—pop, rock, hip-hop, techno, call it what you will—it often comes from the last place people expect. Seattle, Scandinavia, Osaka, Detroit… The reasons are clear. Ultimately, someone looking towards music to help them escape or explain or expose their humdrum, utilitarian existence is not going to find solace in music put together by teams of advertising executives attempting to second-guess emotions they lost track of years ago. Artists need time to develop: what better place than the USA's Gun Capital, one of the few cities left in America where it's still possible to buy a pre-WW2 skyscraper for under $1 million?

"The auto companies have damaged this town almost beyond repair," sighs Dirtbombs singer Mick Collins. "It could never be a nice urban area like Cleveland or Toronto. It's the only big city east of the Mississippi that doesn't have a mass transport system. Ten years ago, maybe, it

Left: Iggy Pop & The Stooges, 1974 (Michael Ochs Archives/Redferns)

Right: MC5 circa 1970. (LFI)

could have been different. The good thing is that Detroit had a gigantic economy in the Fifties but when that all went away there was nothing left. There are not enough non-retail office workers downtown to support the city the size we have. Detroit is two-thirds bigger than it should be. There's always the hope that we'll get another five companies the size of Compuware to move downtown with retail outlets like Border's and Hard Rock Café inside its building, but who are these stores helping? Not the people who live there."

Detroit has long had a reputation for great music—insurrectionary music, even. Some of it was born straight off the factory production line (the inspired harmonies of Motown, techno music pioneers such as Derrick May and Jeff Mills): black music repackaged back to the more affluent whites. Some of it was inspired by the riots and even caged for helping fan the flames (John Sinclair of the MC5[i]). Ted Nugent[ii] is from Detroit. So is Alice Cooper[iii]. So were the Pleasure Seekers, the all-female Sixties band that spawned Suzi Quatro, the leather-clad precursor of Joan Jett. Bob Seger's working class creeds of dissent have their base in this depressed, rundown, racially segregated city. Eminem notoriously took the title of his hit movie from the 8 Mile highway that divides city from suburbs, underprivileged black kids from pampered white.

The goddamn kings of garage rock, Iggy Pop And The Stooges are from nearby Ann Arbor, for Chrissakes! How much more of a musical lineage do you need?

Yet until The White Stripes came along, Detroit rock was given short shrift by the mainstream music industry. As their singer Jack White remarked in the sleeve-notes to the 2001 compilation, *Sympathetic Sounds Of Detroit* (an album he recorded on eight-track in his own house, featuring likeminded bands such as The Von Bondies, The Dirtbombs, The Detroit Cobras and Bantam Rooster): "No suit from LA or New York is going to fly to Detroit to check out a band and hand out business cards"—a statement that holds true today, even in the wake of the Stripes' success.

"Detroit's horrible," remarks local producer and bassist Jim Diamond. "Every time I go out of town I come back and say, 'This place fucking sucks. I hate this.' You know, there's some one-legged guy outside my door saying 'Gimme some change' and I go 'All I have are euros and pounds' and he says, 'I don't care', so I give it to him anyway. But yeah, it's just really ugly here. And depressing."

One-third of Detroit's residents live below the official poverty line, according to a 2000 census, conducted the same year the population dropped below one million for the first time since 1920. The weather veers between freezing cold and unbearably hot. So people party hard when they can. No one's going to pay attention to you, so you just get on with doing what the hell you like.

"Detroit isn't nearly as dangerous as people think it is," suggests local journalist and Paybacks singer, Wendy Case. "There again, we do drive everywhere."

i The proto-punk garage late Sixties Detroit band, best known for its call-to-arms cry of "Kick Out The Jams, Motherfuckers", as since echoed by countless mediocre middle-class rock bands the world over. Their deafeningly loud music and heavily politicised lyrics predated punk rock by a good decade. Sinclair was a founder of the radical White Panther movement, and is a major influence on (and mentor to) Detroit bands such as The Detroit Cobras and Soledad Brothers. Strangely, however, their "Rock'N'Roll, Dope And Fucking In The Streets" credos seems in direct opposition to Jack White's gentile, almost old-fashioned "I'm Finding It Hard To Be A Gentleman" approach.

ii Now, he's a guitar wild man who *really* likes his guns.

iii The 'School's Out' vaudeville freak originally started out as Vincent Damon Furnier, fronting a band *called* Alice Cooper.

JACK'S VIEW

Ben Blackwell: What's your favourite part of Detroit, and what part makes you saddest?

Jack White: My favourite part is that you can do whatever you want. There are no rules. But the sad part is that because of that, the city government is terrible. The employees are raping the city left and right. They have no idea how to run a town. All of the government is insane. They're in such a fix. It feels like it's always going to be that way.

BB: Do you think if it wasn't that way you wouldn't be able...

JW: Exactly. That's the conundrum.

Ben: Jack once said that you could park a bulldozer on your front lawn in Detroit and no one would care. But of course that's the downside as well, all the empty houses and lots in the city that are in limbo. They are trying to make the city better by putting tons of tourist attractions downtown but meanwhile tons of people can't find places to live in for affordable rent. It's easy for the musician class to get by, but there's real poverty in Detroit. The local weekly magazine has gone as far as having an Abandoned House of the Week column. Someone should just turn it all into farmland.

Dan Miller (Blanche): There's a general feeling that living in Detroit is like living in the Wild West. You don't necessarily have to follow the rules of traffic lights—stop signs and one-way streets are more of a suggestion. It's not that different from a lot of cities. There are areas where it's fine to go into where it's safe. But people in Detroit like to perpetuate that myth. The worst thing is that there isn't one place you can just get out of your car and go to a bunch of cool stores. And that's why we've recently been voted America's Fattest City again.

BB: You've lived there all your life, have you at least gotten used to it?

JW: People say "What's it like?" or "I wanna come there" and I always say they're probably not going to like it. When I come home from tour, we'll go to some nice place, like Paris or Amsterdam, and Detroit looks like this grey, sickening thing. Why do I live here? Why? I don't have to live here anymore and I do. It feels like I just can't leave, there's nothing I can do about it.

Ben: My feeling is, if you move out of Detroit you never really lived here to begin with. Detroit is a very broad term to describe this area: the city population is less than a million, but with outlying suburbs it's closer to three million and a half [2000 consensus]. *I could never see Jack moving away.*

BB: It's a weird, almost timewarp city... maybe it was you who said it, but Detroit seems like a Southern city stuck in the North.

JW: That's very true.

Ben: Ever since the civil war, the South has been depressed economically—there's little urban renewal or new buildings—and that's how Detroit is. Detroit and Memphis are sister cities, both through their music and economic state.

The White Stripes play a free concert in Union Square Park, NYC, October 1, 2002. (Dennis Van Tine/LFI)

iv Of course, all these artists lead in a direct lineage to The White Stripes themselves—with a few bluesmen thrown in.

It's long been known among fans of US record labels like Sympathy For The Record Industry, In The Red and Estrus that during the Nineties—at a time when most rock bands were chasing the corporate dollar—Detroit remained true to the wellspring of rock music: the same earthy, gritty, fucked blues and two-minute songs that inspired artists as diverse as Leadbelly, the Stones, MC5, Jonathan Richman, Ramones, The Cramps and Nirvana[iv]. It may only have been a handful of drunks, cheering down the front at Mick Collins' Gories shows: it may only have been a couple of friends recording tracks on their front porch with a snow shovel and a handful of blues licks in between upholstery jobs, but Detroit never lost faith in the rock: the Rock That Knows How To Rock.

"You can't move to Detroit, man," comments Restrepo. "It's bleak, it's ugly—it's not a bad place, but you can't make a career here cos there are no businesses. So why is there such a healthy scene here? I don't know. I was an army kid. I moved around all my fucking life. Detroit was a place I didn't have to move from."

Maybe it's because Detroit is so damn cheap—outside of Pittsburgh, the cheapest town in the States to survive in.

"We have it pretty easy here," The Detroit Cobras guitarist agrees. "We can drink 'til two in the morning, we can have half-jobs. We can have nice places to live... Dave [Buick, owner Young Soul Rebels] couldn't open his own business in New York. Well, he could, but he'd be starving. In New York, nobody's got a place to rehearse and you got no car. Jim Diamond has a studio in Detroit across by the new stadium. That should be really high price property but it's not. They could build a company across the street from me for what it costs to rent the space in LA for a month.

"Also," she adds, "because it's such a small scene, you get influenced a lot by other people's tastes. We're like happy drunks. If somebody says 'listen to this record' we do, because we got nothing else to do."

ALCOHOL

Mary Restrepo: When I do our guest list for The Detroit Cobras shows at The Magic Stick [second-floor pool hall and 600-capacity venue on Woodward Ave], it's like an AA meeting.

Dave Buick (Italy Records): Pretty much every Detroit musician has come to a terribly blurry end passed out somewhere in my house.

Chris Handyside (Detroit journalist): When you drink, all things are level.

Dave Buick: The difference between how people drink in Detroit and how they drink in other places is that elsewhere they're drinking to escape their dismal, lousy jobs and here we're celebrating our lack of... having to work too hard.

"Detroit's got a weird work ethic," suggests Matthew Smith, Detroit musician and producer. "The whole city revolves around people working in factories, and if you're not punching the clock then you're made to feel you're a bum and you're not contributing to society. Anyone who becomes an artist out of Detroit has got an inferiority complex. At the same time, everybody's got this heavy work ethic. It's a schizophrenic paradox. Insecure people working hard on what they're doing."

"Part of it," says Mick Collins, "is the cost of living is so low in South Michigan. If you've lived your whole life paying $300 for a two-bed apartment, you're not gonna pay $1,200. There are no airs. A lot of these bands still know each other. Here, it's not important that I'm somebody famous. I'm still Mick. If I went to LA I'd be 'Mick Collins'—here, I'm just 'Mick, the guy without a car'. The cost of living is extremely low. I can get by without having another job—I suppose if I needed more money to spend on a car or rent, I could get a job but I don't have to. Detroit is isolated that's why there are so many musicians here. There's not a lot else to do. It's more freewheeling around here. People are going to make the music they make and if you like it fine, if not tough."

Detroit reminds me of the International Pop Underground capitol of America, Olympia WA (home to the Kill Rock Stars label, whose bands have often toured with The White Stripes)—from the outside, a half-finished, sprawling ugly dump of a city enlivened by some beautiful, crumbling, three-storey townhouses. Both cities have the same feeling of community among their musicians, the same sense of creating within a timewarp separate to whatever may exist in the outside world, the same wave of creativity, the same... Probably if you look at any musical community outside of major media centres, you'll find a similar feeling, but the Olympia analogy seems particularly appropriate. Maybe it's the fact both communities prefer to look towards the origins of rock'n'roll for their inspiration and favour stripped-back, analogue production and DIY sensibilities. Maybe it's because both communities are limited in their choice of cool places to hang out in, and they believe in the adage that if there's nothing happening you get out there and do the damn thing yourself.

"These are weird times," says Matthew Smith, "and America's more fucked-up than it's ever been right now. This country is becoming just like the Soviet Union but nobody's saying it. If you look at what people are doing musically, nobody has any comment or dialogue about what's going on in the world. On one level, The White Stripes represent rebellious music, on another it's like Norman Rockwell Americana. You're writing a book on the last vestige of regional culture that lives in America. Everything's homogenised. It's mass hypnotism. Right now everything is just so controlled. It's going to be interesting to see where this is going."

DETROIT VS SEATTLE

Entertainment Weekly claimed Detroit was the new Seattle.

Why do you think all this attention's been focused on Detroit?

Rich Hansen (promoter, The Lager House): The White Stripes.

Is that it?

Rich: Maybe people saw a ready-made marketable package; "Look, it's the next Seattle, I already have something to write about". *Sympathetic Sounds* came out before *White Blood Cells* hit big, so there was already a pre-packaged thing with The White Stripes' name on it saying, "Look at how great the other bands in our city are". It wouldn't have taken much research to find out there was a thriving music scene here.

Why is there a thriving music scene here?

Rich: People always attribute it to stuff like, "Oh, I didn't have anything else to do"; like in Seattle they always say, "It rained all the time". But I like to think that maybe those people had jobs and stuff, lived with their parents and were normal people. When I was 16, those people were heroes to me—not just Kurt Cobain. We were all turned on to that music when we were in high school together, and I wonder now if it's happening again with Detroit. I like to think so.

The Dirtbombs

This interview was conducted in February 2002 for Careless Talk Costs Lives, *during the Detroit band's first headline tour of the UK, to promote their second album* Ultraglide In Black. *The line-up of The Dirtbombs is fluid—revolving around the charismatic figure of Mick Collins (ex-Gories, the band whose minimal, no-bass approach during the late Eighties is an acknowledged influence on The White Stripes). At the time, Bantam Rooster and Detroit City Council singer Tom Potter was filling in on guitar (and tour support). For the 'bombs 2003-4 dates to support their third album* Dangerous Magical Nurse, *Tom was replaced by the fiery female singer of Ko And The Knockouts, Ko Shih.*

Left: Mick Collins (The Dirtbombs) (Courtesy of Steve Gullick CTCL Archive)

Give me a definition of rock'n'roll.

"Rock'n'roll is about honesty and expression."

Give me a rock'n'roll experience.

"That would be Mick and I throwing a set of drums down the stairs at our studio," bassist and producer Jim Diamond continues. "Throwing a computer out the window, and recording it. On the ground were two guys armed with baseball bats, who smashed the thing to bits—it's all available on tape."

God fucking damn it all, I want to dance. I want to feel the sweet sensation of the ground moving unsteadily beneath my feet, one leg barely in rhythm with the other, brow covered by a stickiness not caused by alcohol or age, mouth working wordlessly, head bobbing up and down, infused with the exhilaration of knowing that this—this moment, this song, this sudden collision of electricity and melody—is what it feels like to be truly, gloriously, wantonly alive. I want to feel shivers cascading to my heels. I want to keep blasting the volume up and up. I want to be able to leap up on rooftops and shout it in the proletariat and Islington's grey, uncomprehending faces: THIS IS SOUL! I want every next moment to be as glorious as the one before, to listen to the Isleys and The Saints and The Troggs and half-a-dozen motorbikes braying in the deep shadows of night simultaneously.

I want to dress in black, cool, studied, shades a matted mess on my shaking face, life a riot of colour (pink and gold and red). I want to conga with Billy Liar, dance on the graves of given-up friends and shout in their comatose skulls, leaven this existence with an enthusiasm that is all the more wonderful because it is so primal. I want to fuck the world and give birth to nobility, a new strain of life.

I have no sense of cool, no idea what's right and wrong. Just two hours ago, I switched a (classic, but dull) Bob Dylan album for ELO's (wrongly derided) Greatest Hits because the time for poetry and Lenny Kravitz resumes is long past. I want to DANCE! Dance like we do down

BEN'S FIRST DRUMKIT

Johnny Walker (Soledad Brothers): When I was a kid in Toledo I would go to markets, set up and play. It's a great way to learn how to work a crowd. One of the vendors would always give you lunch, a sandwich or something. I wanted to buy a Les Paul with Garbage Pail stickers all over the back from a pawnshop and the owner wanted $750 for it. I was like, "It's got all these stickers on!" He's in a wheelchair, and he's screaming at me and I'm screaming at him, and my ma was totally horrified. We bought that blue satin flame drumkit that Ben Blackwell still plays from that same pawnshop.

Ben Blackwell: It was him, me, Jack and Meg. They wouldn't allow me inside because they were worried the owner would screw me over. I'd saved up a bunch of money and I was ready to buy a drumkit. Toledo's got good pawnshops and good drum shops.

at Chris King's Girl Group night at the Hanbury Ballroom in Brighton, the sweet/harsh harmonies of The Royalettes and The Honey Bees and The Whyte Boots shimmering in the air. Dance, like that time in 1980 at a Ramones show when I pogo'd the entire breadth of the Electric Ballroom to embrace the only other shirtless person present, only to discover it was my brother, the man who'd turned me onto rock'n'roll in the first place. Dance, like there's nothing corrupt in life whatsoever—just sinews and stutters and the occasional bittersweet burst of sex.

Spontaneity is still what matters.

I want The Dirtbombs.

"My name's Patrick Pantano. I'm one of the drummers in The Dirtbombs, also a drummer in The Come-Ons. My definition of rock'n'roll is teenage angst put to beat music and everything else thrown in, just so long as it's got some teen angst. An example of that would have to be this time when I was dancing at a soul music, beat music party and I broke my nose on a girl's forehead while we were dancing. I was bleeding and I didn't seem to care because I was so drunk. I had a great time, but my ass at that time was probably pretty rock."

Pat turns to the rest of the ensemble, and challenges us to disagree. Murmurs of assent come from all around.

"I'm Mick Collins," says the legendary Detroit frontman. "I don't have a definition of rock'n'roll *per se* except that it's music you can dance to that has lots of guitars in it. I used to be part of a teen social club years ago and we threw a party that was 'New Wave' music. There was this weird moment when I realised I was looking at 500 black kids doing the twist to '1-2 X-U' by Wire. That was one of the defining moments of my life."

That must have been a pretty fucking fast dance.

The Dirtbombs, L-R: Jim Diamond, Pat Pantano, Mick Collins, Tom Potter, Ben Blackwell (Courtesy of Steve Gullick CTCL Archive)

"Oh, it was great," Mick nods.

"I'm Ben Blackwell and I drum with The Dirtbombs," says the blue-eyed, blonde-haired boy on my right. "If your parents like it, it's not rock'n'roll. I don't know if I can give you an example involving my parents but last night was kind of fun."

What happened last night?

"We were just trying to have some fun, you know," the drummer explains. "We were falling down on stage and everyone loved it. It's like we've invented rock'n'roll."

"We're not trying to destroy anything," Jim adds.

"I'm Thomas Potter and I play guitar," states another voice. "My definition of rock'n'roll is unbridled rhythm."

"Can you give an example?" asks Mick.

"Of what?" asks Mr Bantam Rooster, confused. It's a confusing situation. Seven of us round a small table, pre-show in Highbury's Garage venue, no beer and the whiskey long since disappeared. None of us can figure out the lack of alcohol. These Detroit rockers have driven all the way from Birmingham where due to a calamitous misunderstanding they were served vegetarian fare, and they're thirsty God damn it.

"A defining rock'n'roll moment," Mick clarifies. He's sharp, Mr Collins. He likes to have his affairs in order—at least, until the booze hits.

"That would be the times my wife had to drive me home from shows in a trailer while I puked out the window," Tom muses.

"Do you have an affinity for ditches?" I ask, remembering the time I deliberately sought out one in Melbourne having read John Steinback's *The Grapes Of Wrath* a few weeks before.

"There aren't too many ditches where we live in Detroit," replies Pat, "but if there were, Tom would be..."

"I'd be leaping in," the guitarist interrupts. "Rock'n'roll!"

I was introduced to the music of The Dirtbombs a short while ago.

GHETTO RECORDERS

Jim Diamond's Ghetto Recorders is situated in Cass Street, Detroit—just round the back of the State Theatre in a (relatively) affluent downtown area. It's composed of one big white concrete room and one smaller one inside a crumbling warehouse—posters cover holes in walls and a faint smell of paraffin masks everything. There are no modern amenities like a shower, TV or leather sofa—just a filthy coach and a couple of overflowing ashtrays. Huddled up in between the BTO and Foreigner records are a bunch of mono Rolling Stones records and first edition Velvet Underground sides, and Jim's self-penned book of poetry.

"I started listening to rock'n'roll music in 1969," says Jim. "The Beatles made me want to play guitar—them, and Shocking Blue and Creedence Clearwater Revival—also Steppenwolf cos they scared me. I took classical guitar lessons when I was a kid, and saved up my lawn-mowing money when I was 14 to buy a Vox 12-string. In 1978, when I was 13, I bought an electric bass and joined a junior high band called Inferno. We did Ted Nugent, Kiss and Aerosmith covers."

Tell me a story from your childhood.

"In '68 I was at a Brownie meeting... I was three, I was pretty excitable and there were these girls talking in this church basement, my sister, my mom, they're all going 'blahblahblahblahblah', making all kinds of horrible racket. I was playing with a wooden train set and couldn't stand the way they sounded like yapping crows, so I stood up and screamed, 'SHUT UP!' And everyone was silent and my mom took me upstairs and spanked me."

What is your motivation?

"I like having a decent car that is not falling apart and I would like to buy a '69 Alfa Romeo at some point. But my motivation is to make records that I like and to work with bands that I like."

Do you want your parents to be proud of you?

"I'm lucky because my parents have always been supportive, even though they don't always understand what I do... I had a 48 input Neve board in a studio in Austin, all computerised and the faders would move. My dad was like 'Whoa Jimbo! This is like a rocket ship in here! You know how to operate this?' I always liked messing around with microphones and recording things as a kid. But I had these horrible bands to work with when I got out of college, Christian metal. I never really produced anything. I would just go, 'Does that sound OK?' I wanted to get my $6.50 an hour and go home. Owning my own studio sprang from that frustration."

Ghetto Recorders is laidback. Loose. It's not a purpose-built recording studio and two million dollars were not spent on making it look like your standard place with wood on the walls, and sound diffusers, and an isolation lounge with lovely soft lighting and someone running round getting drinks. It's a studio for people to make music in. There's a small room and a big room. If you're looking for Electric Ladyland, it's not that, and it's not Trident or Olympic either. There's just Jim and a converted chicken processing plant.

Dave Buick: Jim used to have a punching bag hanging up on a big industrial spring. Jack White ran up to it and grabbed it, and it went "boing" and rolled off. Jack was like, "Aw".

Mick Collins: In late 1995, I was asked to help remix a Bootsey X And The Lovemasters album. So I go down to Tempermill Studios and the engineer is Jim Diamond, just moved in from Austin, Texas. He tells me he has an eight-track studio downtown. I'm like, "I'm supposed to be doing these recordings for Warner Bros but we had a tiff and I spent all the dough". About six months later, they call me up to ask where the demos are, so I take a tour of Jim's studio. The front part is his apartment and his kitchen. There're some cool funky pieces of musical shit lying around—old gear, instruments that don't work properly.

Jim: I had a painting of dogs playing roulette on the wall. That was what really attracted him to the studio.

Mick: I noticed the Arthur Sarnoff painting and it was the only one I'd ever seen that had female dogs in it. I thought that was a good omen.

Dave Buick: One of the important roles that Jim Diamond played was that he took the burden of recording off the band. Before he came along, a lot of bands were doing their own recording—and that can be a very tense, unpleasant experience. He's super relaxed.

Jim: My massive porn collection consists of an overflowing milk crate filled with Seventies and early Eighties *Playboys* and *Penthouses*, the stuff that accompanied me well beyond puberty.

Mary Restrepo: If anybody deserves a prize for Detroit rock, it's Jim. He puts in a lot of hours for his friends. He's always on the computer looking at porn. I'll come by, he'll be like, "Look at this, Mary" and then he'll hear the music stop and he's like, "Try that one again, that sounded pretty good". Porn makes him relax when he's recording. The thing about Jim is, he can capture the sound of a band recording live.

Marco (Rocket 455): When that whole Seattle thing happened I felt those guys were stealing Detroit's thunder. They took the whole Detroit rock aesthetic and had the advantage of centralised recording—and even photography—so people could latch on to it. Until Jim Diamond came to town, Detroit lacked that. Guitar players are not engineers. The product just didn't come through.

Jim: I've been pretty lucky, because everyone I worked with never had much money because they would get those Sympathy [For The Record Industry] deals. They'd get like $2-3,000 and go "Oh my god, we gotta make a record!" And I'd go, "OK, I'll charge you $35 an hour". I started at $25, and inched it up to $30, and then $35, and you could make a record for $2,000—or like $1,300 as in The Clone Defects' case. So that got me to do it really quickly but well at the same time. People go, "How many records have you made? A million?" I go, "I don't know... 50." Everyone would only spend a couple of weeks on each one."

Their singer, Mick Collins I already knew something about. He's a 38-year-old dude, with a chequered past. I used to search out seven-inch singles from his bugged out punk band The Gories during the early Nineties, usually to little avail. The Gories were damn *crude*—a Detroit three-piece with no bass that ripped up the garage rock rulebook and barely bothered to staple the pages back together. Songs were dedicated to Thunderbird wine, nervous breakdowns and relentless three-chord thrash. Those singles have long disappeared in a haze of Riot Boy largesse, gone to some damn druggie hipster's room with my third Ramones album and Go Team singles. Sigh.

Among others, Mick has helped out that demonic and unsavoury distillation of music's misogynistic core Andre Williams. (Sample Andre stage banter: "See that pussy there? That's some mighty fine pussy there.") He was also in Blacktop[i]—a killer, Birthday Party-inspired, outfit who released one album, *I've Got A Baaad Feelin' About This* (In The Red, 1995). Mick is great at tearing it up to a heavy motor city beat. He possesses an energy, a naivety that is central

Above: Jim Diamond at Ghetto Recorders Studio (Pat Pantano)

to all great rock music—The Langley Schools Music Project, Them, James Brown, Meg White. Mick understands the need for simplicity, for some raw. Some nights, his guitar won't even be plugged in.

Fuck, don't you wish other bands... Limp Bizkit, U2... would take a tip from that?

Bassist Jim Diamond I knew about. Working out of his Ghetto Recorders studio, he's engineered and produced many great Detroit punk records of the past five years—Slumber Party, The Von Bondies, the terrifyingly great Bantam Rooster, the sweet, sweet female-led sassiness of The Come-Ons, The Go, The Volebeats, The Gore Gore Girls, The Clone Defects, The Hentchmen, The Dirtys, The Witches, The White Stripes and many more. He's stocky, full on and ROCKS.

... Oh yeah, and there's all the rest too.

After the interview, Ben (who by some considerable distance is the baby of the band) thanks me for introducing him to Nirvana. His email address boasts the moniker SUBPOPFAN1. But shit, time is wasting away and I need to give you a warning. 1998's *Horndog Fest*, the debut Dirtbombs album originally conceived as three seven-inch singles, recorded with Jim at the controls before he joined the group full-time, sports a dire "funny animal" sleeve (what sort of retard cartoonist invests animals with sexuality?) and that in itself should be enough to alert you. Not that it did me, of course. I was committed. It's not that the album is bad. Sure, it has balls. Just that it pales next to *Ultraglide In Black*, and why settle for second-best, ever?

i Mick: "We played Costa Mesa as Blacktop, at a cool club that was formerly a Chinese restaurant. Earlier that day a Himalayan cat mauled me, and I'm allergic to cats. By the time we get to the club I can't see straight and am getting puffy, so we find some strong allergy medicine and I take about five pills, and I'm only supposed to take two. All of a sudden, everyone's moving way too slow for me... On the very last song, I start swinging my guitar around and by the end there's nothing left. It was a first year edition of the '71 Univox High Flyer, similar to the one Kurt Cobain played, but with different electronics. And I'm just standing there, vibrating. I go backstage and go straight to sleep behind a black lacquer Oriental screen."

"The first time I realised I wanted to play rock'n'roll," recalls Tom. "Was when my mother bought me a Music Machine single, 'Talk Talk', when I was five. That was such a gnarly song it really got me going. When I was in fourth grade, some friends and I dressed up like Kiss and mimed through a talent show. All the kids at school were going crazy. I'm like, 'I can live with this.'"

He smiles, shows his teeth. Someone has found the rider, sorted the band out with a Heineken, but not the critic. Fuck man. I'm the most talented one here.

"Whenever I had to go to the dentist, my father would bribe me with a comic," Pat recollects. "That progressed onto the Top 40 singles behind the counter at the store. I remember getting 'Love Machine' by The Miracles and thinking the drums were great."

He chuckles at the memory. "Later, these kids at school were saying 'we're going to put together a band' because one kid's older brother was in a band and they had all the equipment at his house. I said, 'I want to play the drums.' We planned all week that on Saturday we were going to practice. We showed up at this kid's house to pick up these instruments that we'd never played before, and these four girls showed up with soda pops and pizza for us. We made the connection that there is something immediately and strangely attractive about someone playing music."

Everyone nods, knowingly.

"Soda pops and pizza has evolved," smirks Jim.

"It's still the same thing," Pat counters.

"They're still bringing it," laughs Mick.

"I never kissed those girls," Pat sighs.

So what about you, Mr Collins? When did you first realise that rock'n'roll was going to be your life?

"I don't have a moment," the singer replies. "I knew that I wanted to play music. I don't know that I ever really wanted to play rock'n'roll. It's just the music I play. I was watching KC & The Sunshine Band on the Orange Bowl Jamboree, 1975. Orange Bowl is a college football game. Every night before the game, they had these extravaganzas or variety shows. So I was watching this four-piece horn section, doing their synchronised dancing. This was the greatest thing I'd ever seen. I'd never heard of lip-synching. So I begged and pleaded for a trombone and I got it. Of course, the next year, Kiss did 'Rock And Roll All Night' but I already had a trombone..."

"I was probably about nine," recalls Baby Ben, "hanging out with my uncle who everyone here knows. He was playing a Deep Purple record. There was me, my brother and my uncle sitting there, we weren't even playing music but I just had this idea that this was what it was like to be in a band, and we should be in a band. I never did anything musical until I heard Nirvana, though. I slowly got into it."

Ben pauses, takes a gulp from his bottle.

"In high school," he continues, "I said to my uncle 'all my friends are playing guitars. I want to do that.' He said, 'fuck guitar. There are 10 guitar players on your block already. You should play drums.'[ii] He gave me a drum set and later that week I was in my basement, just messing around with it. And the same thing... girls showed up. It was totally unplanned but girls from down the street were like, 'Hey, how's it going?' Yeah, sure, check it out."

"What was the question?" asks Jim.

The voice of order booms through.

"When did you know you wanted to play music, the defining moment?" says Mick.

"I never had a defining moment," his co-producer states. "I was born to rock. In 1970, when I was five, I hung out with the older kids down the street who showed me dirty pictures: 'Hey Jimmy, what do you think of these *Playboys*?' I was like 'oh, nice tits'. The older kids and I would get guitars, and we'd pantomime Beatles songs to the neighbour kids on the street."

Pat has another zeitgeist moment he wants to share with his buddies.

Above: Dirtbombs guitarist Tom Potter. (Doug Coombe)
Below: Mick Collins. (Courtesy of Steve Gullick CTCL Archive)

ii This story coincides with Ben's earliest memory of The White Stripes—going to his Uncle Al's wedding, where Jack told him that he and Meg jammed in their attic. "So I started practicing," Ben recalls, "Later that summer, we were up in his attic and he told me to play a drumbeat and he busted into '1969' by The Stooges."

MICK COLLINS

Ben Blackwell: Describe Mr Collins.

Jim Diamond: Mick Collins is talented with... you know, there's some parameters there, I'm not gonna say "Oh my god! Mick Collins is a genius!" Mick Collins is a musically talented guy and I'll tease him about this as long as I know him that he's the inventor of punk-blues. And he'll hate that and he'll claim that he's not garage.

BB: If Mick isn't a genius, who would you claim is a genius?

JD: No one I know.

BB: Give us a genius on any level.

JD: I don't know if there are any.

BB: Would you say Paul McCartney is a genius?

JD: No, I think he's a good musician, he writes catchy songs... I guess Einstein is a genius.

Dirtbombs releases, L-R: 'Brucia I Cavi' 45, 'Maybe Your Baby' 45, *Horndog Fest* LP, 'Stuck Under My Shoe' 45

"My mother told me this," he says. "She bought me a toy drum for Christmas when I was about three, and I was really excited. She said that within an hour of getting it, I took a cinder block and threw it at the drums. It went through the head and that was the end of it."

"That's a Dirtbombs rudiment right there," Jim points out.

Tell me a few more.

"We used to joke that you can't be in The Dirtbombs if you've got less than one thousand LPs," Mick recalls. "I've got seven thousand, Jim's got one, Tom's got four, Ben's got about two thousand. I've been buying records on my own probably since 1974 and in that time I've only ever sold two records and I'm sorry I sold them."

"I was working in a record store and I quit my job so I decided I would sell half my record collection," sighs Pat. "That was the only time. Our collections mean we have incredibly diverse interests. Our comfort music is stuff that none of the others like."

So what is your comfort music?

"I like soul and jazz kind of beat music from the Sixties," Pat replies.

"I like Seventies funk and hip-hop," Tom counters, "and things like Rose Tattoo."

"Rose Tattoo and AC/DC," agrees Ben. "I like listening to girls sing, The Crystals, The Ronettes or newer stuff. I like Queens Of The Stone Age, but that's not comfort music. I have a big affinity for Kim Deal. Her voice puts me at ease."

"I go through phases," Jim chimes in. "A lot of time I don't listen to music at all but I like a lot of Fifties and Sixties Mexican music."

"For me, it's jazz and classical," finishes Mick. "I like a lot of the romantic classical music."

The Dirtbombs bass player Ko Shih live at the Siren Fest, 7/03 (David Atlas/Retna)

Back in the early Nineties, a line in the sand was quickly drawn when it came to grunge music. (I'm a big fan of hype, but you have to learn how to separate The Small Faces from Spencer Davis, The Gories from Jon Spencer, Ramones from The Clash.) On one side were bands with passion, instinct and soul—Nirvana, Mudhoney, (early) Afghan Whigs. On the other were Pearl Jam, and others far too heinous to name. Commentators and fans became confused, thought that one was the other and that the line was unnecessary. The line is always necessary. Radiohead may very well be well meaning fellows with their record collections in the right place but, fuck, do they make a God-awful noise. I have heard only one Andrew WK track, and that's enough to assure me that he has as much to do with rock music as Busted. I do mean Busted, don't I? That pre-packaged boy metal band. Or is that The Vines? It's so hard to differentiate.

So we come to Detroit and New York City, and the fact that—because of the media's tendency to only go for the

Above: Both flyers are for the same 03/04 New Year's gig. The one on the left is by Chuck Sperry, the one on the right by legendary Grande Ballroom poster man Gary Grimshaw.

people that cosy on up to it—NYC (like London and Sydney) finds it very difficult indeed to produce a half-decent rock band, because no one's given any time to develop.

On the one side of the divide is The White Stripes and the righteous Detroit clan, led by the Dirtbombs and of course *Ultraglide In Black*, a collection of soul covers originally done by folk like Stevie Wonder and Curtis Mayfield and Marvin Gaye, strained through the most intense guitar distortion and purified by noise, and why the *self-billing invoice* haven't you bought a copy yet? Stop reading this now...

...And on the other are The Strokes.

It's that simple.

"I was thinking the other day of how The Strokes always come up in conversation because they've got this big popularity now," begins Pat, "and everyone in this band is confused as to why. The reason I dislike them—and this may sound like a compliment—is because the music sounds like a conscious decision on their part. They could have sounded like anything. It's not pure. All of us, maybe not Jim who's pretty versatile, but most of us when we play and get in a room, it sounds like The Dirtbombs. So you could run an Otis Redding tune through us and it's going to sound like us, no matter what we do. We filter all these diverse genres through this mess and it comes out sounding like us."

"I don't know," mulls Jim. "It's having fun, you know, it's not like we're saying, 'It sounds like this.' We just play and fuck it up, see what happens. You see bands on stage like The Strokes or The White Stripes (even though I love them) and it seems like they're too serious. They could be having a great time but the demeanour on their faces is like it's World War III."

"Whereas," chuckles Mick, "with The Dirtbombs, I love when Jim is playing a bass part and it fucks up and he turns around and... "

Jim shoots Mick a glare.

"I don't fuck things up a lot," the bassist complains.

Mick Collins (left) and Jim Diamond (right) at The Lager House 9/02. (Doug Coombe)

"I'm not saying it happens often," Mick agrees, "but when it happens, you turn around and you and me just look at each other and laugh. I have a feeling that if I were in the crowd and I saw a band that were laughing and smiling and enjoying themselves, I would feel that they were doing something right."

"I'm generally laughing the whole time," admits Jim.

"Sure," agrees Tom. "Like 'man, we suck. Woo hoo!'"

"The concepts behind the band just evolved," Mick explains. "What I like about The Dirtbombs is that I can pick a genre or something, I can say, 'Let's do a glam rock single' and the band will be like, 'Sure'. Or, 'Let's do a whole album of soul covers I liked when I was a kid' and they're like, 'OK. We don't care'. They're willing to go any place."

"It's never contrived," Pat states with finality. "It's always pure. It's always going to sound like us. The Dirtbombs is just a beautiful mess."

MICHIGAN

Little Rooms

THE WHITE STRIPES

Monday, November 12, 2001

Left: The White Stripes at Brighton Concorde 2, 11/11/01 (Steve Gillett)

Last night I saw The White Stripes play Brighton. The buzz was palpable, friends coming up the whole time, thrilled to be seeing such a passionate, rockin' band, energised by the hype created by John Peel and the press. People dressed in red. People dressed in white. "Hey Everett," cried one friend, bedecked in both colours, "I've decided I'm The White Stripes Number One fan after seeing them on TV last week. There is something so cool about the way that woman plays the drums." Something so cool? Meg White plays with childlike ferocity and clarity, like she's possessed by the spirit of Mo Tucker (the androgynous-looking female drummer for The Velvet Underground)—head tilted to one side, no fancy fills, no inveterate trickery, just a solid understanding of emotion and the power of silence and pigtails. I danced, sideways—two steps away from another friend, moshing on a chair at the back. A man with two giant tufts of hair sprouting sideways rushed up to me, shook my hand vigorously and ran away again. My fiancée and I kissed passionately to the sounds of the righteous music. A hipster lounged at the bar and demurred that perhaps the Stripes weren't too bad after all. "Do you think they are brother and sister then?" some other acquaintance asked, breathlessly. I didn't give a fuck for any of them: I wanted to rush in and shake the world by its neck—"Look, look! Life is such fun. Stop being so damn cool. Stop it. Stop it."

I'd tried my hardest to dislike the third White Stripes album, *White Blood Cells*, of course. Wouldn't you? Never trust a person paid to write about music.

Never trust someone who thinks they're cool.

(Careless Talk Costs Lives 12)

GROWING UP

Ben Blackwell: "I grew up on the east side of Detroit—I've always lived in this house. My mom is 21 years older than her youngest brother, Jack. Like everyone else, playing music is a result of teenage boredom—that 15-year-old sexual frustration, masturbating 10 times a day. My parents have always been supportive. My mom works the night shift, and one of the most selfless things she ever did was to tell me we could practice in the basement even though she sleeps during the day. She still comes to shows and helps run my record label [Cass]...

"I went to Catholic school, kindergarten through high school, and then college, where I majored in journalism. I drank a little when I was 15, 16. The first hangover was on some stupid rotgut, Mad Dog 20/20... trying to get into shows, they assume that every underage kid wants to drink, so if you don't you stand more chance of being let in. People ask how I can put up with

Jack White, 1998
(Ko Shih)

being around drunks all the time. I'm so used to it. The biggest anti-alcohol message you'll ever need is hanging out with a bunch of alcoholics.

"I've known my uncle Jack all my life. He went first to Catholic school and later to a public school. Right from the time he opened his upholstery shop in '96, when I started high school—we were hanging out then. For the first year or two, I would have to get rides or he would pick me up cos I couldn't drive. He kept telling me I'd have to learn how to take the bus. He'd take me to concerts: he took me to my first ever show—Foo Fighters and That Dog, March 30, 1996—and stuff I wanted to go see, like the Melvins. He'd sneak me into shows, Two Star Tabernacle and The White Stripes. You need someone around who knows how things work, so you know where to park so your car doesn't get busted into and all that crap. I'd liken it to having a big brother.

"I hardly ever saw him drink—even now, it's far and few between. I don't know if that was him knowing I was looking at him… certainly if I'd seen him getting drunk all the time, then I may well have been more prone.

"He probably wouldn't like me saying it, but yeah I was in awe of him. He was doing such different stuff from what you're told you can do as a freshman in high school: he'd started his own business, owned his own house, didn't go to college. In America, you become so indoctrinated that you need a college degree: 'One out of four jobs require it.' No one else was doing what he was doing.

"My uncle Jack was quick to hand me a copy of The Gories' *I Know You Be Houserockin'* when I was 15. I think I was lazy about listening to it. I probably didn't even bother—but it was the fact he cared. It wouldn't be until I heard The Gories album *Outta Here* that I got it, probably a month later. Jack never had a little brother, and I would hope to say that he cared for me, like he didn't want to see me listening to bullshit. It doesn't take much to push somebody in the right direction. One album could be all it takes.

"It's just a really close family. You talk to someone in it, aside from your immediate relations, once a day. I probably saw him once a week. From a kid's perspective, someone who's seven years older than you is going to be cool, and for me Jack will eternally be cool—he'll be wearing silver glitter moon boots just when I think I'm about to catch up with him. I spent so much time with him that his music's influence has become ingrained."

Jack White (née John Anthony Gillis) was born to Gorman and Teresa Gillis on July 9, 1975, in the working class area of southwest Detroit known as Mexicantown, the youngest of 10 children by seven years.

Both parents worked for the church: his father as a maintenance man and his mother as a secretary to the archdeacon. He has fond memories of visiting apple orchards where they made hot cinnamon donuts, and eating Coney Islands (hotdogs) right by his parents at a place called Duley's when he should have been attending church. His favourite toy was "anything to do with war, grand battles with toy soldiers or building forts in the backyard" (Mojo, 2002). The soldiers were hand-me-downs from seven different brothers.

Steve Nawara (The Detroit Cobras): "When Jack and Meg first went on the road, I went over to Jack's house and I saw a picture on the wall of the Pope blessing Jack when he was a little kid, with his hand on Jack's forehead."

The event happened when the Pope was visiting the States during the Eighties—because of Jack's mother's job, she was aware of the seating arrangements and got them both places on the aisle. The Pope loved kids, so there was every chance he would stop and bless Jack.

MegWhite, 1998
(Ko Shih)

Johnny Walker (Soledad Brothers): "He said he was really nervous when it happened. He thought you weren't meant to hug the pope."

Jack first got the opportunity to play drums in front of his peers at a Montessori elementary school—"The kids were passing a bongo drum round," he told *Rolling Stone*, "and when it got to me, I played 'Shave And A Haircut, Two Bits'. Blew the crowd away at five years old."

Two of the first songs that thrilled Jack, according to an article in *Hotdog* magazine in 2000, were The Who's 'My Generation' and Johnny Cash's version of the old Leadbelly song, 'Rock Island Line'.

Inspired by the example of his brothers' band Catalyst who were playing local venues such as the Vietnam vet bar, Old Miami, and Paycheck's—and also by classic rock groups like Led Zeppelin and The Stooges—Jack acquired his first drum kit at the age of 11. Self-taught, he played the drums for four years, before switching to guitar[i].

Dave Buick (Italy Records): "Jack liked Led Zeppelin, even though it wasn't a willing influence of his. It was something he couldn't escape, like being from Detroit."

Chris Handyside (ex-Dirtbombs/Hentchmen): "A bunch of brothers growing up in the Seventies and Eighties, it was inevitable."

John Krautner (The Go): "I met his brothers at a show. They were talking about Jack and they were going, 'Yeah, I was the one that played him Deep Purple first'. 'I was the one that played him Led Zeppelin first'."

In fifth grade Jack was wearing Doors T-shirts: a year later, Pink Floyd and Zeppelin. He would make rough tapes of himself playing guitar and drums on a four-track reel-to-reel, and ride down to Dearborn on his red bike with his friend Dominic Suchyta to buy equipment—riding back loaded up with hi-hats. Jack was an average student at Cass Tech High School, an institution where the majority of kids were into hip-hop—a music that Jack's not particularly fond of. He wasn't too fond of school either: at the end of each grade school year, he would walk outside and kiss the ground like he was the pontiff himself.

i Some guitarists who started off on drums: Dave Grohl, Dick Dale, J Mascis, Evan Dando, Mick Collins, Joey Ramone.

Above: Blanche L-R: Patch Boyle, Dan Miller, Tracee Miller (Doug Coombe)

Right: Dave Buick (Italy Records) and Ben Blackwell (Cass Records), 2000. (Steve Shaw.)

Jack White: "The school was Mexican and black and they were all into rap and house music, which I couldn't stand. I had such a stiff upper lip about it for 18 years. The good stuff is underground. I love OutKast and Wu-Tang Clan, but I can't stand those videos over and over again, the same gold chains and cars and hot tubs. There's been 15 years of that stuff, and it needs to go away. It's teaching kids the wrong ideas about aspirations and life. It would have been easy for me to give up and listen to house music and techno. At least then I would have had friends."

He wasn't very fond of Motown, either: something that amounts to sacrilege if you live in Detroit. He just wasn't into the production style.

Ben Blackwell: "Some people like Motown more than The Stooges, some people like techno. If you're from Detroit, people will try and tie you in with what happened before. Yet John Lee Hooker played stuff in Detroit and that doesn't get mentioned too often in connection with The White Stripes."

Jack was very influenced by the perspective he gained during childhood—as he told *Sonic Magazine* in 2003: "I like to imagine that children come into the world all innocent and kind-hearted and then slowly realise how hard and tough the surrounding world is. I am saddened when I see bad and arrogant people who are 'uptight' the whole time, when they were once completely different from that. The worst is that most people seem to think there is no other way. That is as good as continuing that meaningless search for a lower ideal, like money and all that other material crap. But I believe that one can work to become better, to become kinder and more empathetic."

According to *Rolling Stone*, when Jack White was a teenager, he wrote a poem called 'Image Can Kill Love': "I like looking at things from a child's point of view. Children who are really young don't lie. When they get older, they start being untruthful, start dressing how everyone else dresses, start worrying about what everyone else thinks. I like those periods of life before it gets to the point where other people are corrupting your viewpoint."

Ben Blackwell: "What's your most vivid memory of the Detroit River?"

Jack White: "I decided I was gonna go fishing by myself. I don't know how old I was... eight or nine. My brother told me that I was gonna go, I guess, 'cause by the time I walked all the way down to the river with my fishing pole my dad came walking up. He didn't say anything. He just took me back to the car and took me home."

Ben: "Jack's a Detroit man. The river is an important part of the city. I know the exact spot where Jack went fishing. It's kind of nice. It's always in the back of your mind that Canada is there and you can look across and see it. Jack once said a great thing, you can go to Toronto which is five hours

Above: Goober And The Peas from the film *Le Ballon Rouge* (Courtesy of Metro-Goldwyn-Mayer Studios)

from the border and the stores will take American money, but you can go two miles this side and try to offer Canadian money and the stores will fucking spit at you. Toronto is where The White Stripes played their first ever out of town show. It was supposedly terrible—10 people there, and of course now any number of people claim they saw it and it was great. The river is no more than a mile or two from where Jack grew up."

BB: "Have you ever been swimming in the Detroit River?"

JW: "No (pauses). Well, I guess so. Yeah, at Belle Isle when I was a kid. That's the Detroit River. Technically not a river, it's actually a strait."

Ben: "Belle Isle is a 970-acre island in the middle of the Detroit River. It was originally a leisure place. In the 1900s, people would go there, row canoes, go ice-skating, but it's long since fallen into a weird state of limbo, in disrepair. Folk go there now to get rowdy and fire guns. People do still argue it's the jewel of Detroit, however, with lots of wildlife and lakes and rivers. The MC5 once conducted a famous photo shoot there. In the Sixties, they held the Detroit love-in there."[ii]

ii Ben's first band, Hell's Belles—who also featured Dave Buick on guitar—were originally named after the AC/DC song, before changing their name to Belle Isle.

In 1991, when he was 15, Jack started working at Muldoon Studio, an established upholstery business. Its proprietor and family friend, Brian Muldoon, was 16 years older than Jack, and also a drummer. He passed along his passion for furniture and acted as White's musical mentor. Jack apprenticed for Brian for three year or so—while creating his own found material sculptures—rennovating mid-century modern furniture like Noel and Herman Miller, before moving away to work in Beaupre Studios in the suburbs. An independent spirit, Jack started his own upholstery business at the age of 21 in a warehouse that contained some artists' studios (who gave him his first commissions).

Jack worked on mostly antique furniture—settees, chaise lounges, for older people who can afford it. Initially, he thought he'd be able to sort out his friends who'd got cool stuff from Salvation Army thrift stores, but it proved to be too expensive: it costs $1,000 to reupholster a couch.

Jack preferred to see upholstery more as an art form than a business anyway. His whole shop was painted in just three colours—yellow, black and white. As were his tools. As were his business cards. His van was a yellow Ford bought at a used car place for $1,200 with borrowed money. He built a huge fabric table with one of his brothers, with Styrofoam underneath the cloth of the table—yellow and black. It's now in his basement.

Jack (to *The Believer*): "I started trying to make an art form out of giving someone a bill, like writing it with crayon on a piece of paper, or having a yellow piece of paper with black marker saying, 'You owe me $300'. People would be like 'What the hell is this?' [They] just didn't dig it. It was two different worlds colliding."

Inspired by Brian's passion for mail art in the Seventies, Jack slipped poems into the back of chairs he repaired, waiting to be discovered in future years by other upholsterers. He had cards—"Third Man Upholstery"—and a slogan—"Your furniture's not dead", and splattered blood red paint on each card. His clients weren't amused. He was often broke. The shop remained an ongoing concern until August 1998.

Brian Muldoon (to *Detroit Free Press*): "[Jack] told me one day he was starting to play guitar. Within a year, he got really good. At the time we had another kid from Cass Tech—Dominic Suchyta—and we played together. Then Dominic went off to school in East Lansing, so Jack and I went on as a two-piece, from the fall of '93 through '96. We were very serious about the sound. We were very determined about the way feedback should be. He was never just goofing around."

The duo was called Two Part Resin and, later, The Upholsterers, playing live once. As The Upholsterers, they released a posthumous record on Sympathy For The Record Industry, the 'Makers Of High Grade Suites' seven-inch (it sounds similar to early White Stripes, only with a more conventionally proficient drummer).

Thanks to Muldoon, White—who'd previously been into typical 17-year-old male fare as Helmet, AC/DC and Led Zeppelin—became fascinated with Dick Dale, Flat Duo Jets[iii], The Stooges and The Gories. Also, Rob Tyner's singing with the MC5 was a major influence. It wasn't long before Jack started writing his own songs.

Ben: "I remember hanging out at his upholstery shop—there was a lot of Flat Duo Jets, Love[iv], The Cramps[v], and Frank Black[vi]'s early solo stuff... whatever album had 'Los Angeles' and 'Teenager Of The Year'. He had a collection of maybe 20 CDs to pick through, so stuff got repeated often. He had the *Back From The Grave*[vii] stuff. He also had the Johnny Cash box set. The sheer fact he was broke meant he borrowed everything from Brian Muldoon."

Dan Miller (Blanche): "He was also listening to a lot of early blues stuff. I remember him buying a Tampa Red[viii] CD around that time. Also, he really liked that old cartoon with Cab Calloway singing 'St James Infirmary'—that old jazz stuff."

Ben: "Listening to his early songs, you can definitely hear his and Brian's Flat Duo Jets influence but a little more punk. Substitute the Flat Duo Jets' Fifties influence for the Gories power chord influence."

Did the upholstery business do well?

Ben: "It got too much with him and the various bands he was in, so he started doing odd jobs around town—cleaning gutters and walking dogs."

BB: "Brian was playing me some stuff that you did with him in The Upholsterers, stuff like 'Eyes Of White, Blue And Silver'..."

JW: "Yeah, that's old. I forgot the name of that song."

BB: "... or '3', 'Nine Foot Two By Four' and 'It's Nine, Let's Go'. '3' just seems your thing. Is it too obvious to do that one?"

JW: "That may have been the first song I ever wrote. It was definitely one of the first. It was just an instrumental, though. I never felt it was ready for The White Stripes. Now we'll have to try it out sometime."

BB: "'Spitting Tacks' is the other one that comes to mind, that you would play constantly. I heard it all the time and now it's like, 'What did happen to that?'"

JW: "I dunno, they go away sometimes. There are songs on our albums that I really like that don't go over well live. They're slow... people don't respond to them. It's a shame that I can't play 'A Boy's Best Friend' or 'Sister, Do You Know My Name?' often because they stop the show in a bad way or something. It's hard to sneak them in. I try to sneak them in every once in a while."

iii Flat Duo Jets are a minimal, rockabilly-tinged duo from Chapel Hill, North Carolina—early Stripes material does indeed sound similar to the Jets' early Nineties output, albeit with a less revivalist flair.

iv Their *Forever Changes* is one of the quintessential late Sixties psychedelic albums

v Perhaps the most undervalued rock'n'roll band of the past three decades, The Cramps sparked any number of musical styles through their glorious, fetishistic goo goo swampabilly muck. Led by Lux Interior with his high heels and manic stare, and latex heartthrob Poison Ivy on guitar, their late Seventies albums *Psychedelic Jungle* and *Songs The Lord Taught Us* still serve as the blueprint for every psychobilly, primal, bass-less band that followed—Billy Childish's Headcoats, The White Stripes and International Pop Underground torch-bearers Beat Happening to name but three. The highly influential compilation series, *Songs The Cramps Taught Us* and *Back From The Grave* also came about as a direct result of the NYC group's fevered existence.

vi Frank Black is the former singer with surreal and tempestuous late Eighties Boston rock band, the Pixies. 1994's *Teenager Of The Year* is his second solo album, far superior to the first.

vii Ongoing series of compilation records released during the Eighties by US label, Crypt featuring unknown Sixties garage bands inspired by groups like The Kinks, Troggs and Them.

viii During the Twenties and Thirties, Tampa Red was called "The Guitar Wizard"—his speciality was slide blues on electric or steel National guitar, played down venues on the Chicago vaudeville circuit. Also known for his kazoo solos!

In between learning his trade, writing songs and doing the odd job, Jack briefly attended Wayne State College.

BB: "You went to a semester of college?"

JW: "I had to pay for it myself so one semester was all I could afford."

BB: "Weren't you saying that it felt like high school all over?"

JW: "Totally. I hated that. I thought something was going to change and nothing did. People were still ignorant and stupid. I was in a film class studying *Citizen Kane*. I loved it and I was learning a lot, but people were there just because they thought it was an easy course to get an A on, you know? I'd sneak into other classes to find out what other teachers were saying about *Citizen Kane*, and all the other kids wanted to do was to watch Bruce Lee movies."

BB: "Do you know your school, Wayne State's claim to fame in blues music?"

JW: "Yeah, of course. Son House[ix] was a janitor there."

BB: "When did he die?"

JW: "I think it was around '88."

BB: "Yeah, Son House was a janitor there. That's where I'm going to school now, and it definitely makes me take a second look anytime I walk by maintenance workers."

JW: "That's hilarious. I don't know why no one cared about that. Maybe they did, that's bizarre. Son House is a huge idol of mine. Recently, I got in touch with his manager, Dick Waterman, trying to find out what happened with his guitar in Detroit and he said, 'I doubt he owned a guitar while he lived in Detroit'. He'd always sell his guitars or pawn them for alcohol, but supposedly, as Son told him, he'd given four of his guitars to a business owner of a clothing shop in Rochester, New York to hold for him, gave some money to him to hold them, and then he moved. So he's gone and searched Rochester all over, trying to find this guy and can't find him, where his guitars are. Also, his family who's getting their royalty checks from his estate sent a thank you note over to me because the royalties have been real big checks lately because of us covering his songs. They wanted to say thank you, so that's pretty great. Son House's family thanked me."

BB: "Well that's almost like Mick Collins telling me, 'Say thanks to your Uncle Jack' 'cause he got his biggest Gories royalty check ever."

JW: *(laughs)* "It's funny."

BB: "It's true."

Wayne State is a college in the—quote, unquote—cultural centre of Detroit. It's a school where 90 per cent of the students registered are commuters. From a rock'n'roll standpoint, almost anyone who plays in a band has dropped out of Wayne at some point. There's a building built in early 1900s that serves as a focal point—other buildings are from different eras, a law school, a school of pharmacology, etc.

Ben: "When I was going there, for the longest time it felt like I was in high school. There was an arcade in the student centre basement where I'd go and play pinball. That was about the only difference. The joke about Wayne State is that your admission test is someone feeling your pulse. During my early classes I never felt so smart before in my life because of the dunderheads around me. Son House probably never owned a guitar while he lived here. There's a record store in Rochester called House Of Guitars and its owner is this old guy called Armand and he talks about how Son House supposedly washed dishes at a Howard Johnson, and he'd come in and buy guitars with a cab waiting out in front. It wasn't unusual for him to go out and find Son asleep in a big snow bank after a heavy fall—but that's another typical Detroit thing, that Son House could be mopping floors at Wayne State and no one cares."

Above: Tampa Red
(Michael Ochs Archives/Redferns)

ix Torn between the sacred and the profane, Son House was a major innovator of the delta blues. His Thirties sides for Paramount remain some of the scariest, most primal music extant: and, as a main source of inspiration for men such as Robert Johnson and Muddy Waters, you could say he pretty much invented modern music. Yet he didn't even pick up a guitar until the age of 25, unable to stomach the way it was played. He developed a liking for corn whiskey, and later shot a man dead in Lyon during a drunken brawl.

Two Star Tabernacle poster, 1998

Around this time, Jack became close friends with Meg White.

Megan Martha White was born on December 10, 1974 to Catherine and Walter White in the affluent Grosse Point suburb on the east side of Detroit, the youngest of two sisters by 10 years. She attended Grosse Point North High School, where, by her own admission, she didn't have too many friends: "I never got into too much trouble," she told *Mojo*'s Andrew Male in 2002, "and didn't have too much confrontation because I was super-shy. And I never really had much direction. I went to high school. I went to college, and then I went to culinary school for a year. I liked going to school a lot but I just didn't have much thought about what I actually wanted to *do*."

To help pay her way through college, Meg took on various bartending, line cook and waitress jobs—including a stint working at the Memphis Smoke blues bar in Royal Oak, alongside Corey from Electric Six.

The future drummer's favourite childhood pastime was reconstructing the Fortress of Solitude from *Superman*: "I would shovel all the winter snow into a big mountain and then tunnel all the way through. I was obsessed with it. It was the best." She also enjoyed roller-skating in the basement while listening to Steve Miller's 'Abracadabra'.

The pair married on September 21, 1996 in South Lyon, Michigan—upon betrothal Jack took his wife's surname. When his parents moved out of their home, he and Meg moved in.

Meg: "I've always been obsessed with colour. Even as a little kid all I would draw was rainbows all over everything. But it does have a big affect, even down to what you wear, what's around you, the colour of your walls."

Greg Baise (promoter, The Magic Stick): "I've been acquainted with Meg longer than she's known Jack—she used to come into Car City Records, at 8½ and Harper, where I worked in the mid-Nineties. I vaguely recall her coming in with her sister Heather and her mum, and buying Beatles records. They lived in the neighbourhood. I might have turned her onto Love. One day she showed up with her boyfriend—or fiancé. He had really curly, blond hair. They did what everyone does at Car City: scour the vinyl bins looking for good records."

Jack White in Two Star Tabenacle with Dan Miller (left panel), 3/99 at Paycheck's, part of the Blowout (Doug Coombe)

DAN MILLER

Chris Handyside: "We'd hang out at Dan Miller's house and sit there and sing songs on the porch, 'Wayfaring Stranger' and classic hillbilly music like that. People would sit around wanting Dan to sing and Jack would step up instead, and it would be like, 'Oh, well, Jack's singing'."

Brian Muldoon: "Jack learned a lot about being on stage while playing in bands with Dan Miller—how to present himself, how to dress himself."

BB: "I remember you saying about Two Star Tabernacle when The White Stripes first started playing: 'I can see us getting really huge, maybe we'll do a record or two, be some kind of cult band'. It's kinda changed since then, don't you think?"

JW: "I don't remember saying that, but I guess it's just the opposite. 'The Two Star 45' is a cult thing. The White Stripes have become some sort of insane institution."

Ben: "Two Star Tabernacle were a band that Jack played guitar for, while Dan Miller, who's now in Blanche, played guitar and sang lead. It was like country music, with a punk nihilistic edge. It sounded creepy and it didn't fit in with anything else. It was definitely oddball. In true Detroit fashion the only release they ever did was a single, 'The Two Star 45' (Bloodshot, 1998), with Andre Williams[x] of two cover songs.

"Dan's always been around. In 1994, he and Jack put together the earliest incarnation of Blanche (Dan's current band)—'We did a five-song cassette,' he recalls, 'all covers of songs by dead country stars, and played at a senior citizen jamboree and they didn't like us very well.' Before Two Star, he played in Goober And The Peas, a cowboy punk band—five guys dressed in George Jones-style suits, kicking hay around on stage. Dan is one of the best talkers you'll ever meet. He could talk his way into a nun's pants, and he's not slimy either, but genuine."

Greg Baise: "You could tell by the name that Goober were kinda hokey, but they could also be humorous and beautiful. Something people don't realise about Detroit is that there are no brand new bands here. All these bands have a history. They have several albums' worth of material, and

x Legendary Chicago character fond of lavender suits, sometimes referred to as the "father of rap" because of his licentious, libidinous greasy voiceover on 'Bacon Fat' (1956). Also co-wrote several major R&B hits, including 'Shake A Tail Feather', and was signed to Motown in the early Sixties. Mick Collins and Two Star are among many Detroit musicians who've backed him up in recent years.

xi Early Eighties LA punk/blues hybrid, led by the startling and unpredictable former president of Blondie's US fan club, Jeffrey Lee Pierce: similar in tone and fervour to The Cramps and X, their 1981 debut *Fire Of Love* is a major influence on the Detroit bands of the last Nineties, particularly The Von Bondies.

years of playing live. Goober became Two Star Tabernacle who threw up Blanche and The White Stripes. Whenever a new record comes out, it seems like there's a song on it I've been listening to for five years."

Dan Miller: "When I was in 3rd grade there was a play about getting sick in school. My role was to play sickness: my lyric was 'Hooray hip-hip, I'm post-nasal drip' but it was a fill-in part. My main role was that of the female teacher who got mad at the post-nasal germ. So I switched into a skirt and a wig, and when I came out all the kids laughed, and I thought 'yeah that's funny.' Then they made fun of me all day for being so stupid. And that hurt my feelings. Also, my dad died when I was 14. So that's the sad part of my life. It's a winning combination."

In late '89, Tom Hendrickson and Dan Miller felt that punk shows in Detroit were getting a little tired. They loved the way old country stars dressed in suits, and—with a view to winding up the punks—decided to form a band that looked like Hank Williams and play music that veered between slow country and more frenetic stuff. Goober And The Peas was born. The biggest problem was that they couldn't find a live drummer: they went through 15, and each time they held a new audition another 15 would show up...

Dan: "Our biggest inspiration was The Gun Club[xi]. Musically, we were all the way over the map—we put out two albums in five years [the first recorded with John Wesley Harding at the controls] and everyone assumed the final one was country because of the way we dressed, but it wasn't. Jack was our final drummer, and of those 225 [15 x 15 x 15]auditions he was by far the best. He wasn't technically great, but he had the right spirit. It was great to see somebody with that kind of passion for music. The first show he ever played with us was in St Joseph, Michigan, 1994—a weird little resort town about an hour outside of Chicago. For the encore, Jack sang an Elvis song and it was pretty great."

BB: "I remember him saying he played 'Electric Funeral' with you, the Black Sabbath song—and that he played guitar."

DM: "No. It might have been 'Paranoid'. Jack was really odd, for somebody so young, he was really focused and driven. I remember him saying, 'I really want to be proud of everything I do'. At that time, with the band having been around for so long, we took things for granted and he still really questioned things—and that's carried through with everything he's done. He's a really thoughtful person."

BB: "Everyone talks about the haircut where it was dyed blonde and shaved on the sides, but this was before that—that was about '96."

DM: "So Goober came to an end, which was sad but good because after touring a lot—in Europe and United States—and selling out 1,000 seat places, it wasn't inspiring anymore. So I worked at an impound lot for cars, then I was a substitute teacher for a while..."

After Goober, Jack and Dan started Two Star Tabernacle with Miller's wife Tracee on bass, and Damien Lang (ex-Goober) on drums. Their first show was in February '97. And just once, when Damien had broken his foot, a Chicago club owner was kind enough to let a 16-year-old Ben Blackwell sit in.

Dan: "Two Star Tabernacle was a misfit band—from what people tell me, we were either really great or really pitiful. I was writing drone-y, country-ish songs, and Jack was coming in with songs that were phenomenal, faster and more energetic. It was a weird mix. I sang half and he sang half, and neither of us had sung harmonies before. We would do old gospel numbers, 'Just A Closer Walk With Thee'... we recorded it in Jack's basement and realised how hard it was to do old gospel songs."

Two Star never recorded an album or released any original songs. Their one recording was the Andre Williams seven-inch.

Dan: "We met down at Jack's house and did three songs, one of them 'The Big Three Killed My Baby'[xii] that Jack wrote for Andre, wanting something controversial... then Andre said he'd give us a gift, the song 'Lily White Momma And Jet Black Daddy'. So we worked that out. We did 'Ramblin' Man'... I'm not sure Andre was as familiar with the song as he led us to believe. I remember telling him that each time there was a key change he needed to change the lyric—he said, 'I see what you're saying, it's like when you're in jail you can go anywhere you want in jail

The White Stripes 03/01 (Courtesy of Steve Gullick CTCL Archive)

but you're still in jail'. Two Star was a lot different to what was going on Detroit—there are a lot of straight ahead garage bands there. We recorded some stuff in our basement but never finished it. We had 'Hotel Yorba', 'Now Mary', 'The Union Forever'... we played 'Same Boy You've Always Known' at the last show... Blanche songs like 'So Long Cruel World', 'Who's To Say', 'Garbage Picker'... We also did 'Wayfaring Stranger'—oddly enough when Jack auditioned for *Cold Mountain* that was the song they requested he sing."

Two Star Tabernacle stopped in March 1999 because by that point Jack was in three bands: them, The White Stripes and The Go... The Go had gotten signed, and The White Stripes had been given money to record an album for Sympathy For The Record Industry.

Jack: "With Two Star, we kinda didn't know what we wanted to do. We were going 15 directions at once. I had just started The White Stripes and we didn't really have a direction."

Dan: "It had become a little bit excruciating. I knew I wanted to take the band in a certain direction—I didn't want everything as loud and fast. Jack was really excited to be playing in The White Stripes and The Go: being in three bands was too much. It ended well. Damien was playing drums for The Detroit Cobras simultaneously."

xii The "Big Three" referred to in the title are the big three Detroit automobile companies: Chrysler, Ford and General Motors.

RHYTHM & BLUES MAYHEM!

I THINK I'VE HAD IT

APPEARING WITH

ALEX CHILTON

MAXWELLS-MAY 11 KNITTING FACTORY-MAY 13,14

The Gories

Left: Gories poster

OK. Listen up. Can't say I'm too down with the blues kids myself: the reams of worthy, waddling men paying tribute to a spirit they probably never understood first time round. But fuck. Who am I to criticise someone else's taste? Music resonates through the ages down to the individual, or it doesn't. I'm way more into the Pere Ubu and Devo and Wire and Jam shit that Mick Collins first got into when he discovered punk rock in 1980—all those serrated powerchords and staccato rhythms, bursts of frayed energy—than the old Chicago Thirties guitar rag stuff, and I dig The Cramps and Ramones foremost, but I gotta tell you something. Found me a Tampa Red CD, nestling among my Residents long-players just now—*Bottleneck Guitar 1928-1937* (Yazoo, 1992)—and it moves me mightily. It's simple, direct and playful, and has a small glass bottleneck guitar on every track. Sure, the recordings are scratchy—but nowadays folk like Moby spend small fortunes attempting to duplicate that sound with Pro-Tools in hi-tech digital studios. Every cut sounds live—and almost certainly was. Tampa understood that what matters is The Song, The Voice and The Guitar Tone. Fuck fidelity.

Before Tampa, I'd been listening to the two Gories reissues albums on Crypt, solid—particularly *I Know You be Houserockin'* with its primal cover of Louis Jordan's 'Early In The Morning', and downright *nasty* 'Nitroglycerine'. Peg O'Neill's drums are all clatter and thump, unsophisticated perfection that has nothing to do with her sex and everything to do with the thrill of forming a band for the first time: my main man Mick Collins' vocals are a raw Mod delight, all R&B rasp and amphetamine buzz: Dan Kroha's guitar as basic and lo-fi and mean as The Sonics. These kids learnt the lessons of Tampa and John Lee Hooker and the garage bands of the Sixties well... but they're not difficult lessons to learn, not at all. Rock music should be kept simple, with a strong melody and abrasive sound. That's it. Learn your three chords one day and go out and write 50 songs the next. It's that simple.

Ben Blackwell: "How much do you think The Gories embodied that Detroit feeling, and how much do you think you drew from them for The White Stripes?"

Jack White: "The Gories super-embodied the Detroit sound for the entire Nineties. It took years until things like Rocket 455 were coming around. They weren't really popular at the time, but I was super-influenced by The Gories when we started the band. We were trying to do something deeper and more primitive and simple, and The Gories were an easy litmus test—they were an example that was already set, from Detroit as well. It was, 'We can feed off of this, but take it and move it into our own direction'. We didn't want to copy them. I mean, even they were copying or ripping off everybody—it's a standard thing in garage rock, most of the bands do that... like Billy Childish. I didn't want to do that. I didn't

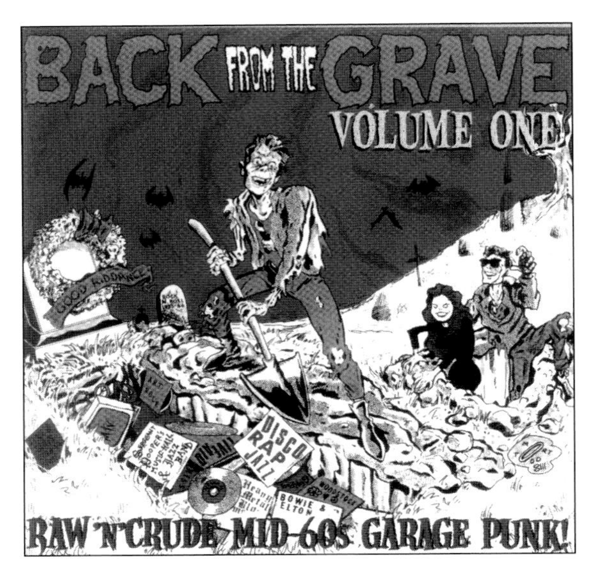

want to rip off other people's music and call it my own. We have a lot of songs that sound like something else..."

BB: "I could tell you all of them if you want[i]."

JW: (laughs) "You can't get away from that, no doubt. But I've never sat down with an old obscure record and said, 'I'm gonna take this lick and write a new song with it'. Covering music is better. You're carrying it forth to a new generation and keeping songs alive, but also paying respect to the people who wrote them[ii]."

i Ben: There's just little things—for example, 'Red Bowling Ball Roof' [B-side to 'The Big Three Killed My Baby']. Jack told me it was a homage to AC/DC's 'Have A Drink On Me'.

ii Ben: "Jack was in awe of The Gories. One time, he bought a Broad Appeal record and Mick was behind him in line. Jack was like, 'Mick Collins is behind me!'"

"I'm Danny Doll Rod, known as Dan Kroha in The Gories days.

"I was born in 1965 on the north side of Detroit. I was introduced to Parliament at an early age. Around 1970 my neighbourhood was 75 per cent white. Once Detroit got a black mayor, Coleman Young in '74, he said, 'If y'all white people don't like it, y'all can hit 8 Mile Road and get the hell out of here'. So they did. Black culture was a big influence on me. I'm sad to say I can't say culture in general, because Detroit is racially segregated. Even though I grew up here, it's still not 'people'. It's still 'black' and 'white'. We'd come home talking black English and my dad would get real upset because he didn't want us talking like that. My mom wanted to move out to the suburbs, but my dad didn't want to because he was starting a business.

"When I was at high school, a kid from England told me I looked like a Mod. I was getting into early Kinks and Who records at the time. There was a big garage revival happening in the early Eighties that has since been forgotten—The Fuzztones, The Vipers, The Cheepskates, Hysteric Narcotics, Tell-Tale Hearts, Unclaimed, The Pandoras... I thought it was cool. I began to discover that the Mods were into obscure American rock'n'roll and soul stuff. I'd check the credits on Yardbirds songs, and see they were written by guys like McKinley Morganfield and Chester Burnett... and so I found out about Muddy Waters and Howlin' Wolf, the original Mods.

"Around that time I met Mick. My friend Tom Lynch met him at a big concert downtown where one of the guys was wearing a Martha And The Vandellas T-shirt, and I found out he lived only two miles away from me. He rode his bike over to my parents' house. He impressed me as an imaginative, interesting guy with wide-ranging musical taste. He really liked the Mod thing and knew firsthand a lot of the soul and

BACK FROM THE GRAVE

Mick Collins: The Gories' debt to Crypt records is tremendous, inasmuch as we had any rock influences at all—Crypt's *Back From The Grave* series and the Chess library were our inspiration early on. They were the only songs easy enough to cover when you have no music aptitude. In America, we lost rock'n'roll around '61, but The Pretty Things, the Stones and The Yardbirds brought it back. Suddenly, every town had 50 bands, and half of them got one 45 out, and then just as fast they were gone... maybe it was Vietnam. Or maybe it was the lack of commercial recognition. Only a few got on the radio, and that was all local. Let us not forget '96 Tears' was recorded on a patio in Saginaw, Michigan.

The same thing happened after punk in the Seventies: everything got real complicated and baroque. So when we heard *Back From The Grave* we were like, "Holy shit, these guys were making records like this when we were in our diapers! These guys are playing Chess blues and if they can, we can"—so we got a bunch of Chess records and figured out how to do it. People may have thought we were musical geniuses, but all we did was found songs we could play—John Lee Hooker stuff only has two, maybe three notes.

We always thought that was how The Gories would end up—with our one 45 turning up on a compilation 20 years on. We'd do our one single—'Thunderbird ESQ' on the A-side, whatever on the B-side—drop out of sight and never be heard of again.

Above: Gories records

blues stuff I was discovering. I turned him on to The Small Faces, and some soul I'd collected. And he had a compilation called *Demention Of Sound* (Feedback, 1982) with real obscure but heavy, wild Sixties Mod stuff. I had a Muddy Waters album I'd borrowed. He turned me on to a lot of Sixties instrumental stuff. We started going out record shopping together."

Mick Collins: "Dan Kroha was the first person I met who had a real scooter. He has a Vespa T-100."

"I met Peggy in a record store and we ended up dating soon after. This would have been around 1984. The three of us, and the Hysteric Narcotics' crowd, would go up to my room and play records. Mick was like, 'These songs only have three chords in them. We could do that'. He had all these great ideas for bands in his head, complete with album covers, videos, whatever. So I said, 'I'm ready'. Peg had never played drums before, but that didn't matter. We didn't wait till we got good. We started playing shows real early on."

The Gories' first show was in the autumn of 1986 at St Andrew's Church on the Wayne State University campus: Peg was 19 and tripping on psychedelic mushrooms: Dan was 21, reasonably drunk and churning out gutbucket Sixties punk riffs on his cheap guitar: Mick was 20 and completely wasted on Thunderbird ESQ, the drunks' drink (cos it's cheap, sweet and gets you fucked up real quick). For support, formerMC5 singer Rob Tyner ran through a two-hour set of Vietnam vet songs played on auto-harp.

"It was part of a community concert series run by Rob and his wife who did catering for rock concerts. It was the only place we could get booked, because it was a free for all. We barely got through five songs—a few covers, a few originals. There were two or three of our friends there. It was fun. We really liked what we were doing, that was what we wanted to hear.

"From the beginning, it felt like something good. Gories live shows were very often a shambles, very rickety, barely getting through it. Peg has a volatile temper and every time something she didn't like happened she'd quit the band. A lot of people didn't get it. [One place even got closed down after Gories performed, because the landlord took offence to the crude sound.] I found a 45 by a Fifties R&B group called 'You Little Nothing'. I thought the title was great so we wrote a whole other song round it. We wrote a song about a psychic from the *Weekly World News*. One time, Peg was talking about all the kids in the neighbourhood running around like feral dogs. She said it would be a good idea for a record. Mick said, 'I'm already working on it'."

After three years playing to about 10 people—including Steve Shaw (original Detroit Cobras guitarist) and Chris Handyside (original Dirtbombs drummer)—Len Puch, owner of Detroit label Wanghead, invited The Gories to his out-of-town studio to record their debut album. The band decided they wanted to use the massive Nissan hut where Puch stored half-assembled engines instead (Dan had previously worked in his dad's car parts factory). The result was *Houserockin'*, a complete commercial failure.

Below: The influential Billy Childish. (Hayley Madden/Redferns)

PROFICIENCY

Ben Blackwell: A lot of Detroit music is based on not being technically proficient—The Stooges, The Gories, The White Stripes…

Mick Collins: It's a good thing we have a city full of bands that don't feel you have to be Jesus to play guitar. Part of it is cos we're isolated, we don't care—if you're a good band you're a good band. We have a different aesthetic about rock'n'roll here. We just want to hear a heavy beat and it doesn't take a lot to pound a heavy beat out. We like it pretty loud and it apparently helps if you can sing a bit. It's unlikely that any of the bands that got big in Detroit with the exception of The White Stripes would have got any recognition in any other city—they would have been regarded as a bunch of talentless drunks, but here we're all talentless drunks altogether. I'm one of the worst guitar players I know… God forbid the drummer should play a fill. The song would be over. We don't like a lot of time changes in Detroit—even with Motown songs, the beat is steady all the way through. I'm the same way. Don't be arsing around with sudden breaks to sing about unicorns or whatever, just play the fucking beat.

Steve Shaw: The Gories are like the Ramones in that a lot of people who might not have thought they could start a band saw them, and realised they could do it too.

Dan Kroha: We were so bad. And we had the gall to get on stage being that bad.

What made you want to play drums?

Chris Handyside: I was a complete spaz. It was the only instrument that was basic enough for me to learn, and instant enough not to lose patience with.

You have to be really together to drum.

Chris: Not at first you don't. It's nice if you are, but you don't have to be. Until I joined The Dirtbombs I didn't use a hi-hat. I couldn't use my left foot, so my left foot was always flying out and kicking stuff, and my right foot was going crazy on the bass drum. That whole "coordinated" thing's a bit oversold.

I'm glad to hear it. You sound like my favourite kind of drummer.

Chris: It's a matter of being able to hit things hard and loud and play music that's rudimentary. Learn by listening to The Mummies[i] records.

Do you think that's a key to the Detroit aesthetic—drummers lacking in technical proficiency but with plenty of heart?

Chris: It pops up every once in a while. I always thought rock'n'roll was better when it was chaotic, and the best way to be chaotic is to have an uncoordinated drummer.

Was Peggy like that in The Gories?

Chris: No. Peggy was fabulous… There's also the "play live as practice" idea. People have started bands for no other reason than to play a gig with their friends, and then decided it was fun enough to try again.

Julie (Slumber Party): I played my first show five days after I joined the band, and the first time I played drums was the day I joined.

Dave Buick: I played my first Go show three days after my first practice. It was my first time playing with a drummer.

i Killer minimal, trashy Eighties garage trio. Check out their "raw, totally uncooked" 22-track compilation *Death By Unga Bunga!* (Estrus, 2004)

"There was a fair amount of tension in The Gories, but it wasn't a motivating factor. We just loved what we doing, and no one else was doing it apart from Thee Mighty Ceasers[iii]. By the end, around '91, people finally started coming to the shows, but we were burned out. We couldn't go any further. Tim at Crypt offered to get us a European tour. Alex Chilton thought we would go down well over there. [The former Big Star singer had produced The Gories' second album, 1990's *I Know You Fine, But How You Doin'*, after hearing their record at a New York party]. So we reformed and toured Europe in May 1992 to promote *Outta Here*. It was a disaster, but kinda fun."

Matters came to a head the night The Gories played Orleans, France. Dan's former girlfriend [Margaret, who now plays in his post-Gories band, Demolition Doll Rods] started stripping—a point of contention. Peg cut the set short, and Mick and Dan sent her boyfriend out to get her: cue massive barney on cobblestone street outside.

Mick: "That was the last straw. I was fully determined to kill Peg that night. I was going to beat the life out of her with my guitar. I had the guitar raised up over my head… But I'd read a little about the French penal system and decided she wasn't worth it."

When The Gories returned to Detroit, Peg was out of the band. Other drummers were tried, but didn't work out. The Gories were done by '92.

iii Featuring Wild Billy Childish—later of Thee Headcoats and The Buff Medways, and mentor to Holly Golightly (guest vocalist on the Stripes' fourth album). South Londoner Childish is the king of primitive, emotionally direct, three-chord garage rock and has served as primary inspiration to virtually every Nineties US band worth its garage/grunge credentials (Mudhoney, Nirvana, The Gories and The White Stripes being not the least among them). He's produced several books of poetry and woodcuts, and released over 100 independent records released since '79. "We don't want to hide behind volume and monitors," the Chatham poet wrote in 2002, "We want to close the 15 feet between us and the audience, and have true communication."

Wendy Case (The Paybacks): "There's nobody who would dispute that The Gories introduced the concept of do-it-yourself rock to this city. And they did it in a really innocent way, too. They did it because they loved records."

Dave Buick: "The first time I saw The Gories they were opening for The Laughing Hyenas on Halloween, and there wasn't many people there. My high-school girlfriend had just dumped me, and my buddy Gus was like, 'Come on, we'll dress up, it'll be great'. I didn't feel like dressing up, but he wanted to so I taped a bunch of spoons and crap to my head and wore a robe. Gus was a burglar, so he had black jeans, a black jacket and a black cap on. We get there and nobody else was in a costume. The Gories came on and Danny had no shirt on with a dog collar, Peggy was on the drums, and I'm in this goofy costume with spoons taped to my head. It didn't make no sense to me. Courtney Love was at that show too."

Steve Shaw: "I remember being downstairs at Dan Kroha's house in the mid-Eighties, and he'd be picking on a guitar, putting records on and figuring stuff out. He was a cocky kid."

Dan: "I've mellowed out since then."

Above: Flyer for the last Gories show ever, a reunion gig, 7/93

Steve: "I loved them. The word that comes to mind is immediacy. I guess I like R&B. I like the blues, too. Mick could sing R&B. That was a big part of the charm. They were haphazard in their approach. That could be amusing. I thought The Gories were the shit and anyone who couldn't see that had their head up their ass."

Mick: "We were liked, but not by very many people. That's what gets lost in translation. We would do shows and people would come, but only a few. What's the biggest myth about The Gories? That we did it all on purpose. We had no plan. We had no bass because someone had to play solos, someone had to play chords, and so the bass got dropped. We played the blues because we were Mods. We did what we did because a) we were bored and b) we had this idea of music that we wanted to hear that no one else was doing and to that end I think we failed. We weren't good enough to play it. When we heard the Seattle band The Nights And Days[iv] we were like, 'That's it! That's what we want to sound like!' If we'd heard them first we wouldn't have formed."

Dan: "I can see why people say The Gories are the biggest influence in Detroit. When we were around I thought we were the last word in the genre. I called it grunge[v] before the Seattle thing got big ."

iv Eighties garage-punk band who appeared on the pivotal *Sub Pop 200* (Sub Pop, 1988), the 20-track compilation that helped launch Seattle on an unsuspecting world. The Nights And Days recorded an album with Jack Endino, but it never came out. Shortly before release, the drummer got offered a job as a bank teller, causing the band to split.

v As did Art Phag, a mostly forgotten, but totally rockin', Pussy Galore/Cramps-style Detroit duo who released an album entitled *Gods Of Grunge* (Vinyl Drip, 1989).

Ben Blackwell: "Did you ever think The White Stripes were taking too much from The Gories, or did you feel humbled because it was someone who really got you were doing and evolved it?"

Mick: "They took a similar physical idea, but Jack explores different musical territory to Gories. Gories were based in Chicago electric blues, and The White Stripes are more country blues, more Memphis than Chicago. It wasn't until people started pointing it out me I started to make the connection. Same with Deja Voodoo [Eighties Canadian duo], but they were purely Link Wray rockabilly, in a Duane Eddy vein, that is different from both The White Stripes and Gories. I'm pleased that Jack acknowledges a lineage there, but at the same time I'm gratified it's not just a slavish copy. You can take the same elements and do something different with them. I don't think Jack is an imitation at all."

METR

Detroit Rock City

During the early to mid Nineties, while most of the music around was techno and an overspill of shoegazing groups from Chicago, a handful of bands from Detroit and nearby towns kept the garage flame burning—The Hentchmen, Rocket 455 (who included Dan Kroha for a while), The Witches, Dan Kroha's own glam rock outfit Demolition Doll Rods, Godzuki, Mick Collins' Blacktop and Outrageous Cherry among them. A common shared aesthetic was a love for alcohol, a good time, zero musical bullshit, and the dirty grungy guitars of the Sixties garage rock. If two chords were good enough for John Lee Hooker, and three for the Ramones, then they were certainly good enough for Detroit. This was unadulterated male party music—music that could be played while chugging a beer (Dave Buick's party trick while playing bass in The Go was to keep a bottle clamped between his lips while playing an entire song).

Round about 1996-7 came bands like The Dirtbombs, The Babykillers (later to change their name to The Von Bondies), The Sights, The Go and the almighty garage soul band The Detroit Cobras. Most of the line-ups were fluid, with musicians often in three or four bands simultaneously.

Wendy Case (The Paybacks): "The Hentchmen are definitely a loggerhead for the current scene. But Bantam Rooster were also influential—we'd all seen Flat Duo Jets, so they weren't the first blues-based aggressive rock duo around, but they made a real impression. The Hentchmen were instrumental because they were so loved and visible. And the Doll Rods have had a much greater influence than people recognise. They're probably the most overlooked band in this whole scene. Peaches[i] and Jon Spencer drop their name as a major influence, but they're not reaping the rewards they're due. Rocket 455 were instrumental because they were so brutal, ballistic and explosive, and they don't get the credit they deserve either. It's probably their own fault—they just didn't seem interested in making really good recordings. Get Hip! put out a Rocket compilation, but it doesn't even come close to what they were capable of."

The scene was self-supporting: it supplied the necessary core of musicians, audience and drinking buddies. Steve Nawara, for example, played guitar or bass in Detroit Cobras, Rocket 455, The Wildbunch (nee Electric Six), The Dirt Eaters (also featuring Sixties style chanteuse, Denise James), the Andre Williams band and, for one show only, The White Stripes. As he puts it, "I've been a band slut for many, many years now. You've got to keep your fingers busy." His former comrades in The Wildbunch—an inspired, near parody of Seventies mid-American rock with songs written about storming fast food places and starting nuclear wars in discos who later turned into Electric Six—take up the story.

Left: The Wildbunch guitarist Anthony Selph at Paycheck's, 3/99 (Doug Coombe)

i She's naaaaasty! This forceful rock/electronic female singer's live show gives a whole new meaning to the expression "cock rock". Has duetted (brilliantly) with Iggy Pop.

BANTAM ROOSTER

Tom Potter

"When I was five, my mom would take me out to flea markets. My first records were stuff like 'Roadrunner' by The Gantsi and 'Chapel Of Love' by The Dixie Cups. My mom was like, 'Well, it's like 10c a piece, I'll just buy him a little stack'. My kindergarten teacher told my parents I might have disabilities to the level that I might always be retarded... but I was already reading, so my mom was like, 'Bullshit'. I got given this hip, young teacher in first grade who was really hot, plus her name was Miss Lick. She was like, 'Tom's very creative, he just doesn't have time to think about all the stuff that you and I think about'. Suddenly, I'm taking private art classes after school with this quasi hippie small town artist, and then I'm like, 'Drums are cool' and—bam!—that Christmas I get a set of bongos.

"I played drums in bands in junior high. I got my first guitar when I was 11 or 12. I was born in Detroit but my father, being a cop, got the fuck out during the late Sixties, so we moved to a farm town out in the middle of Michigan. The place where I got my guitar was a combination Christian bookstore, used guitars, dry cleaners and stuff like people doing rock polishing. But he had two racks of cruddy-ass used guitars at $40-$50 a piece. Now, it's all totally boss-ass collectible shit. After that, I played for a while, and every couple of months I'd go to the store and trade in one guitar for another. My first guitar was like a Teisco Delray. I had the diamond shaped one. It was bright electric blue, and it had a billion switches, with three of those cruddy pick-ups with the screws. Of course I paid $40 for it... actually, my dad did.

"My first band was called My Pet Dog Road Grater. None of us could really play, so our main influence was Flipper. That was when we were 14, 15. We did a couple of shows up in Lansing. It was the closest town where there was something going on—The Meatmen were from there, and The Crucifucks.

"When we formed Bantam Rooster, we were living in Lansing. Eric [Cook] was the first drummer. He was in Gravitar at the time, this snarly noise. So we started playing together as a two-piece and kept it like that because we couldn't figure out how to write any other way. After all, people danced to Leadbelly—and he only played guitar.

"Our first tour, the soundman would be like, 'Oh, we gotta have a soundcheck, the bass player better get here', and we'd be like, 'We don't have a bass player', and he'd be like, 'Yeah, that's cool, but the bass player better get here'. Shit like that. And then you always got the dude coming along saying, 'I play bass, you gotta get a bass player'..."

i Sixties garage band from the Deep South. Their sole hit, 'Roadrunner' (a Bo Diddley cover) made the Top 50 in 1965.

Bantham Rooster at Paychecks in Hamtramk, 03/99. (Doug Coombe)

Surge Joebot (WB): "There was this guy Matt Smith who was in Outrageous Cherry and The Volebeats. He would do a lot to drum up stuff and put on shows. That was the first time I got the sense there was stuff going on here."

Outrageous Cherry started around '92, inspired by late Sixties psychedelic rock: "We had an audience of 20 people back then," Matt recalls. "It was, literally, the other bands—Rocket 455, The Hentchmen, the Doll Rods. I can't remember anyone else being there. One time I was on stage screaming, while Mick Collins used power tools to smash records. I don't know what that was about."

Anthony (AKA Rock And Roll Indian, WB): "For Godzuki's record release party they had a whole bunch of different support bands do one of their songs—Godzuki, Rocket 455 and The Volebeats. A group of people all doing the same thing. Rocket was the main draw. Then the scene started melding into us, Bantam Rooster, The Hentchmen and Rocket 455. After every show, we'd have a huge party."

Steve Nawara: "It was the realisation we could invite chicks back to our house! That's how everyone got to know each other, partying, getting fucked up. Joe put his hand through the window, I would talk to Jeff Meier from Rocket 455 and everyone became friends. There were two regular party-throwers—Dave Buick and us."

Joebot: "Demolition Doll Rods were huge. We'd tape their show and listen to it while we were landscaping. They were a big deal cos they made it to California. Any inkling

THE WILDBUNCH

Steve, Anthony, Joe

Steve Nawara: I'm 28 years old, a musician born and raised in Detroit, Michigan. My first sexual experience was due in part to Anthony. We were all at this homecoming dance. After the show we went to the park, drinking beer, getting stoned, all laid out on these blankets. I leave for a second with this girl, come back and he's mysteriously taken our place. So I had no choice but to go to his station wagon and get rug burn. The same girl also introduced me to LSD, which I'm fairly thankful for.

Tell me your aesthetics of rock'n'roll.

Steve: Keep it simple.

Because you're drunk?

Steve: Well, that too—but there's only so much your hands can do. If you just play a barre chord over and over it's easier.

You can rock out harder?

Steve: You can move your hair around a lot more.

Anthony AKA Rock And Roll Indian: I'm half Indian, half German. White kids have surrounded me all my life. I needed attention badly. So I got onstage. I first started playing music with Joe when we were in high school together. That was in the suburbs of Detroit, near the old headquarters of the KKK, where Rob Tyner retired. We were into the same kind of music: Mudhoney, The Stooges—all that shit. Steve was a couple of years younger than us. He was 15, playing shows with the post-Descendents hardcore band, All. This was 1990.

Surge Joebot AKA Joe: I was so pissed. Kingdom Come was out, the big Led Zeppelin rip-off, and I was like, "How come nobody rips off The Stooges"... and then he brings in Mudhoney. I was like, "Wow, this is great, this sounds just like The Stooges", but he was like, "No it doesn't! Who is The Stooges?" So I brought in a tape and he was like, "Wow, this is pretty good. They should change their name, though."

Steve: Everyone from The Wildbunch went to the same high school, although Corey [drums] and Tyler [AKA Dick Valentine, singer] were way older than us. Joe and Anthony came up to me and said, "You have to hear this song Tyler wrote called 'Gay Bar'". I jumped in the car, listened to it, and thought it was pretty good. So I decided to play bass with them. We thought it would only last a couple of shows. Tyler was going to weatherman school, and that would be the end of it. We went up to Ann Arbor thinking we were going to start up this great band, and there was nobody there. It was a dead-end college town.

Joe: Everyone was into Phish and The Grateful Dead. When I was kid, Detroit was the forbidden zone—like *Bladerunner*. My dad was like, "Don't go down to Detroit".

The Wildbunch in some weird line-up without Steve and before the name change. (Pat Pantano)

THE HENTCHMEN

Johnny Hentch

"This is John Szymanski, also known as Johnny Hentch from The Hentchmen—and The Paybacks."

You've had 26 singles out.

"We've had over 20, certainly—from '93 to present. We put one out just this year."

Why so many?

"They just snowballed. We put two out ourselves to get our name out there and get people into hearing our music. The next thing you know, about a dozen little labels wanted to do a single over the next couple of years. Then we signed to Norton, and they put out 45s regularly. We didn't plan on putting out so many records, but it's hard to stop doing it. If someone wants to put out a single, you don't say no."

You started The Hentchmen when you were 19.

"We were just out of high school."

What made you start? Had you been in bands before?

"We'd been in a ska band. Chris Handyside was our first drummer. Tim [Purrier] was the guitar player. Me and Tim and Chris were all in the same class together. Tim played sax. My dad was a piano player, so I got a little keyboard. It took about a year before we got sick of that. We were growing musically and getting into old rock'n'roll, the good stuff. That was when we were in Northville, Michigan—I moved to Detroit when I graduated but we're pretty much a Northville band."

What was Detroit like when you started?

"The most noteworthy band was The Gories. There wasn't much of a scene at all. We met Wendy [Case, Paybacks] and some of the Ann Arbor folks, and played some shows out there. It seemed like there was more of a communal rock'n'roll scene out there so we moved out for a year and a half. I commuted to college in Detroit from Ann Arbor. We moved next door to each other, near where Iggy's from. 1993 was our summer of love. We played all the time, partying, turning each other on to music."

What were the aesthetics of rock'n'roll that interested you?

"We liked Chuck Berry, the production values of the Sixties, early Rolling Stones records. That Sixties garage band sound is the greatest stuff in the world. It was an immediate, genuine reaction to the Stones and The Beatles. We loved the crudeness of the instrumentation and the lyrical content: snotty, frustrated high-school kids—which we all were, anyway. Which we still kind of are."

Were you surprised when people started paying attention to Detroit?

"Yeah. We moved back to Detroit from Ann Arbor in '96. Chris left the band and we got Mike [Latullipe]. Mike was the drummer in that ska band I mentioned earlier. Chris wasn't in that band. He was in high school. All three Hentchmen now are from that band. Which will remain nameless."

Why did you move back to Detroit?

"We got bored of Ann Arbor quickly. I don't know... There was a time when we were going to leave Detroit. We met some girls so we stayed. The scene started to get better around '98, the bands that had been around for a few years were getting better, like Rocket 455 was really strong, The Wildbunch had just started, The Sights, The White Stripes, Soledad Brothers had all just started, The Garden Bowl became a hangout. It's the oldest bowling alley in the country, but before '98 it wasn't a hip place to hang out. Ko [Ko And The Knockouts] bartended, and she pulled a lot of people in. The bowling league started, bands playing on the lanes in the bowling alley. The Magic Stick had been around for about a year upstairs. It got really fun in '98. And there wasn't any attention on Detroit yet from the outside. There were a lot of all-night parties. Everyone moved to the Commonwealth area downtown. I guess that was enough energy to create a scene."

Were you surprised when outside people started paying attention?

The Hen
(Kelly Cas

The Hentchmen 10th anniversary show with Jack White guesting, at Jacoby's, 10/02 (Doug Coombe)

"Well, when The White Stripes started getting good we all knew if anyone was going to make it, it would be Jack. We figured he was the guy who had the aesthetics we liked but could also be commercial. I remember seeing him do a solo show and thinking, 'That guy will be on MTV some day'."

How would you describe Detroit to an outsider like myself?

"Shohola. There's nothing to look at, but there's a lot of great people and it's easy to get on."

How big an influence has it been on your own music?

"I don't know. We've had opportunities in this town. We've met a lot of real geeky musicians and record collectors. I'm not sure if that's indicative of working class environments or not. It may have had something to do with Detroit. I love Detroit music but I don't think it's that big of an influence. I love soul, Motown and The Stooges but my songwriting isn't inspired by them."

Do you see elements of The Hentchmen in other Detroit bands?

"Every band sounds a bit different. Do you agree?"

There's a common aesthetic.

"People compare it to Seattle but I thought a lot of the Seattle bands sounded the same."

To my mum, all rock music sounds the same.

Chris Handyside

"I asked my parents for a set of drums every Christmas since I was three. I was like the kid who wanted the puppy dog. When I was 15, my parents got me a guitar. I started taking lessons, I was horrible, I stopped. Then I started asking for drums again. I eventually gave up when I moved out of the house, when I was 18. It was around that Christmas that John and Tim of The Hentchmen said, 'Go buy some drums and play rock'n'roll with us'.

"The first Hentchmen show was a complete and utter train wreck, but it was the most fun I've ever had in my life. My main influence were records by The Mummies, The Sonics[i] and The Trashmen[ii]. The Milkshakes[iii] were what I aspired to, but I still can't play that well. Beer was a good facilitator. I was still underage, it helped me be illegal. John made a really good mix tape which ran the whole gauntlet of what he wanted The Hentchmen to be. I listened to it for two weeks straight. By '94 we'd played in Detroit at least once or twice. At Penny's, the old Miami, and Zoots[iv]. I remember it being really quiet. Everybody I met I was intimidated by, because they were older or had a connection to The Gories.

"We straddled Ann Arbor and Detroit for a long time. We played at Cross Street Station a lot, which was college drunks, and The Blind Pig. We would play with The Monarchs and other old bands. We'd play with Couch, or other noise and performance bands that would alienate everybody, then we would go up and they would think that we were doing it on purpose, that we were trying to be a noise band, and we'd be like, 'No! We're trying to sound like The Trashmen'. People would laugh and tell us we sounded like The Doors [because of the keyboards, presumably, because The Hentchmen sound *nothing* like The Doors—Ed]. They heard us as two opposite things—The Doors and a noise band."

i Savage young Sixties garage band from Tacoma, WA. Should've been mega. Weren't.

ii Demented surf band from Minneapolis, best known for their 1964 Top 10 hit, 'Surfin' Bird'—as beloved by both The Cramps and Ramones.

iii Billy Childish's pre-Caesers, post-Pop Rivets, early Eighties, Kinks-influenced Medway band. Classic.

iv Chris: I remember Zoots being a really cool, diverse place. Everything from film nights to acoustic shows to touring bands like The Make Up and stuff.

DEMOLITION DOLL RODS

Danny Doll Rod

"Jack White really learned well. He studied everyone that was happening. He studied the Doll Rods and The Hentchmen and whoever else were playing at the time. He was a really good sponge. The Doll Rods were wearing matching outfits before anyone was wearing matching outfits. When we first started out—'93, '94, '95—even though we didn't wear much, what we were wearing matched.

"We went out and bought these skin-tight see-through black shirts that said 'babe' in silver across the chest, with silver mini-skirts. We all bought the same outfit and we'd wear that. We started wearing less and less clothes, to the point where we would tape things to our chest with duct tape. We'd have little toys. On one outfit we had little plastic racing cars taped to our chests, and wore plastic kids' racing helmets with a stripe down the centre. We'd wear little panties and g-string thongs and matching boots. We had this whole packaged concept. And we were very minimal. We had a very simple drumkit. I know that was an influence [on The White Stripes]. And I remember there was a point where we didn't play that well, so a lot of our songs were slow. After one of our shows, Jack said, 'That was really dirge-y', and then I saw The White Stripes a bit later and they were very dirge-y. They had these songs that were plodding. People thought that Margaret [Doll Rods guitarist] and I were brother and sister. He picked up on all that stuff, and Bantam Rooster, too.

"Jack did a great job of incorporating all those things. He had the whole concept package together where they wear matching outfits. He'd set up this table onstage with a red tablecloth, and Meg had the white drumkit with the candy on it. Jack learned a lot from Dan Miller in Goober And The Peas. Dan and his band would always mess with that kind of stuff. They would pretend to have a manager and a booking agent, and make it look like they were big. They had the balls or craziness or whatever, to pull off that stuff.

"Jack is an intelligent kid, and he's a talented player and songwriter. He did a smart job of learning from everybody. I remember John Hentch saying that all Jack talked about 24/7 was music and doing a band. He was totally obsessed with himself and what he was doing. It shows you the power of dreaming."

that bands could get out of here was a huge deal. The idea was to do something unacceptable. There was this orthodoxy that you didn't rock out. Techno was so huge then, the sheer act of playing rock was taboo and foolish. It was self-defeating."

Jeff Meier was a major influence: not only were his band reckoned to be the Greatest Live Detroit Band of the mid-Nineties, and he was also in the original line-up of The Detroit Cobras, but he engineered the debut White Stripes single up at Jack's house. He first met the future Stripes singer at a concert in New Pontiac, at a senior citizens centre, where old Fifties country music and honkytonk singer Kitty Wells was playing—right in the middle of a suburban neighbourhood. Jack was one of the five people present under 65.

Jeff also produced the Two Star Tabernacle/Andre Williams single: "Everybody was overwhelmed because Andre was one of our heroes, he had this mystique," he told journalist Martin Roach. "And here I was getting to record him! We used my portable studio. I took all my gear over to Jack's house in the Mexican quarter. Jack's house was weird, but cool. He didn't have a whole lot of records—maybe 30 or 40. He was really into Love and Dylan."

Jack spent a lot of time trying to convince Andre that he should record 'The Big Three Killed My Baby' but the wily old R&B singer wasn't having any of it: "It was worth a try, and I admire his persistence," commented Jeff. "That's the kinda guy Jack was."

ROCKET 455

Marco Delicato

"In 1989, I was going to school in East Lansing. That's when I first met Tom Potter from Bantam Rooster and Jim Diamond. They lived in a house off-campus and started a basement bar to have punk bands come and play. I saw Scream [Dave Grohl's pre-Nirvana band] in their basement. Their modus operandi was to bring the music to the people as cheaply as possible, underground and lo-fi.

"The first thing I did when I joined the original line-up of Rocket 455 in 1992 was to get rid of the mounted tom to make sure I didn't try to do anything stupid, like a drum fill. And I stayed drunk most of the time, which helped. When we first started, having Dan Kroha in the band attracted The Gories crowd. That helped immensely. So I'm in Rocket, and I get Steve Nawara in the band, and he's 21, and we got Kenny Tudrick [Detroit Cobras drummer: also The Go, Electric Six] in the band, and he's 21, and the first time we play they're talking about their alcoholism and medical maladies, and they're like peas in a pod. Steve's been diagnosed with cirrhosis, and Ken... he was working in a furniture shop lacquering wood, and the doctor said, 'You cannot continue doing this, this stuff is ripping apart your insides, and your drinking and smoking is killing you'. They're getting off on their medical problems, and they never stopped.

"After I left the band for a year, I returned playing guitar in '94/'95. I stayed with Rocket until the New Year of '99. For a few months I filled in on keyboards, there are some photos of me wearing a yellow space helmet you should get hold of. I also played lead guitar with The Go. When The Go started they were playing at The Gold Dollar. What was striking was that they had no lead guitar. It was all rhythm, a very stripped down rock'n'roll band. Without that lead you could really focus on that rhythm. As it turned out, they loved Rocket. I played with them for several months, played some great shows.

"Detroit musicians play with lots of different bands. The plus side is that people get to play lots of different kinds of music. They get to be on stage more often. The bad side is that you don't get to concentrate, as you may need to. I could never handle more than two bands at the same time, which is why my stints in The Wildbunch and The Go weren't very long. Before Rocket broke up, Wendy Case approached me for a band. I was sceptical, but she'd put a band together for a prom night show at The Gold Dollar and it was fantastic. So we formed The Paybacks. We had Marc Watt from The Dirtys playing bass and Pat Pantano playing drums, eventually replaced by John and Mike of The Hentchmen. I did that for three years and put out a wonderful record. I'm floating around right now.

"Rocket was fuelled by the British invasion, American garage, and Stroh's beer. It comes in a 30 pack, for $9.99, I've been drinking it since high school. The aesthetic was always lo-fi, and to play the type of rock'n'roll that we would stay up to four in the morning listening to, drinking beer and having fun. We set a beer-selling record in Lily's. I would walk on stage stone sober and walk off drunk as a skunk. I'd like to think that everybody else in the bar did the same thing. Tyler [Electric Six singer] once said he would play a half-hour show and celebrate it for 10 hours afterwards. That's the kind of town this is."

Greg Baise (The Magic Stick): "The first time I saw Rocket 455 was in the summer of '92. They were on a bill with Laughing Hyenas[ii] and Couch. They covered 'Guess I'm Falling In Love' by the Velvets, and I was stunned. Rocket 455 carried on the legacy of MC5 and The Stooges, but not in a slavish way. It was just great rock with energy."

Dave Buick: "I've loved Rocket 455 since the first time I saw them. It doesn't translate on 45, but if you know anything at all about them, you'll know that as Jeff Meier is playing his guitar leads or whatever, Mark [Walz, vocals] has got his face right at the guitar, screaming. I always liked the way he'd yell at the instruments—or strangle himself with the mic cord."

Godzuki were one of the bands inspired by Rocket 455's energy.

Dion Fischer (guitar): "Although we got called indie rock, or science rock, we were totally garage rock when we started. We were loud and noisy, but we had a girl singer, with elements of K Records[iii] and stuff. We just did whatever we felt like."

The Hentchmen were a trio of Northville High teens who played raucous, organ-fuelled, three-chord garage songs: songs dedicated to the three Gods of Garage—to chicks, cars and beer. Twelve years on, and they still bring the party with them[iv].

John Szymanski (Johnny Hentch): "When we started, in '92, there wasn't any Detroit scene to speak of—the people we were hanging out with in Ann Arbor were much more into authentic Sixties garage and surf music, not Iggy or MC5. It didn't take long for us to put some singles out—Norton Records in NYC liked our demo. So we started recording trashy basement four-track material. Then, around 1995, Detroit started picking up, so we returned."

Marcie Bolen (The Von Bondies): "I saw a Hentchmen show at The Gold Dollar that was pretty amazing. They had all these Leslie speakers spinning all around them and everyone was dancing like crazy all over the place."

Dave: "The first time I saw The Hentchmen was in '93, at this place called Penny's on Woodward Ave. It must have been their third show, and I was floored. These three nerds who couldn't play blew me away. I've loved them ever since. They're an important Detroit band. For

Left: Demolition Doll Rods (Doug Coombe)

ii A tormented bluesy post-punk Ann Arbor group formed in 1985, fronted by the demonic John Brannon.

iii K Records—home of the International Pop Underground, run by the charismatic, deadpan Olympia, WA performer Calvin Johnson (Beat Happening, Halo Benders, Dub Narcotic). Kurt Cobain once had a small K, with its trademark surrounding shield, tattooed on his arm.

iv 1994's energetic 16-track LP *Campus Party* is entirely recommended.

THE GOLD DOLLAR

Amy Abbott

"Heather White [Meg's sister] came into the Cass Café where I was bartending and asked if I would be interested in bartending at The Gold Dollar. As I was used to bartending at rock clubs when I lived in Chicago I jumped at the chance. I went into the Dollar and met Neil. The interview was relatively informal. I was hired on the spot and we went to the Temple Bar for drinks. My first show was on March 14, 1997—The Detroit Cobras.

"I started out bartending on the occasional busy show and was given Thursday night, poetry night. That got pretty old, pretty quick. Once Heather left I took over on weekends, and helped Neil with staffing, scheduling, opening and closing, running things when he wasn't around and, of course, bitching. We were pretty particular who got to work there, as it was such a small establishment. Neil had started the club with altruistic ideas and I kind of pushed him in a money direction.

"The Gold Dollar was dingy and dark with worn reddish carpeting that retained a smoky, stinky odour. When you walked in, you faced the soundboard—and the bar was on your left hand side, while the stage was to the right. There were stools lining the bar and a mirror behind it—if you weren't ordering a drink you had to watch the band. The stage was about 12 x 14 and about 18 inches off of the ground. Minimal stage lighting, probably eight lights, and the board was a 12-channel. Neil was very handy with things and made a lot of the stuff. Capacity was 107, though we could have as many as 250. The women's bathroom was usually clean, though the ladies didn't treat it right. The men's room smelled of urine and urinal cake—it was foul. It was just before the back room.

"The back room was nearly the size of the front—except it was perpetually leaking when it rained, or smelt of tar when it was really hot. There was a deep freezer in the back where we kept bagged ice, which we always ran out of—and a back door that led to a fenced-in backyard. The band room was stellar. It used to be a drag bar for many years, so it was painted pink and had show light type mirrors for the drag queens -which can be seen in the *Ace's High* video [a documentary about Chris Fachini's Kiss cover band]. We had three security cameras that monitored the parking lot—on dead nights we would just watch the cameras. Oh yeah, and the walls were painted black around the stage and panelled throughout the club. There were mirrors behind the stage.

"Behind the bar there were two cash registers and old-fashioned coolers. Neil liked to carry a lot of quirky stuff so we had, like, 30 beers from $1.50 Stroh's to $11.00 Chimay's. We carried Faygo pop—and for the first few years had to mix drinks with litre bottles of soda, tonic or cola. In the final years we had a proper soda gun.

"The staff generally got along like a dysfunctional family. Our favourite activity revolved around setting up early. Usually we would get there at 7:30 for an 8pm opening. If we set up quick enough we would sit outside drinking coffee—we called it 'coffee on the veranda'—and watch the prostitution stings going down. The unmarked squad car would sit in our lot and we'd watch the police plant lure the johns in. Sometimes they would attempt

to flee, other times they would give in. A lot of times the prostitutes would ask to use our restroom to clean up.

"For a while we had a fondler in the parking lot that would run up to girls and try and grab them. It happened a few times—so once Katy Potter (who worked the door and was bad ass) and I grabbed blunt instruments and ran out to look for the guy. We saw him and he saw us, so we thought he would stop. He did it again and Katy went running after him—when he realised he was being chased by a girl he stopped and asked, 'What are you going to do?' She thought about it, and turned around—but he never came back.

"A lot of the time it was up to the girls to defend the place.

"People used to sit on the bar and watch the show, so there was a tier of people standing, then sitting on stools, then sitting on the bar. It made serving drinks easier because it helped block you from the animals, but occasionally someone's ass would take out a whole row of drinks.

"Bartending can get boring so I would occasionally have a theme night. I think I was channelling a polter-transvestite. There were characters that I would come up with—like alcoholic housewife, Sixties Italian film star or Catholic Schoolgirl. It was a way to keep it interesting and fun, and I like to think it was fun for the patrons as well.

"That bled over into a prom. The Empty Bottle in Chicago used to do a prom when I lived there, and Neil had the idea simultaneously, so we had a prom the first year I worked there—the theme was 'Purple Rain', there was a committee to decorate (tin foil was our main source of décor) and all the musicians formed cover bands. There was Moustache Ride, Surge Joebot had a band, and Tyler from The Wildbunch went on as Bryan Adams. Rock And Roll Indian was prom king—the queen escapes me. The next year we had 'Night On Disco Mountain', the year after that we hit a low with 'Porno Prom' and finished up our last year with 'Xanadu'. We also had a Night Before Thanksgiving party. Usually, The Wildbunch would play. They were like a house band.

"There were too many great shows to mention, but a good time was always had when Bantam Rooster played, it would end with either myself or Tom Potter, or both of us, dancing on the bar. We always tried to encourage gentlemen to take their shirts off. Local shows supported our bar entirely, and when we didn't have a lot, we didn't do as well. That was the only problem. People wouldn't come there to hang out. They would only come to see shows.

"I don't want to be biased, but The Gold Dollar was the scene. There was a sense of community that other clubs in town haven't been able to match. It enabled a lot of bands to play and get exposed that wouldn't normally have had the chance. There wasn't a lot of ego going down and you felt like you could do whatever you wanted. We didn't have mean or intimidating security so people felt sort of free. While the larger rooms are important like The Magic Stick, they just don't have the sense of belonging that the Dollar did. Neil did a good thing, he gave people an environment where they could flourish, and bands always got 100 per cent of the door. No other bar has ever done that.

"Unfortunately, the bar climate kind of sucks now, as there hasn't been a suitable replacement for the Dollar. Because everyone is trying to capitalise on a good thing all these clubs are booking rock shows, but the people that are turning out now are the suburbanites and the college kids and they have no respect for the way things were. Going out to shows isn't nearly as fun—they are selling out (which is good for the bands) but the drinks are costly and the vibe is altogether wrong. Anyhow, the Dollar was the cornerstone of it all."

a while they were the only ones playing, and they'd have parties at their house, and play down in the basement."

Dion: "They're a Detroit institution."

Dave: "They put out three or four amazing singles. They did a tour of Europe. By the time 1996 rolled around they'd already done four US tours, with John shotgunning beers across the country. They're a fun band."

Independent US record labels like Get Hip!, Crypt, Sympathy For The Record Industry, In The Red and Estrus began signing Michigan bands. And more out-of-town groups—such as Lansing's full-blown dirty-ass rock duo Bantam Rooster and Port Huron's vicious punk rockers, The Dirtys—started relocating to the city.

Above: Surge Joebot at The Garden Bowl (Courtesy of Dave Buick)

Left: Photocopied handbill for The Gold Dollar advertising The White Stripes first two non-open mic night shows

v Blag Jesus of Dwarves used to delight in pissing over the front row of audiences. Their sexploitation classic, 1990's *Blood Guts & Pussy* was one of Sub Pop's early best-sellers, helped no doubt by gratuitous nudity and gore on the sleeve.

Joebot: "The Dirtys were the scariest group of guys. We were dating the leader's wife's friend. There was this huge rivalry between the two bands, but they were a big deal. They were going to Europe, and Crypt put out their record. The guitar player put the other guitar player in the hospital when they were touring Europe. They refused to let him back in. The guitarist was hospitalised and later died one night while hanging out with us."

Anthony: "We were drinking with him and he died."

Joebot: "The next morning he was dead."

Anthony: "He died on the table and I carried him outside."

Joebot: "Terrifying stuff."

Anthony: "They were loud as hell. But they were a great punk band."

Steve: "I saw them empty out The Gold Dollar. They'd sell the place out, but the amplifiers would literally push people out the door it was so loud. They were like the Ramones, but dirty. So it was Mark Dirty, Joe Dirty, whatever. They were the Dwarves[v] of the Detroit scene."

Anthony: "Except without the humour."

Joebot: "It wasn't much fun. Terrifying."

In 1996, Jim Diamond moved down from Lansing, and started Ghetto Recorders. The Magic Stick, located in the Majestic Theatre complex on Woodward Avenue, became a focal point—with free shows taking place in the bowling alley downstairs at The Garden Bowl.

"We were supposed to open up for The Hives or International Noise Whatever at The Shelter, basement of St Andrew's Hall, and our crackhead bass player is late," recalls Eddie Baranek, singer with poppy Sixties-heads, The Sights. "He eventually shows up, and we're like, 'Let's get the PA and we'll go play The Garden Bowl tonight'. The whole room is just swarming, people climbing on tables, breaking chairs... There's no stage, you're playing on eye level and the girls are dancing right in front of you, and there are people hanging on the steps to go up to The Magic Stick. Every week there'd be a bowling ball in the toilet. The whole world was a circus, a carnival, with all these different characters—the first time I saw Tim, singer with The Clone Defects, he was like, 'My guitar doesn't work, I don't have a strap', and he wouldn't play the show. I was like, 'Fuck man, that's so great. I didn't know you could just be a dick'..."

Other venues such as Paycheck's, Old Miami's, Zoot's and The Magic Bag also provided outlets for garage bands. But it was a seedy, former transvestite bar, located in the Cass Corridor a five-minute walk away from Ghetto Recorders, that became inexorably connected with the emergent scene. Owner Neil Yee's policy of giving 100 per cent of the door takings to the bands, and the venue's intimate, cosy surrounds meant that The Gold Dollar ruled everyone's ass.

Neil Yee: "I moved here from Wisconsin in 1990. In Madison at the time, Butch Vig [producer of Nirvana's breakthrough album *Nevermind*] was running a little studio out of his house, and the guys who ended up running The Knitting Factory in New York were trying to start a label. From the Fifties through 1987, The Gold Dollar had been a drag show bar, but since 1989 it had been empty. Drug users were living in the building, but I figured it was usable, so I bought the interest in January 1995 and spent all that year cleaning the place up. A lot of the amps and stuff I bought into the club had come from when I used to do sound for other bands... I rebuilt everything. The monitors worked. Usually. I also wired an eight-channel

OUTRAGEOUS CHERRY

Matthew Smith

"I've been in a million bands, I currently play in Outrageous Cherry and The Volebeats, I sometimes play in Monster Island, I play guitar with Denise James[i]. Occasionally people ask me to produce records for them, so I've produced for The Go, Slumber Party and Denise James. I've also made records with Kim Fowley[ii] and Andre Williams and I've played on stage with... oh god, who knows. Yeah. I've played a bit.

"Everyone I know was playing in bands in the Eighties and it was horrible. There was no scene or anything. There were a handful of bands that stood out—The Gories and The Frames...

"I started Outrageous Cherry in 1992, the same time as Rocket 455 and The Hentchmen. We'd play these little bars together, to about 10-15 people. Then this coffee house called Zoot's started attracting all these kids from the suburbs and Wayne State University, and all of a sudden bands started converging on this place, and it was a scene that lasted for a few years through the mid-Nineties. It came and went: because it was in Detroit no one covered it. It remained underground. People in the audience started bands like Adult[iii], and you name it. So I was playing with Outrageous Cherry and The Volebeats [Detroit pop-country band] and all of a sudden this scene sprung up around me. The first band that I recall looking like breaking outside of Detroit was The Go."

i Sultry Sixties-style dream-pop, somewhere close to the engorged harmonies of Slumber Party and Françoise Hardy's whispered enchantments.
ii He's 64. He writes songs that lift from T Rex and extol the virtues of teen love. He discovered The Runaways. He sings like Lou Reed, only seriously perverted. He's had 43 gold and platinum records over four decades. He's the Creepiest Man In Rock Official, given to making five-hour phone calls at three in the morning. He's a goddamn fucking genius.
iii Electronic Detroit duo specialising in sleazy old school glam stomps played on analogue synths. Known in some quarters as electrocl$sh.

recording system into the place so I got a lot of great live recordings. Our first bar person was Leah Smith, then it was Heather White [Meg's sister] for a couple of years, but our main one was Amy Abbott. She'd show up in odd costumes and wigs. She was a personality. Most of the staff were in bands or were artists themselves."

Despite reports to the contrary, Jack White did not carve The Gold Dollar sign when it first opened—he offered, but didn't get round to it. Neil designed it. It was supposed to be temporary, but remained in place—like much of The Gold Dollar.

Neil: "Nowadays The Gold Dollar is known for the whole garage scene and The White Stripes but at the time it was known for out-there, experimental music. Immigrant Sons and Frank Pahl from Only A Mother were big draws—he'd play Vivaldi using a conch shell and doorbells. Gravitar[vi] were great, live. You never knew quite what they were going to do. Geoff Walker was always around. He brought in a decent number of people. His brother Mike Walker [Detroit City Council][vii] was also in that band. Or we would book two punk bands and put on a magician in between them.

"Duos were reasonably common: Bogue, Bantam Rooster, Chris Handyside's Fighting Pinheads[viii], Scmods, my own band 249. In fact, we used to bill The White Stripes as "one of southwest Detroit's better two-piece bands"—and talked about doing a festival of two-piece bands. Then there was a guy from a Canadian radio show called The Hearing Trumpet who'd bring in crazy Japanese noise bands. I'd always book his shows even though only 20 people would show up. We didn't need to worry about the money because we could just book another Detroit Cobras show and everything would be fine."

Right: Jack wrestles with a guitar superglued to the floor. (Andy Willsher/S.I.N)

vi Darkly experimental jazz-noise-fuck group, like My Bloody Valentine with some Carcass thrown in.

vii Tom Potter's full-on 2003 rock extravaganza. Billowing grunge, like she ain't be wrote for way too long now.

viii Later called The Night Moves—more comedy than a serious proposition, according to Neil.

This was the Detroit that Jack and Meg started playing shows in: a load of loud, rambunctious garage rock bands, experimental outfits and trend-chasing indie groups competing for space in the same few venues.

Matt Smith: "I miss The Gold Dollar. It was an anomaly. It was definitely a place you could go and feel comfortable knowing that you didn't know what you were getting into. It wasn't The Detroit Cobras playing with two other garage bands. A lot of the time they'd be sharing a bill with a computer band and a performance artist. We'd sit out front in the car and smoke a joint, and the cops would drive by and be like 'Yeah, whatever', and keep driving."

Dave Buick: "The one thing I don't miss about The Gold Dollar was everyone's car being broken into the whole time."

Rich Hansen (promoter, The Lager House): "The Gold Dollar was a dive. It was a dumpy place. I've been in many conversations with people looking back on it with rose-colored glasses, but it had a lot of problems. It didn't always sound good, it was always packed, it was sweaty. Sometimes, you just didn't feel like going there. That aside, it was pretty magical. Neil did a great job booking that place, and Amy Abbott remains the best bartender I've ever experienced. The White Stripes, The Wildbunch, The Hentchmen, Rocket 455, The Go... everybody who's functioning now and isn't brand new had their first show at The Gold Dollar."

MEDAL IN HEAVEN

LETS SHAKE HANDS

BIG 3

WASTING MY TIME

RED BOWLING BALL

SUGAR NEVER TASTED

☆ ONE MORE CUP OF COFFEE

★ DO

LETS BUILD A HOME

LITTLE RED BOOK

WHEN I HEAR MY NAME

SCREWDRIVER

CANNON

LAFAYETTE BLUES

SUCKER DRIPS

10/23/98
GD w/HENTCHMEN
"LAFAYETTE BLUES" RELEASE
☆ - INDICATES STEVE NAW
PLAYED BASS ON SON

Let's Shake Hands

Ben Blackwell: "Jack has always been two years ahead of himself with his ideas. Before the first record was even out, he knew what the second album was going to be. I was around before they played shows and they were practising and I remember them coming up with the name The White Stripes. I was worried people would think they were a skinhead band. Originally, they were thinking of using Soda Powder or Bazooka, so maybe it wasn't such a bad name after all. Meg came up with it—the old story about how they got it from the candy may be true, but there were also some bricks in their garden, in front of their house, that said 'White' on them. It never seemed that conscious—like, 'This is a band, we're going to wear red and white, and we're going to play like this'. The further along it went, the more that happened. The two-piece thing was deliberate, though. Jack wanted that childish aspect to it—he obviously wasn't playing guitar childishly. There has to be a balance. So have Meg approach the drums like she'd never played them before."

Greg Baise: "You know the story, right? One day Jack was playing in the attic—Meg told me this herself—and she sat down at the drums. They were jamming on 'Moonage Daydream' by David Bowie. That's the thing about this music. It isn't about virtuosity. It's about feeling and instinct—and that's how it should be."

Meg's rudimentary clatter provided a neat counterpoint to Jack's more schooled guitar. At the time, Meg was a waitress in Royal Oak: Jack was playing in Two Star Tabernacle, and occasionally would get up by himself and perform at the Planet Ant[i] coffee house. So The White Stripes formed—no great master plan, no months spent honing their craft in a rehearsal studio before they played live. And that's how it should be. Spontaneity is at the heart of all great rock music. Without tutorage, Meg understood that what matters in rock music is emotion, not fancy footwork—and that silence is a rhythm too.

Dan Miller: "Things just clicked. Everything seemed so natural for The White Stripes. I remember thinking that this is a band who—if they keep it together, play for the right people could go somewhere. Even from the first, Jack knew what he wanted—a lot of The White Stripes aesthetic comes from his interest in modern furniture. Even for the first show he was like, 'I don't want it to look like a regular show with amps' so he covered up the amps [with a red tablecloth]. Ben had a cassette tape of it, and hearing that without seeing them, we could see how it held up: his voice was so powerful. There were ragged parts to the music and everything, and Meg was still learning to drum, but it was so driving."

Jack (to Andrew Male, *Mojo* '02): "When we started the band it was a way of getting back to childhood without it being a comedy act. It was about how kids look at things. There's a sense of humour that is deeply buried under everything. I'd kind of like it if people saw us and halfway through the set started laughing."

Left: Set list for the 23/10/98 show at The Gold Dollar, the 'Lafayette Blues' record release show. The songs with a star next to them indicate songs that Steve Nawara joined the band on bass for. This is handwritten by Jack White. (Courtesy of Ben Blackwell)

i An arty Hamtramck hangout that under-21s would frequent, due to the lack of alcohol. The performances would usually be acoustic. Jack played at Planet Ant about three or four times. It was the only Detroit coffee house he played.

Jack White talks to Bobby (The Go) while Steve Shaw (The Detroit Cobras/The Fondas) poses with the second White Stripes single, probably in 1997.
(Ko Shih)

Jack's strong sense of style carried through to The White Stripes: he saw the number three (taken from the number of staples required to upholster the cushions on a chair) as being vital to his vision for a band—three instruments (voice, guitar, drums), three songwriting elements (rhythm, melody, storytelling) and three colours (red, white, black).

Marcie Bolen (guitarist, The Von Bondies): "They're strong iconic colours. They contrast with each other very nicely. It seems like everything in his band is based on three. Everything fits into this perfect mould. His house is not red [as has been reported]. It's big and white."

On July 14 1997, Bastille Day, just two months after Meg started drumming, The White Stripes played their first show at one of the regular open mic Sunday nights held at The Gold Dollar. There were about a dozen people present. According to a Jack White interview in *Rolling Stone*, the band played three songs, one of which was a cover of 'Love Potion Number 9'.

Neil Yee (proprietor, The Gold Dollar): "The first time they actually played wasn't really a show. At the time Jack and Meg were married, and Meg's older sister Heather was a good friend—she was helping me bartend. Jack told me he was trying to put a new project together, just the two of them, and asked me to record the band for him. We had some regulars there. It was interesting, but it wasn't that impressive. Jack was always good, but Meg couldn't keep her drumming steady—and I like simple drumbeats. Her tempo was completely off.

"As payment for the recording, Jack reupholstered an old rocking chair for me. I don't know if Ben's mentioned this, but it's the only recording from The Gold Dollar that I can't find on multi-track right now. Also, Jack wanted a couple of chairs that my brother had reupholstered. That was part of the deal somehow—we were trading back and forth. We never exchanged money in all our dealings. He actually varnished all the wood on the frame as well. He did a really nice job. Unfortunately, I don't have it anymore. It left at the end of a relationship. She got the chair.

"Their first few official shows weren't that big a deal. Some people liked them but no one thought they would make it big despite what people may say now. They came in, played a few

CASEY COSTON

Southern-fried soul

SOUL ON A ROLL

The **Soul Food Cafe**, looking to jump on the soul food gravy train, threw open its doors for a special preview party last Tuesday, with **Mayor Dennis Archer** cutting the ribbon on this promising new restaurant on the western edge of Greektown.

The speakeasy-style joint was packed with local luminaries, but maybe they should have delayed the party a bit, given the amount of work yet to be completed on the restaurant.

While the appetizers were delicious and plentiful, a key problem here was no bar facilities whatsoever, other than some tepid sparkling wine. Even a cold drink of water was nearly impossible to obtain, a bit of a downer on such a sweltering day. Combine that with some problematic air conditioning, and you get partygoers strolling down the block to **Bennigan's** for a cool beverage.

These are bugs that can easily be worked out, however, and the place will surely be a destination for local movers and shakers, particularly the fat cat VIP cigar room, with private humidor lockers at $750 a pop.

The triumvirate behind the cafe is auto dealer-superstar offspring **Michael Farr, Dr. Andre Singleton** and **Dean Adams. Mel Farr** himself was on hand, along with fellow sports-star-turned-business-titan **Dave Bing**.

Also in search of a cool beverage was **Kathy McKee**, who hosts "Kathy McKee's FYI" every Thursday at 4 p.m. on **WPON** (that's 1460 on your AM dial). She'll be chatting with **Peabo Bryson** on her show this week, with upcoming interviews with **Bill** and **Camille Cosby, Warren Beatty** and many more. Check it out, kids.

WEEBLES WOGGLE

An intriguing melange of hipsters, musicians, record store inhabitants, thrill seekers and an odd hoedown participant or two converged on the **Magic Stick** last Tuesday night for a scintillating sonic doubleheader featuring the **Woggles** and **Southern Culture on the Skids**.

The Woggles, hailing from Athens, Ga., evoke a frenetic '60s garage-rock sensibility which is oh-so-in-vogue these days. As always, these types of bands are HUGE in Japan, but around these parts often find themselves competing with, say, the **Red Wings** playoffs.

Indeed, the last time the Woggles played the Magic Stick, it was the same night the Wings clinched the Stanley Cup. Suffice to say, many folks had their attention focused on TV screens rather on the Magic Stick stage.

This time, despite game six of the playoff series with the **St. Louis Blues**, the crowd took heed as mad master lead singer **Manfred** bounced off the stage and gyrated onto the dance floor, leaving a slick spray of perspiration in his wake.

In speaking with him after the show, he observed that while the band's van was rocked and tousled by delirious Wings fans last year, he harbored no ill will toward Detroit fans and found the Stanley Cup crowd comparable to last Tuesday's teeming masses.

Breaking away from our conversation to wipe Manfred's sweat droplets off my glasses, I piloted my way through the cavernous pool-rock emporium to the stylish 45-spinning DJ prowess of **Off the Record** offspring **David Italy** and cohort **Johnny Hentch** (of the **Hentchmen**), who was chatting with devoted Woggles fan **Erin Bomb** (of the band the **Girl Bombs**). Bomb

Johnny Hentch and David Italy

had made the long and torturous trek from Toronto to see the show.

Also in the party mix was Hamtramck gatekeeper **Scott Ross, Motor Lounge**-meister **Dan Sordyl, Ritual Productions**' den mother **Diana Frank** and counterpart **Perry Lavoisne**, a **Detroit Cobra** here and there, and **Car City Records/WDET** man **Willie Wilson**, who's positively giddy about the upcoming show at the Stick featuring the **Kaisers**, the **Neanderthals** and the **Volcanos** on June 20.

ALLEY OOP!

The Magic Stick crowd really picked up as Southern Culture on the Skids hit the stage with their overalls-clad, Southern-fried musical irony.

Armed with such crowd-pleasing tactics as throwing fried chicken to the hungry audience and doing the on-stage limbo, the band rarely disappoints ... and they also don't sit down, which includes the tireless drummer as well as the **Junior Samples**-sized keyboard player.

The floor almost seemed to buckle under the weight of a few corn-fed bouncy fans, as the band raced through its set with equal amounts of "Hee Haw" humor and stellar musicianship.

CORRECTA-MUNDO

Not one to play fast and loose with the facts (oh, heavens, no), and in response to the screaming protests of thousands of people (actually two), I feel compelled to make a few minor corrections to a piece a few weeks back about the resurgent **David Whitney Building** in downtown Detroit.

One, the beauty portraits studio is *not* being run by Birmingham makeup-man-to-the-stars **Todd Skog** and photographer **John Lieckfelt**, but rather by celebrated Detroit photographer and Ford Escort aficionado **Lisa Spindler**, who is subletting from Skog and Lieckfelt (which would make sense — isn't Skog's Birmingham salon, like, booked until the year 3000 for all except those special clients?).

Two, the techno company is called **Bang Tech 12** and not Tech Beta 12. Moving on.

C-MART SURPRISE

Not one to say I told you so, but some time ago I reported a rumor going around the development community that the **Kern Woodward Group** had the downtown **Campus Martius** project in the bag. Well, lo and behold, Mayor Archer revealed his choice last week, and — surprise — it's Kern Woodward. Just a lucky guess on my part, of course.

Invites? Gossip? Scandalous stories? Call FOW's tip line at 313-962-5281, press star (*), then dial box number 8056. E-mail Casey Coston at metrotimes@aminc.com.

Detroit Metro Times, May 27 1998

songs… I was more impressed when he'd show up occasionally at open mic nights and play drums. He was more of a stand out as a drummer."

The White Stripes' first booked appearance was a month later, supporting The Hentchmen and The In-Sect at the same venue on August 15, 1997. Right at the last minute, however, they got added to another Gold Dollar bill, the night before, supporting Rocket 455 and '68 Comeback. Dave Buick was among the handful to witness the pair's (second) debut.

Dave: "I remember Jeff Meier [Rocket 455] going, 'Yeah, it's my friend's band'… trying to explain, or something like that. Not apologising, but… They were interesting. Obviously it was a little more primal. There were more kids hanging around outside the venue while they were playing than watching them. There were maybe 20 or 30 people inside."

Steve Nawara (The Wildbunch): "I watched them support Rocket 455 thinking, 'Man, they're fucking great. They've got real slow songs, great heavy songs. Man, they'll never ever make it out of Detroit. Never.' You have to understand that at the time techno music was huge. Meg was horrible, though. It was like someone handed her the drumsticks for the first time right before they went on."

Surge Joebot (The Wildbunch): "I thought, 'Wow, that guy has some balls to sing like Geddy Lee'[ii]. He dressed up the stage with different colours—red and white, I guess—and furniture and stuff. I think they were wearing red and white as well. Jack had his head shaved at the sides, with this weird red concoction on top, like a rooster. There was an element of the cartoon-like to their image and sound, but in a good way. Bands from Detroit can be too similar sometimes—these kids seemed like they were from another planet, with Jack's absurd voice and haircut, and the simplistic drumming."

Meg took her cues from Jack: during most of the early White Stripes gigs he'd direct her from on stage—much to the amusement of the other Detroit musicians, who also approved of the roughness of the shows.

ii Ridiculously high-pitched singer with Seventies Canadian arena rock band Rush.

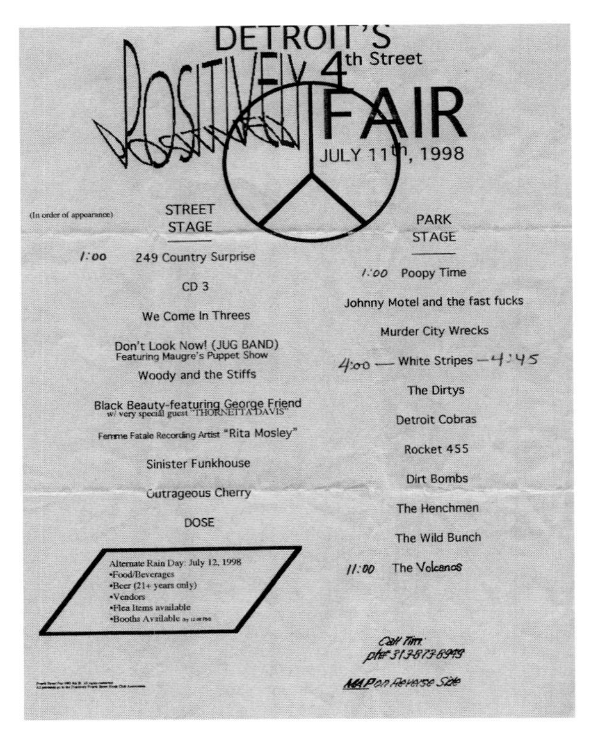

Above left: 4th Street flyer, 1998. Ground zero for the scene? Above right: June 6, 1998 flyer designed by Jack White at his upholstery shop, Below: The White Stripes early performance at The Magic Stick, showing their early stage set. (Courtesy of Dave Buick)

The White Stripes/Soledad Brothers at The Gold Dollar. February 7, 1998. This was the Stripes' first hometown headlining show.

Rock And Roll Indian (The Wildbunch): "They played 'Sugar Never Tasted So Good' and I was like, 'This is a really catchy song'. They played songs like 'Let's Shake Hands' and stuff. Jack scowled at Meg the entire show. I thought they were a Gories rip-off..."

Joebot: "He'd yell at her, but you could never tell if it was part of the shtick... or if he was yelling at her."

Rock And Roll Indian: "...and they were married. I was like, 'They're married? And they're in a band? No way in hell is this going to work'. Meg's sister Heather worked at The Gold Dollar, so I figured it was nepotism that they were even playing the show. I didn't think they were even worthy of being up there."

Joebot: "You're going to be so happy when this book comes out."

Carrie Smith (The Von Bondies): "We all thought Meg was blind cos she kept looking up at the light. She looked like Stevie Wonder, waving her arms around on the drums."

Chris Handyside: "The first time I saw Jack White he was draping that red stuff over the little table he used to put the speaker on. I was like, 'What the fuck is he doing and what is going on with his hair?' I liked them a lot, but only because I couldn't quite puzzle out what they were trying to do. He was then, as he is now, a really intense performer. Meg was unsure. Rudimentary. She was a Detroit drummer, playing first and asking questions later. Or asking questions during. I never thought of her as a bad drummer. She didn't strike me as any better or worse than any other first time drummer I've seen."

Dave: "Even the first time, when there was nobody there and it was totally low budget, the visual concept stood out. After three shows I was a huge fan and knew all their songs."

Dion Fischer (Godzuki): "They had a certain musicality that wasn't being emphasised in the city at the time. Other bands could be fucking awesome live, but weren't as concerned with songs. For a while, I'd stopped going to Rocket and Cobras shows, so I was happy to see a song band I liked. And the guy sounded funny, a bit glam-rock."

Ben: "I got Neil to make me a copy of the tape of that first show and listened to it forever. I would sing 'Screwdriver' and 'Jimmy The Exploder' over and over. By the time the first record

ITALY RECORDS

"I'm David Dunbar Buick... some relation to the car. I'm ex-The Go, ex-Belle Isle, currently in The Wolfman Band, and a couple of other goofy things. I'm the head of Italy Records, and co-owner of Young Soul Rebels Records And Tapes[i], a record store in Detroit. I grew up about 20 miles north of here, in the suburbs. But I used to come down to Detroit all through high school, watching Laughing Hyenas and The Gories and stuff like that. It's a nice town; the stop signs are all shaped like traffic lights.

"Bobby [Harlow, The Go singer] talked me into playing the bass for his band, and I'm glad he did. Originally, I didn't want to be in a band. I just wanted to put out records. But I had good shoes, a cool hairdo and a good jean-jacket and Bobby thought I'd fit the bill. Tons of things have made me want to play rock'n'roll: Ramones, The Who, The Clash, Devo... everything. XTC, even.

"Italy Records started in 1997, and I decided to put out records when I saw The Dirtys play up in Jim Diamond's studio. There was talk of a record coming out on Crypt and I thought it was a shame that such a good Detroit area band were gonna come out and people probably wouldn't realise they were from the Detroit area. So I asked them if I could put out their single before the Crypt record came out, and they said yeah, and that was going to be the first release on Italy. They ended up taking their time and Rocket 455 was my first release. And then I just started putting out other things. I'd drive around and pedal the singles at local stores. We had some distribution. It's not an exclusively Detroit area label. I've put out several non-Detroit bands as well—Whirlwind Heat are from Grand Rapids, The Fells are from Arizona, and The Greenhornes are from Cincinnati. Italy Records has kinda stopped now[ii]—although some records are still available from the website.

"My flatmate Dion [Fischer, ex-The Go, Godzuki] also used to put records out, on Go Sonic—and so we started the Young Soul Rebels record label together. We're putting out the third Slumber Party[iii] full-length on vinyl, and this old Seventies Detroit punk band called The Denizens. And we did a Transistors single."

i Named after *Searching For The Young Soul Rebels*, the debut album from inspirational early Eighties UK group Dexys Midnight Runners.
ii The full catalogue runs as follows: Rocket 455, The Dirtys, two White Stripes singles, The Hentchmen with Jack White (single + full-length), The Fells, The Soledad Brothers, two Clone Defects singles, The Greenhornes, Whirlwind Heat.
iii Excellent melancholy all-female Detroit band led by Aliccia Berg Bollig: their three Kill Rock Stars albums gently straddle the line between The Velvet Underground, the somnambulist pop of NYC's Galaxie 500 and the sheer fizz and sparkle of Eighties Scots band, Shop Assistants.

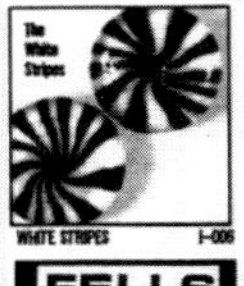

WHITE STRIPES I-006

CLONE DEFECTS I-010

GREEN HORNES I-009

HENTCHMEN w/ JACK WHITE I-008

THE FELLS w/ J. HENTCHMEN I-005

SOLEDAD BROS. w/ JACK WHITE I-007

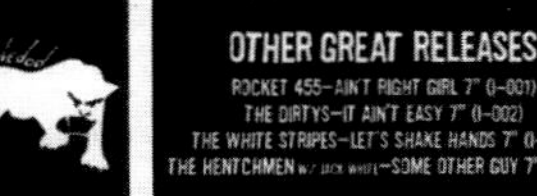

EVERYTHING $4 PPD. (US) • $6 PPD. (NON-US)
EXCEPT HENTCHMEN 9 SONG MINI LP $7 PPD. (US) • $10 PPD. (NON-US)
MAKE CHECKS PAYABLE TO DAVE BUICK
DISTRIBUTED BY REVOLVER, GETHIP & SUBTERANNEAN

came out, I was tired of the songs because I'd been listening to them for two years. Jack had a video of the first show, and one time we were sitting round watching it. Someone said Meg plays drums like a little kid and Jack was like, 'Thank you. I've been waiting for someone to say that the whole time'."

The next night The White Stripes got the chance to divide more of Detroit's rock cognoscenti.

Johnny Hentch: "I saw Jack walking down the street and he said, 'Hey! You're in The Hentchmen'. He was like, 'We're in a band and we'd like to start playing out and I'll play with you guys one of these days'. And he hadn't played yet. He gave me a card for his upholstering company with his number on. A couple of months later we had a gig coming up and we needed an opening band. It's always fun to try a new band out, so I pulled that card out and gave him a call. To this day, if a kid comes up on the street and says his band wants an up, I'll give him a chance. That was the kind of thing. They played that show with us and, to me, it was their first show, but technically it was their second gig [or third—Ed]. I really liked the T-Rex quality to it. They had a couple of show tunes. It wasn't mind-blowing but it was good. Meg was terrible, but in a good way. We weren't offended by it, but she was [hums out-of-time drumming]. It fit, though. He was helping her keep time and that was part of the charm even back then. Even though at first you thought maybe he should get a good drummer! The crowd was split. A lot of people thought it was crap. Afterwards, we threw a party and Jack came by with his Chihuahua. They started doing a lot of shows with us after that—at least 10 or a dozen in the next six months."

Dion: "The first time I saw The White Stripes was with The Hentchmen on the Saturday. I'd seen Jack play with Two Star Tabernacle and I thought he was a really good guitar player and he had a great singing voice. He had a really dumb haircut—kind of New Wave—but nobody else was sounding like that, so I started going to see them. Meg was bad. Now she's like John Bonham."

Tom Potter (Bantam Rooster): "It was charming as fuck, that's how you'd describe Meg's drumming at that point."

For the first year or so, The White Stripes would play first on the bill (out of three) and there'd be hardly anyone there. Jack was also still playing with Two Star Tabernacle—the two bands sometimes shared bills—and would guest with The Hentchmen on occasion.

Marcie: "The first time I saw Jack play, he was a guest in a Hentchmen show. He had this amazingly high-pitched voice, almost falsetto, and was playing this giant hollowbody guitar. Me and Jason [Stollsteimer, The Von Bondies singer] were like, 'This is insane, but it's cool'. He didn't really fit in. He had this whole different aura. I saw The White Stripes after that. I liked the raw guitars, and I was impressed with Meg. I thought it was cool that she was like, 'OK, I'm going to play really simple drumbeats and I'm going to be proud about it'. It was really punk rock."

Eddie Baranek (The Sights): "Ben Blackwell and I had been friends for about a year before The White Stripes came along. He came up one day and said, 'My aunt and uncle are in a band'. I think they were playing a festival in Pontiac. I was like, 'What do you mean your aunt and uncle, where's the rest of the band?' And he was like, 'No, that's it'. That would have been late '97, right around the time my band was starting, and it struck me as funny that it was just two people. When you're 14, like I was, your band is supposed to be two guitars, bass and drums—I thought us being a three-piece was being pretty minimal, but fuck!"

Ben: "I told Eddie he had to go buy the Italy single because he already had the one that Jack played on with The Hentchmen ('Some Other Guy', 1997). His band were freaking out how good it was, cos they were totally into the British Invasion stuff. They were like, 'You heard this?!' I was like, 'Yeah, that's my uncle'. They were like, 'Bullshit!' They were more impressed he was on The Hentchmen single than that he was in The White Stripes, because The Hentchmen's sound is easier to get when you're a teenager, singing about girls and parties and cars which every town needs."

During the first year, almost every single poster and newspaper ad misprinted the band's name: White Stripe, or White Strike, or White Strikes. One time, when they opened for Two Star Tabernacle in front of 10 people at Frankie's in Toledo, they were billed as The White Lines. Not as bad as the time they played The Magic Bag under the name The Light Strikes.

Italy Records founder Dave Buick

At the end of 1997, Dave Buick asked Jack White if he fancied recording for his fledgling Italy seven-inch label. Buick's motivation for asking Jack was simple: The White Stripes didn't have anything out. Jack's response was, "I can't afford it". He didn't understand that Dave was offering to pay for it.

Ben: "I got involved with Italy through The White Stripes. Jack had finished the artwork for the first single and we drove to Dave's to drop it off—the big thing about that day was I'd just gotten into collecting records, mainly Sub Pop stuff, and as we were leaving Dave's house, Jack asked if he had any. Dave pulled out this drawer in an old cabinet and it was full of all these records I'd only ever read about, or seen on the Sub Pop poster. It was as close as I'll ever get to a treasure find... I got the Soundgarden single, Big Chief, an autographed Smashing Pumpkins record, Reverend Horton Heat. There were probably 15 singles, and Dave charged me 20 bucks. The Smashing Pumpkins single alone is worth at least three times that.

"I so wanted to fold sleeves for Italy Records. It was like my perfect job as a teenager with nothing to do. It took two years to get round to it, essentially round the time he repressed The White Stripes singles in 2001—I called distributors and took orders for him. It never went beyond that. I got a key to Dave's house. That was probably the best part of it all—I could go over, watch some porn, maybe fold a few singles while I was waiting for him. Dave was very casual in his approach to putting out records: he'd hear about a band through friends, check them out and if he liked them, offer to release a single. He did a Hentchmen single [the one with Jack singing on] and they told him about The Fells[iii]—and he ended up putting their single out, too. He usually only released records by bands who'd played in Detroit—whether they were local or out-of-town, like The Clone Defects[iv] and The Soledad Brothers."

The first White Stripes single—'Let's Shake Hands' b/w 'Look Me Over Closely' (Italy 003)—came out in April 1998 (not late 1997 as reported elsewhere). Recorded in Jack White's living room by Jeff Meier on his portable recording studio, it bears all the hallmarks of The White Stripes' later work—distorted guitar, rudimentary drums, screams into silence, the odd blister of a bluesy guitar solo and a killer sense of timing. It's gnarly and abrasive. It shreds. Meg's minimal drumbeat provides a perfect counterpart to Jack's controlled, compelling guitar lines and words.

The B-side is even finer: a chilling cover of the Terry Gillkyson/Mitch Miller song, originally recorded by torch singer Marlene Dietrich in 1953, guitar all spooked menace and staccato thrust, the percussion kept to a sparse smattering of cymbal and bass drum. Again, Jack evinces a great sense of the theatrical in his spacing out of the music: the version almost verges on camp but somehow keeps it together. It's a smart song to cover: subtly swaggering yet vulnerable—almost at direct odds with the Rocket 455 consensus ruling the roost in Detroit '97.

Ben: "I was surprised they were going to record 'Let's Shake Hands' as their debut—even though I still reckon Jack's guitar solo to be up there with 'Whole Lotta Love'. Back then I

iii Another great noisy Estrus band.

iv Detroit's answer to The New York Dolls—trashy, jerky and volatile. Their 2003 album, *Shapes Of Venus* (In The Red) is crucial.

THE BLUES

Jack White's musical epiphany came at 18 when he heard 'Grinning In Your Face' by Son House, the Delta blues pioneer. He became obsessed with both the music and lives of such early 20th Century performers as Leadbelly[i], Robert Johnson[ii] and Charley Patton[iii], voices from a distant past that spoke with far more clarity to him than any contemporary sounds.

"At that point I was like, 'What have I been doing?'" the singer told *The Guardian*'s Keith Cameron in 2003. "'Why have I not been paying attention to this music'? It was that honesty, bare bones, to the minimum, truth. The more I thought about it, it was the pinnacle of songwriting. Easily accessible to people because of the repeating lines you could sing along, very easy to play for the performer. It's extremely simple but extremely emotional at the same time. You could go to see a glam rock band and say this is really exciting, but that's far from honesty. If a musician calls himself a musician and listens to Charley Patton and doesn't hear anything at all, I don't think they should call themselves musicians, because they're obviously just looking for fun and kicks and a good time out of it."

"When I got out of high school," he revealed to *The Onion*. "I went to college for one semester, and I was so upset that those kids acted exactly the same way they did in school. I thought you wouldn't have to deal with that crap anymore, peer pressure and people judging everyone. My way to deal with it was to try to relate to older people and get away from that. Their turning me on to the blues made me so happy. I felt like I'd left so much behind after getting involved with that."

Until that point, Jack had only "dabbled" (his words) in more recent bluesy music like Howlin' Wolf, Cream and Led Zeppelin. Son House made him realise he'd been missing something...

"[The blues are] so truthful, it can't be glamorised," he went on to tell *The Onion*. "I'm very sceptical of musicians who say they love music and don't love the blues. It's like someone saying they don't like The Beatles. It makes you think they're in it for the wrong ideas."

This last quote reminds me of an impassioned late night conversation I had with Meg White in The Blind Pig, Ann Arbor, where she was trying to explain why she felt betrayed by the attitude of Olympia's bluesy Riot Grrrl band, The Gossip—a former White Stripes tour support. "They were trying to tell me that they'd never liked AC/DC or Led Zeppelin," she exclaimed, visibly hurt. "That they'd never really listened to them. How can *anyone* not like those bands? They're such an important part of my life."

Ben Blackwell: "From hearing The White Stripes covers you discover some great music—like 'Small Faces' by Public Nuisance, 'Jack The Ripper' by Screaming Lord Sutch, 'Boll Weevil' by Leadbelly, 'I'm Bored' by Iggy Pop and 'Looking At You' by the MC5. The first time I heard them do the Burt Bacharach song 'Little Red Book', I thought they must have written it."

There are still plenty of other styles of music that Jack loves. His favourite rock'n'roll record is Iggy Pop's *Fun House*, his favourite Coasters song is 'Riot In Cell Block #9', and his favourite Led Zeppelin album is the first. His ex-wife favours the second. He's also on record as loving Johnny Cash and Cole Porter. But it all comes back to the blues...

"The blues is holy, a perfect creation," he told Lennart Persson of *Sonic* magazine. "It is everything that music should be. It contains so much that I almost don't dare to mess with it. But I must. I can lie in bed in the middle of the night and feel an ice-cold wind flowing through my body, which makes me start to shake uncontrollably. Then I have to get up and hear Charley Patton or Robert Johnson. Everyone should regard the American South as holy land. Everything that is worth anything comes from there. If I was only playing music for myself, then I would be playing the blues."

i Legendary American folk singer who learnt his craft in the early 1900s, through the oral tradition of songs being handed down—his style actually predates the blues. A troubled adult life included several prison sentences for assault and stabbing: some of which he "sang his way" out of.

ii The tormented, almost mythical, Mississippi singer who famously exchanged his soul with the Devil (so the story runs), whom he met at a plantation crossroads at midnight, in exchange for the ability to sing the blues. Generally acknowledged as the Greatest Delta Blues Singer Ever, he died young, poisoned by a jealous girlfriend at the age of 27.

iii Major influence on Son House and Howlin' Wolf, Patton—AKA, The Masked Marvel—beat his guitar for percussion, and stamped his feet to create counter-rhythms. He possessed the heart of a bluesman, which he mixed with vaudeville flash, several decades before Hendrix. His metal Paramount masters—some 60 tracks—were sold off as scrap after his death in 1934, some to line chicken coops.

Above: Robert Johnson. (Deltahaze Corporation/Redferns)

thought they had far superior songs—'Jimmy The Exploder' and 'Screwdriver'. Jack told me they were saving them for an album. I just figured you should be putting out your best song as your debut single, but as ever he was thinking ahead."

The red and white Xeroxed cover is a photo of the couple holding a giant White Stripe sweet, taken by Heather White: on the back sleeve, The White Stripes contact address is reproduced, alongside that of Jeff Meier and Italy Records. The credited publisher is Peppermint Music. Inside the sleeve, Jack and Dave Buick inserted a George Washington quote explaining the meaning of the American flag: "We take the stars from the blue union from heaven, the red from our mother country, separating it by white stripes, thus showing we have separated from her, and the white stripes shall go down to posterity representing liberty." The initial printing of 1,000 copies was pressed on red vinyl (Jack did not ask for red and white, as reported elsewhere).

Dan Miller: "Once, a journalist asked Johnny Cash if he felt it was an honour that a certain artist was so obviously influenced by him. The country star replied, 'I wish he would develop his own style, because that's just mimicry'. And that's what kills a lot of music scenes. That's what happened with rockabilly and the lounge acts. It becomes an exercise in branding and that's what happened with Detroit garage rock as well. There's a small scene of people who think that's cool—other people from other countries think it's a unique Detroit thing. But do The Stooges feel the same way about Detroit bands that Johnny Cash thought about his imitator, I wonder? People labelling The White Stripes as garage rock were wrong. I was so happy when Jack said the flipside of 'Let's Shake Hands' was 'Look Me Over Closely'. It wasn't your standard macho garage crap about some girl behaving badly. It was honest and emotional. *Maximum Rock And Roll* [the US hardcore punk bible] said it sounded like Edith Piaf. I'm sure Jack took it as a compliment. When things are a little confusing that's good—that's the spirit of rock music. Robbie Robertson may once have said if there's not a threatening aspect to a band it's not rock'n'roll."

Ben: "It's definitely about that feeling of fear or danger."

Dan: "Or at least ambiguity and uneasiness. That's what keeps rock'n'roll from dying. Jack was genuinely surprised that someone would pay to put out his music. It really touched him, because when you get to that point, it shows that your music is connecting in some way."

The second pressing of 2,000 copies in mid-2001, just before the release of *White Blood Cells*, contains a false 10-second start that stops just as Jack reaches the first "Oh" of the opening line. "Jim Diamond assured us that the DAT was exactly the same," Dave Buick explains, "so we just shipped it off and didn't check it cos we were pressed for time. It almost works, if only it stopped just before the vocal."

Unsurprisingly, the single failed to make any impression commercially—although it went down well enough among the small coterie of Detroit musicians.

Above: Jack White 1998
(Ko Shih)

Dave: "It got reviewed in *Maximum Rock And Roll*, *Flipside*, and maybe *Thrasher* skate magazine wrote about it, but we didn't do any press on it, really—just local papers. I'd imagine Chris Handyside wrote about it. He'd started working at *Detroit Metro Times* right around that time."

Dave was correct. "The crunched-out, Cramps-worthy riffage," wrote Chris, "that the song is built upon is segmented by Jack White's plaintive, natural-as-breathing falsetto and the crashing waves of Meg White's cymbal, snare and bass drum punctuating the tender ruckus. In stark contrast, 'Look Me Over Closely' finds the Whites bending show tune convention to their own specifications. Jack sings as though possessed by an aging Hollywood diva. It's eerie and fascinating in a Sunset Boulevard kinda way! The tale of cautious nuptials takes an air of menace as built around The White Stripes' skeletal piano, guitar and drums framework before the requisite 'big finish'."

Ben: "The first time that single went on sale it sold three copies. And one of those sold because the guy who bought it thought that Terry Gilkyson (the writer of 'Look Me Over Closely') was in Black Sabbath. There was a local, photocopied fanzine called *Black And White* that did an interview with Jack at the time—possibly the first Stripes interview. He was asked for his best record-find ever, so he told the story of finding the first Stooges record in the garbage. I remember the *Thrasher* review, because my friend was a skater, and we were like, 'Whoa! The White Stripes are in here!' It was one of those occasions when I thought they'd never get any bigger than that... [Mid-West magazine] *Noises From The Garage* said it sounded like The Oblivians."

Below: Charley Patton
(Rue des Archives/Lebrecht Music)

The Oblivians were a gritty Nineties garage punk band from Memphis. In a strange twist, Jack White later bought his trademark cherry red and white Airline guitar from Oblivians guitarist Jack Yarber. The instrument was originally made for the Montgomery Ward mail order catalogue in the mid-Sixties, but Yarber purchased it second-hand from a Missouri music store in 1994 for $200. Five years later, in April 1999, The White Stripes played support to Yarber's new

The Detroit News

PAGE 3F THURSDAY, JUL

Italy Records is kicking up the lo-fi dirt

• **DETROIT**

I've never seen myself dance, but judging from the wounded state my body was in after the Fourth Street Fair on Saturday, it must resemble some kind of hypnotic seizure.

This was my first visit to the annual street fair, on Fourth near the New Center area, and on top of being one big porch party, it was also a veritable who's who of local rock 'n' roll.

BEAT GIRL

WENDY CASE

I showed up just in time to see an astounding set by **Rocket 455,** followed by **Outrageous Cherry, The Detroit Cobras, The Hentchmen** and **The Wildbunch** (I had to split before **The Volcanoes'** closing set).

My dancing partner for much of this rock 'n' roll hoochie coo was a greasy guy in a black T-shirt, sporting big, bug-eyed Andy Warhol shades. This would be Italy Records chief **Dave Buick.** We kicked so much dirt on each other that we looked like a couple of worm farmers.

Buick is fast becoming Detroit's lo-fi love connection. Debuting with Rocket 455's "Ain't Right Girl" last Halloween, the prolific vinyl purveyor has followed with 45s from **The White Stripes,** The Hentchmen (featuring Jack White) and Port Huron's **The Dirtys.**

"I started the label because I wanted to put out a single but I can't play any instruments," Buick says.

Italy's summer plans include releases by **The Fells** and Toledo's **The Soledad Brothers,** along with follow-up singles by The White Stripes and The Hentchmen. The label's catalogue is being distributed by Revolver and Subterranean and is available at finer indie record stores near you.

band, The Compulsive Gamblers, at The Magic Stick. After the show, Jack asked Yarber if he wanted to sell it. "I had no problem with that," Yarber told Andria Lisle in *Mojo*, "because I'd already seen this white Airline with three pick-ups and a big whammy bar which was a step up."

In January 2001, on Yarber's recommendation, The White Stripes recorded their third album, *White Blood Cells*, in Easley/McCain's Memphis studio—with the Airline. "I picked it up and strummed it," recalled Yarber, "saying, 'I never should've sold this thing'. Jack didn't say anything."

A couple of local stores stocked the single, and some distributors. More importantly, it was listed in the Estrus catalogue (from out of Bellingham, WA) as "the best thing in Detroit since The Gories?"—the question mark an attempt to downgrade the hyperbole. The White Stripes camp was thrilled at the comparison, nonetheless.

Ben: "When Mudhoney came to town, Dave took them some copies of the single, and their guitarist Steve Turner remarked, 'I hear these guys are better than The Gories'. We were totally excited. Stuff like that matters when you're just starting out."

The second single followed in November '98, and was also recorded at Jack's house—this time by Jack himself. Jim Diamond mixed it at Ghetto Recorders. 'Lafayette Blues' b/w 'Sugar Never Tasted So Good' was Italy Records 006. Jack's ability to rework his own muse was already becoming apparent: 'Lafayette Blues' (the lyrics come from a list of all the French street names in Detroit) boasts an opening riff strangely reminiscent of his nephew's beloved 'Jimmy The Exploder' (later to show up as the opening track on the band's debut album), and a rockabilly middle-eight. It's sullen, moody and relies on powerchords a little too much: Jack seems uncertain with his muffled vocals. Far superior is the laidback acoustic ballad on the B-side with its tambourine and drumming that sounds like it was recorded on a cardboard box (and possibly was: the song was recorded to one track with one microphone). Even more than the Dietrich cover, it plainly stated Jack White's intentions to put a distance between his band and the Detroit garage scene. You can discernibly taste the influence of the blues.

On the repressed version, the red and white sleeve (two spiral-patterned White Stripe sweets) opens out into a series of pictures of what could be construed as a child's racing card game: all road symbols and headings in French and English. There's also a strip of paper listing all the French street names in Detroit. The original sleeve features pictures of a young Jack and a young Meg.

Johnny Walker (Soledad Brothers): "You can't really argue with 'Lafayette Blues'. It's so simple, six tracks of beating on a cardboard box. What you going to add to that to make it sound better? That song is so fucking perfect—even the packaging, the franc notes [from WWII], based on who Jack was giving the record to. For the family, five Franc notes, for people thanked on the record, 10 Franc... and he had that insert with a quote from the Marquis de Chastellux about the nature of American music. There was also a [photocopied] picture of George Washington shaking the [18th Century philosopher and soldier] Marquis de Lafayette's hand, which tied the two singles together—a nice touch."

Especially as the first single was called 'Let's Shake Hands'...

Ben: "Lafayette ended up giving Washington the key to the Bastille—and the first White Stripes show was on Bastille Day, which was another weird coincidence."

"Whereas most bands would be content to just get the lead out and have items in their bins," wrote Chris Handyside, "The White Stripes have managed to craft a musical and visual ear-and-head-turner. The first side travels scorched-blues terrain and launches into a rave-up capped by Jack White ticking off a dozen or so names of Detroit streets—civic pride rides again! The second side reclaims from Robert Johnson the acoustic blues that Led Zeppelin swiped it from." (In the same column, Handyside reviewed the seven-inch collaboration between Two Star Tabernacle and Andre Williams, the latter "sounding every bit the man your mother warned you about being sweet-talked by—but creepier".)

The cover was designed by Patti, wife and business partner of Andy from another local label, Flying Bomb—she did it in exchange for free copies of the single for the Flying Bomb catalogue. The sleeves actually arrived after the October 1998 gig that The White Stripes had planned to sell the single at. So Jack and Dave spent the final couple of days before the show hand-painting 15 sleeves (the maximum they expected to sell): Jack drew seven, and Dave drew seven, and they

Above: Poster for 'Lafayette Blues' record release party (set list at the beginning of this chapter)

Left: Wendy Case's column for The Detroit News, July 16th 1998

collaborated on one. These, they sold for $6 at the show—and made a clear $90 on the merchandise that night.

The initial 1,000 copies pressing was supposed to be on white vinyl (to complement the first single's red) but the colour got mixed up with red after the pressing plant omitted to clean the vats beforehand—hence the colour changed as the pressing continued, with early copies being totally pink and later ones varying from a pink and white swirl to just white with the faintest tinge of colour. Fifteen were put inside the hand-painted sleeves: 40 came with the French money. There were another 1,000 copies of the single repressed the same time as 'Let's Shake Hands'.

Ben: "I remember thinking at the time that six bucks was a hell of a lot of money to charge for a single but now, of course... Tommy Potter sold his original copy up on e-Bay in March '03 for $750, but since then Eric Silvenis sold his copy for $2,600."

The same week as their second single, The White Stripes recorded 'Candy Cane Children', with its spaghetti western guitar, for Flying Bomb's excellent 1998 Christmas sampler EP, 'Surprise Package Volume 2'. Jeff Meier introduced Andy to Jack White at an early White Stripes show: "He was just a quiet kid," Andy recalls.

Flying Bomb started off releasing records by Bantam Rooster and Chinese Millionaires in late 1995, because they couldn't find anyone else who would. They also released a couple of the early Wildbunch seven-inches, The Dirtbombs and The Blowtops (fuzzy swamp rock). "There were no labels in Detroit to speak of back then," Andy says. "Just us and Italy Records." Flying Bomb pressed up 500 copies of the EP, and threw them on e-Bay when The White Stripes got big.

I Felt Just Like A Baby

Left: Jack jumps at Paycheck's, 3/99 as part of the Blowout (Doug Coombe)

PLAYING OUT

Wendy Case (The Paybacks): "As I saw The White Stripes more and more, I noticed Jack and Meg would communicate with each other in a really intimate way. Jack would make little counting gestures. I was very intrigued by these little signals. Their chemistry together is very special. Nowadays, it's almost impossible to find anything in music that doesn't reek of money. What The White Stripes do is appallingly honest, and it's an anomaly in a world where TV presenters say you have to have perfect tits and a Christina Aguilera arse. Jack and Meg are both extremely beautiful people, and I'm sure that made their entrée into that terrifying machine a lot easier, but it was their honesty that knocked everybody on their ass."

Ben Blackwell: "I saw every White Stripes show from March '98 through June 2000, roughly around 60 in total. They did a bunch of shows in Detroit: The Magic Stick, The Gold Dollar, The Magic Bag... the Old Miami, Paycheck's and the Wayne State Student Union. They played pretty much everywhere you could. They played at The Gold Dollar on June 6, 1998 and they were the middle band. Something about that night put them light years ahead of how they'd been anytime before. Brian Muldoon had a great line that night: 'Jack, that wasn't rock music, that was fucking *art.*' No one even cared about the main band [Dura Delinquent]."

Greg Baise: "The most brilliant day of Detroit rock'n'roll music ever happened in the summer of '98, at the 4th Street Fair. Almost all the great bands played that day. The White Stripes played at two pm, with The Hentchmen, Outrageous Cherry, The Wildbunch, Rocket 455, and it was also the last time The Detroit Cobras played in their original line-up. I went there with this tape recorder my girlfriend had got me. I was going to tape two songs by each band because none of them had a full-length out yet. It would've been the live equivalent of *Sympathetic Sounds Of Detroit*, a year early. The White Stripes' 'The Big Three Killed My Baby' kicked me on my ass.

Dan Miller: "They played 'Sugar Never Tasted So Good'... *'I felt just like a baby until I held a baby'*.... and you could feel the hairs on the back of everyone's necks stand up, unless they'd shaved them. Especially as later that night it turned into a Detroit drunk garage fest... The White Stripes stood out because of the poetic sadness in their songs—but they also rocked hard too. The first time I heard them do 'The Big Three...' it made so much more sense with Meg's stripped-down drumming and Jack's one guitar. When we rehearsed it with Two Star Tabernacle, Damien [Lang] did more regular drumming—the two of them brought the song's character out more."

Johnny Walker (Soledad Brothers): "It was the 4th of July '98 when Jack came down to play drums with us in Toledo—and also played another song as a two-piece with me. He had an

HENTCH-FORTH

How did you come to make that record with Jack?

Johnny Hentch: "We were bowling one night and Dave Buick wanted to do a Hentchmen single. Jack was there, so we were like, 'Let's do a single with Jack'. It was Jack's idea to do British Invasion tunes. Jack said 'Let's do The Beatles cover, 'Some Other Guy''. I suggested 'Psycho Daisies', The Yardbirds tune. We went into his living room. Jeff Meier from Rocket 455 engineered it on an eight-track. He did a good job. Then Dave wanted to do a Hentchmen mini-LP for our first European tour. Jack plays bass on half of it, and some back-up vocals on a song, and he plays some tambourine. It was a real quickie, a day or two. I don't think it sounds as good as the single. We recorded it in a different room, but at the time we thought it was cool."

How would you describe Jack as a person?

"Dedicated, determined. He quit his job before anything happened, just so he could focus on music. He would do whatever anyone asked him to do. We asked him to be on our record and he was over, every rehearsal, with his bass. He's motivated. He's made really smart decisions along the line. I give him a lot of the credit."

What about Meg?

"She's very quiet. A sweetheart, but I don't know her at all. I spent a lot of time with her over the years... They're different kinds of people. So when they were going to get divorced it didn't surprise me. We double-dated a lot and she was very quiet. It seemed like they didn't really... So they divorced and they had a gig and they cancelled it, and then Meg said she wanted to do the last gig anyway. That's when it started taking off, and then I guess she was along for the ride at that point."

Did it surprise you that Jack let her stay in the band?

"It surprised me more that she wanted to stay in the band. At the time I thought Jack would have a hard time getting over her if she was in the band, but they got through it remarkably. It's very unusual."

So Jack really does have 10 brothers and sisters?

"Yeah. He is the seventh son."

Did you ever meet any of the others?

"Leo loaned him the bass he uses on that record. One of his other brothers did a monologue at one of the shows, but I don't think I met him."

His other brothers are in a band, right?

"I don't know. A couple of them are musicians. They're all somehow musically inclined, the dad too."

American flag draped over his drum kit and halfway through he tied it round himself as a cape. Dan Kroha [The Gories] showed up and was like, 'What the fuck?' I was slightly embarrassed about that—and I don't often get embarrassed."

Eddie Baranek (The Sights): "I can remember being 16, 17 at The Gold Dollar... you had to sneak in cos Neil was strict on the under-21 shit. He'd let you in if you played, but you had to shotgun beers in the girls' bathrooms. Jack had the balls to do a new instrumental with an amplified acoustic guitar. I don't think I ever heard it again. He'd wear a white T-shirt, red pants and Meg usually wore the same: simple stage set-up, Meg on drums, Jack playing the guitar through one amp. Then he would put another amp on a table with a sheet draped over it so you couldn't see what was under there... I want to say it was a Silvertone, but I'm cheating because I know Ben."

Dave Buick (to Brian McCollum): "I remember Jack getting so mad at an early show at The Magic Stick, supporting The Hentchmen, and storming off because the light wasn't the right colour or something. Anyone accusing him of getting a big head through fame is wrong. He's always had a big head."

Matt Smith: "The first time I saw The White Stripes, they didn't exactly knock me out. But then I saw them again, at the end of 1998, at The Gold Dollar, and Jack had really gotten it together. He had this Jeff Beck Group guitar tone, and the two-piece was really making a lot of noise. That was the first show I saw where they had that energy."

Mick Collins: "Jack wanted to bring me his first single or something. I was sitting round watching noon TV, and about four o'clock Jack and Meg turn up. Jack's like, 'We just drove from Birwood all the way here' and I'm like, 'You did what?' It's a 45-minute drive down a street that's cut with freeways and industrial estates—he drove it all the way from downtown to where I lived three miles from the border. I was laughing. Meg was pissed. She wanted to hit Jack in the eye. Then I recall getting a call either from him or The Magic Stick, wanting The White Stripes to open for The Dirtbombs—it was us, Red Aunts[i], Doll Rods..."

Ben: "No, it wasn't. The first time it was Paper Tiger, The Hamicks, The White Stripes and The Dirtbombs: the second time was The White Stripes, The Dirtbombs and ? And The Mysterians. It always comes back to '96 Tears'[ii]."

Mick: "When The White Stripes went on, it was still daylight. I'd had a rough day, so I'd started drinking as soon as I got inside. Right when I was starting to feel pretty good they did 'Why Can't You Be Nicer To Be Me'. It soon became my favourite White Stripes song. Now it's 'Fell In Love With A Girl', like everyone else on the planet. Second time I saw them, I was like, 'Oh, another duo'. They were nothing out the ordinary, just Jack and Meg, this dude who drove all the way along Birwood to be at my house. Then I got the first single—Larry at In The Red had one. He asked me what I thought. I said I thought they were OK. He wasn't so impressed."

Ben: "The White Stripes really wanted to be on In The Red[iii]."

i Female hardcore quartet from LA specialising in sharp abrasive two-minute pop songs: *Saltbox* (Epitaph, 1996) comes recommended.

ii A reference to the sunglasses wearing, Farfisa organ playing, Sixties garage rock band's most famous song.

PLAYING AWAY FROM HOME

Jack plays bass on *Hentch-Forth*, the 1998 nine-track 45rpm Italy Hentchmen mini-album[iv]. He'd already helped out on their 'Some Other Guy' Italy seven-inch, released at the same time as

'Let's Shake Hands'—and would later show up on 1999's 'Ham And Oil' Gas seven-inch. Jack's guest appearances weren't anything out of the ordinary. In Detroit, it was a given that musicians contributed to each other's bands when required. Jack had already tried to sell Andre Williams a song: now he started writing songs for his friends. Mostly, these went unused and would later show up on White Stripes albums ('Hypnotize' from *Elephant*, for example, was originally intended for The Hentchmen)[v].

On the back cover photograph to *Hentch-Forth*, a moody White is standing off to one side of the three Hentchmen, holding a cigarette. Seems like he wanted to emphasise the difference between himself and his friends, at least musically. The record itself is good time garage rock—great to turn up loud and party to when the neighbours are out screwing your brother, with a couple of killer old time Chuck Berry-style solos (particularly on 'Me And My Monotone'), and some neat keyboard shimmies. The mood is energetic and unrelenting: thrash one song out and move on as fast as you can to the next. Turn the amps up to full, and throw in a few turbo-charged solos. Trash those drums—they ain't no friends of yours!

Jack also appears on the drawn-out 'Johnny's Death Letter', the B-side of the debut Soledad Brothers single, 'Sugar & Spice' (Italy, 1998), recorded on the front porch of his house playing snow shovel: a beautifully languid blues, all easy grace and space. The scoop itself adds a washboard-style percussive element that is a total delight.

During 1998, Soledad Brothers would come up to Jack's house at the weekend to mess around on his four-track. The rootsy blues recorded their first album in Jack's living room over the course of the year, and Jack appears on the sleeve to *Soledad Brothers*, dressed as Uncle Sam. Meg has also dated their sometime sax-player, Brian Olive (ex-Greenhornes)[vi].

"We'd go up to Jack's from Toledo," recalls Soledad Brothers drummer, Ben Swank, "and hang out and talk about music and play—we were originally just doing demos and then Buick put out that seven-inch. We'd set things up in different places. One time, we did a whole session on the front porch and instead of percussion we'd just stomp. His house had a real natural room separation sound. You can tell from our first record that the more Jack experimented with recording, the better it got. His house was in Mexicantown: it used to be mostly decorated with junk he'd pick up from the big monthly trash day. He liked to garbage collect: there were drums hanging on the wall, sculptures he'd make himself from wood, oversize hammers and lollipops. He had a lot of modern furniture. In the back, there was a big collection of plastic cars that kids ride around in, and lot of junk everywhere, collections of teeth, skeletons..."

Jack has a huge taxidermy collection: among other items listed at his house are a zebra head, two gazelles, an eland, a tiger's head with broken teeth, a kudu and a giant white elk (worked on by Ted Nugent's personal taxidermist). He has also possessed two old jukeboxes, some rusty sculptures made out of bits of car, a battered piano, canaries, a large collection of old and new alarm clocks, chairs and rescued sofas from the county dump, a photograph of Charley Patton's gravestone, white roller-boots, a red umbrella and old arcade games... After The White Stripes toured Australia in 2000, he brought back a stuffed jackrabbit and stuffed partridge through a somewhat lax Customs.

"I always loved his sculptures," remarks Ben Blackwell. "He would only use three colours in each sculpture—different ones each time. He'd saw chairs in half, and toys—for the furniture aspects and the childish aspects. For his planned obsolescence art attack, he sawed a Coup toy car in half, mounted it, and later used it as a flyer for a White Stripes show. These sculptures are pretty big—two by three feet, more like wall hangings. They're pretty involved... as intricate as sawing huge things in half can be. I can think of about five he did. His home was a shambles back then. It felt like a storage space: TV next to amp cases. It was a stop-off point for bands. It was more of a place to keep stuff than to live.

"Everyone has their own strange little peccadilloes," The Dirtbombs drummer continues. "I was with Jack when we saw the goat's head Johnny Walker left there[vii]. It seemed significant, so he took it from there and ran with it. When they played on the David Letterman show, he put his zebra head on top of the peppermint triple tremolo amp. I remember the day before carting around a zebra head in NYC and putting it in storage space in a hotel and the guy just staring... By that stage you pretend everything's cool and you've done it a million times before. That story about everything being red and white in the house—like anything, you take what you hear with

iii Dirtbombs record label, and also home to an array of great, nasty garage-punk artists like Andre Williams, New York's demented lounge act Speedball Baby, Bassholes and the almighty Lord High Fixers. Based in LA.

iv Be warned. The pressing, especially on the A-side, isn't all it could be.

v Ben Blackwell: "He wrote a song for Rocket 455 in '98 or '99 called 'Bone Broke'—it's a typical Rocket 455 rock'n'roll song. They played it live a bunch of times, but they were always slow to get into the studio. As yet, The White Stripes haven't done anything with it."

vi Also plays alongside Johnny Walker in sweaty, Captain Beefheart-influenced, blues band Pearlene.

vii Johnny Walker: "My grandpa was a big game hunter and when I was little he gave me a white goat's head. It was super Satanic-looking. I found it in my dad's attic when I came up here for Christmas so it was in my van—and I left it on Jack's couch just sitting there. He had no idea where it came from. I called up him four days later. He was like, 'Johnny man, someone left a goat's head here'. It's still on his front foyer, but it kind of pales in comparison to the two stuffed lions."

THE GO

John Krautner
"My name's John Krautner. I've been with The Go for five or six years. I started as the guitar player in The Go. Eight or nine line-ups later, I'm the bass player."

Tell us a story from your childhood.

"My kindergarten teacher was an alcoholic who beat everyone in class. Pulled their hair, slapped them. I remember sitting in a circle doing maths problems, and I couldn't do this one problem. She pulled my hair and said, 'what do you mean you can't do it!' I was shaken up. I saw her slap another girl in the face. That was at Parker School in Royal Oak, Michigan. It was a primary school. She was fired. Eventually some kid had the guts to tell their parents the teacher was beating crap out of them."

What made you first want to pick up a guitar?

"My brother. My little brother was playing guitar. He knew all the blues licks. It was always lying around; so I'd pick it up, strum it. Then I went to college, trying to figure out what I wanted to do there, and I couldn't, so I played guitars all day."

Who influenced you?

"I liked Frank Zappa a lot. I was inspired by him as a songwriter, so I tried to apply that to learning chords on the guitar."

What made you want to get up on stage?

"After a while playing in your friends' basement, you've got to do something with it. And it started to sound good. I started to think that maybe we could do something with it. In '98, my brother and I went to Greasefest where we saw Rocket 455 and Bootsey And The Lovemasters. Bootsey got up and said, 'Ladies and gentlemen, we have now reached the adult portion of the show'. For some reason that cracked me up, cos I'd never seen rock'n'roll that way. So I told my friend Bobby [Harlow, The Go singer], and he said 'Let's go to the 4th Street Fair', and there we saw all these bands doing what we wanted to do. That was the moment it started."

When you saw these bands did you have a vision of what you wanted to do with it?

"A real basic vision of change. I still want to change the face of rock'n'roll. But I also think it's fine the way it is."

Dion Fischer
"I sit around in a record store all day and play guitar. I've produced a band or two. I've recently produced *Slumber Party 3* and *Detroit Rock*. I played in The Go for three years, I was in another band called Godzuki, I've done The Wildbunch, The Dirtbombs, The Wolfman Band, The Wails, Princess Dragon Mom, that's about it. Kiss made me want to play guitar."

Tell me a story about Detroit.

"I grew up on a farm in Romeo, 40 miles north of Detroit. When I was five, I found myself attempting to drive a running tractor and I ran myself over. The Wolfman Band were playing with a bunch of other super-scarily bad bands, at a place I don't remember, with cement floors—and I threw one too many beer cups at a bad band and I ended up with several stitches in my head."

Tell me about The Go.

"One time we were on tour and we'd stopped to use a restroom somewhere in southern California and I went to the bathroom and when I came back I didn't have a band anymore, they left me."

Dave Buick: "Me and Marc [Fellis, drums] were stood outside, we were in a bad part of LA and the bathroom said 'Out of order', so we went and filed a missing persons report. They're like, 'How old is he?' and we're like, '28, 29', and they're like, 'How long's he been missing', and we're like, 'Half an hour?'"

Dion: "I actually went to the police and told them that if they saw this ex-hospital bus with rust all over it driving down the freeway to tell them they forgot me."

Dave: "Another time, it was the second show of our first US tour, and we were super excited—we were big rock stars—and our rock star tour bus broke down because it was a piece of junk. Instead of cancelling the show, we actually paid to have the bus towed to the front of the club, and managed to have some ugly groupies have a party for us. And it was rock'n'roll bliss."

a grain of salt. There is a lot of red and white stuff—but the outside of the house is *not* red and white. It's totally purple and white."

Ben laughs. He's not being entirely serious.

Johnny Walker (guitar, Soledad Brothers): "Jack had two little dogs called Jasper and Elroy. Jasper was a Boston terrier, a little guy, and Elroy was a Chihuahua. We were in his living room, Jack was holding Elroy and I was holding Jasper, and we had them right up in each other's faces, barking. Jack recorded it, and we put it at the beginning of one of our songs. Jasper's barks come in right on time on the beat, but that little motherfucker bit me and drew blood. It was the hardest recording I ever did. I guess it served me right.

"When we came up to Jack's, we'd be brainstorming. Sometimes he'd play songs with us, sometimes us with him. One time, we pushed an amp up next to his piano, put a brick on the pedals, a couple of microphones on the strings, and let the piano strings resonate at their natural frequency... it was fucked up, but sounded really good. We used the stairwell a little bit. For 'Little Red Rooster' someone shot a shotgun off in the distance and it came in right on the downbeat. We used a lot of different microphones—bullet mics, harmonica mics. Sometimes we'd shove newspaper behind the speaker to keep the cone in place—that was supposed to be the secret on the first rock'n'roll record of all time, Ike Turner's 'Rocket 88'[viii].

"One time Jack placed microphones on the porch. He crawled underneath the tiles, all dirty and messy... We were like, 'Is this where you played as a kid?' And he was like, 'Yeah, it's my fort'. Then he ran out to the garage and got his snow shovel and started playing it right next to us. It was so loud. All you could hear was that. So he moved 10 feet over and it was still so loud—so he moved way out on the street and started hitting the sidewalk, singing back up. The Mexican guys would be working on their cars with their hoods up, playing Mariachi music. When they figured out what we were doing, they'd turn it off and listen. It's a real cool neighbourhood.

"We weren't aiming at making a record—we were fucking around, like kids do across the country every day. We made it into the Estrus catalogue via Italy, and they put our first two records out[ix]. We had hours of four-track stuff to sift through. We went up to Jim Diamond's to mix it. That took a day. We did five songs with Jim, two in Jack's attic and the rest in Cincinnati during the race riots while I was working in the emergency room patching up kids all day long, pulling plastic bullets out of girls' skulls. It set the tone for that record."

Jack was never a full member of Soledad Brothers or The Hentchmen, though: he had enough on his plate with the Stripes and Two Star Tabernacle... or so one would think. But shortly before the release of the second White Stripes single, he joined another band.

GO BUDDY GO

Ben Blackwell: "No one ever gets this time span right. Two Star Tabernacle broke up in March '99, and Jack's final show as lead guitarist with The Go was in April '99. His first Two Star Tabernacle show was in February '97, and his first show with The Go was in September '98."

At this point, The Go were fast becoming one of the most talked-about Detroit rock bands. Their sound mixed the swagger and sass of the MC5 to the glam stomp of English bands from the Seventies like The Sweet and Slade, with a little mid-American Kim Fowley braggadocio thrown in. Their first gigs were typical Detroit fare. Shambolic and chaotic and no one could give a fuck what the audience thought. Singer Bobby Harlow oozed sex and sleaze unrepentantly. It seemed like everyone who can play guitar in Detroit has been in The Go at some point.

Matt Smith: "I went to see The Wildbunch, and The Go were on the bill. It was a benefit at a Polish social club at Hamtramck—some methadone thing. They totally didn't have their shit together. Bobby was wearing a Mickey Mouse shirt. The minute they went on stage I thought, 'This is the best rock'n'roll band since the Stones'. I remember arguing with Dion. He was like, 'You're crazy, that band can't tune their guitars, they can't write songs', and I'm like, 'No, but when they do, look out man cos this is the real deal'. Marco from Rocket 455 played second guitar for a gig, then I played a couple, and Dion was like, 'You gotta get me in that band'. Instead of getting Dion they asked Jack White instead. And after Jack left they ended up getting Dion.

Left: The Go live at The Gold Dolar. (Doug Coombe)
Below: Soledad Brothers/The White Stripes 1998, early Italy Records press shot. One of many legendary photo booth pix from Royal Oak's Off The Record store. (Courtesy of Dave Buick)

viii That depends on who's talking, of course, but the Jackie Brenston And The Delta Cats cut (Chess, 1951) has all the necessary elements: lyrics about fast cars and women, a beat-heavy bottom section and a repetitive tenor sax.

ix MC5 founder John Sinclair wrote the sleeve notes to their 2000 debut album, after the pair backed the singer in Cleveland.

SOLEDAD BROTHERS

Johnny Walker (guitar)

"When I was about 12, I went to the University Of Toledo Student Union, couldn't get into the show, so I went round the back, shimmied up a drainpipe, found an exhaust fan that was shut off, climbed through it, went through the ventilation duct, dropped down into the kitchen behind the stage and got to see Cheap Trick. I think Rick Neilson would appreciate that one.

"I've always been into the blues. In the Eighties, I moved away from it cos my dad was into it, and started listening to hip-hop and punk rock. Toledo had a healthy punk scene back then: we'd all hang out at this All Ages club. It was pretty foul—the toilet would drain right underneath the building—but it was somewhere to go. As I got older I got into stuff like The Gun Club, music with a blues undercurrent. I was playing in a New Wave band with the drummer from The Necros [who also featured Corey Rusk, founder of Chicago's Touch & Go records, and future Big Chief singer, Barry Henssler], when I saw [future Soledad Brother] Ben in Henry And June. They were playing Keith Richards riffs, and no one else was doing that, so I asked if I could play bass, and started playing the blues again.

"By the mid-Nineties, there was just a small group of people dedicated to playing rock. The same 40 people would be at all the shows, in all the bands. I stayed in Toledo, Ohio, just 40 miles south of Detroit—it's the same distance as Ann Arbor, but with a whole lot less money. I'd drive up a couple of times a week, hang out, then drive home, usually with one eye shut because I couldn't see. Music kept me out of trouble. All my friends who didn't play music ended up doing a lot of drugs and getting strung out or going to jail, or both.

"Henry And June's 'Going Back To Memphis' single came out on Human Fly during my hazy period, '94, '95, the same time as the first Detroit Cobras single, same label. A week after we broke up, we got a call from an agent wanting us to tour with Jon Spencer Blues Explosion [overrated NYC revivalist grunge-blues band, fronted by a trust fund kid]. That's typical Detroit. As soon as you break up, everyone's into it.

"After that, I started a two-piece band with my brother from way back when, Doug Walker, called Johnny Walker. We broke up because it got too volatile. We'd be rolling round in the middle of the set scrapping on the floor. So Ben and I got back together as Soledad Brothers in early '98.

"We opened up for Two Star Tabernacle in Toledo—they missed our set, down the street getting hotdogs. Afterwards, I was in another room playing slide, and Jack was like, 'Oh you guys are a two-piece? I'm in a two-piece, too...what's up with that slide?' So I showed him a few things. The next week we played The Magic Stick, and Jack showed up and said he wanted to record us.

"A couple of weeks later, I saw The White Stripes at The Gold Dollar. It was rough. Meg was really new at playing drums. Jack was a really good guitar player, but he was playing standard punk rock. He wasn't that adept at playing blues—he was into it, but had never played anything except standard tuning so he couldn't figure out how they made those noises. I showed him a few things. Jack and I have always had a semi-friendly guitar-slinger competition—like, can you do THIS? He's kind of passed me up now. Good for him. I'm really proud of what he's done. When he went off touring I went to med school—he got a four-year head start on me.

"Why two piece? It's convenient. It's easier to work things out. There's twice the money and half the bullshit. Also, we were living in Toledo and there weren't that many kids into what we wanted to do. It wasn't because we were into Flat Duo Jets or Doo Rag or any of the other two-piece bands.

"The summer between my first and second year of med school, The Detroit Cobras had been split up for a year, and Damien Lang was talking about getting them back together. I was like, 'Look dude, I'll play bass with you'. We rehearsed all summer, and did some recordings but never played out. Len Puch—the guy who recorded the first Gories record—was playing guitar and building a rocket car. So we had the Med School guy, the rocket car scientist, the cigar smuggler [Damien], Rachel [Nagy, singer] the butcher and Marybelle [Mary Restrepo, guitar] the Panamanian princess. It was a good summer. I was going to med school in Cincinnati and I was set to move to Detroit. Med school fucked me up good. 140,000 dollars later, I was the world's first homeless doctor."

Ben Swank (drums)

"Me and Johnny had different ideas what we wanted to do with Soledad Brothers. I wanted it as stripped down and dirty and fuzzed as possible, but Johnny wanted to make it more of a decent band. The idea was to take away everything and concentrate on the rhythm. A lot of our early stuff is just one riff, like John Lee Hooker, Hound Dog Taylor and Jesse May Hemphill—the boogie blues. People criticise us for ripping off black music, but a lot of blues is played on European instruments.

"Jack's an amazing drummer. He frustrates me. I'll be upstairs practicing and he'll come up and whip out some crazy stuff. He's a properly trained drummer, so he can do all those crazy counter-rhythms and triplets. He's tight. The switch to guitar makes sense: drumming can be limited as far as songwriting goes, that's why drummers often get kicked out for suggesting songs. I liked the simplicity of The White Stripes. I'm very into stuff like The Gories and The Cramps, and there was nobody else stripping it down that far. I'm not sure everyone else liked them right away.

"I like Detroit because I like to party, however trite it sounds. Most of the bars you go to have a good jukebox, there are great breakfast places, and if you like disgusting food then you're fine. Also, the fact it's a poor town means people help each other out—there's a real sense of community. People support each other's bands. I've never been anywhere where people are so into playing music.

"My biggest influences are alcohol and Johnny's warm sense of self-righteousness. Musically, the most obvious ones are John Lee Hooker, the Stones and maybe T Rex and The Velvet Underground.

"Sometimes when I'm on stage I zone out so hard I start to drool. We've had a few fights. We toured the UK with Pearlene. Their singer is a big, hard, smelly, drunken son of a bitch. We called him The Yeti. One time in Nottingham, some guy bumped into me when we were all drunk and dancing, and The Yeti broke his nose. At the Big Day Out in Australia, 2002, I'd been drinking for about 15 hours, and this guy was really hassling Meg. A friend told him to leave and he started punching him—so I jumped in and tried to bust him in the head with a bottle like Lee Marvin in *Point Blank*, and put my fingers in his eyes. We're not big fighters, though—whatever Johnny may've said..."

"The second time I saw The Go, they had these biker-chicks or prostitutes at the side of the stage, and this woman goes, 'Look at those guys, they look like the fucking Easybeats'. So I call up Kim Fowley[x], and he's like, 'You gotta get me a tape, The Easybeats[xi] are my favourite ever band'. The Go ask him to produce them, but he thinks the cymbals are all over the place... and so I ended up producing them.

Bobby Harlow: "John [Krautner, guitar] and I saw Two Star Tabernacle one night. Jack had a great stage presence. He wasn't a phoney at all. Later, Jack was over at Dave's house—they were best friends—so John and I went over there: 'Hey, Jack, we've got a question for you'... And Jack said, 'Yes, already, wanna join, count me in'."

Dave Buick [bassist, The Go]: "I'd already put out the Stripes single and Jack had started coming to see The Go. So we asked Jack if he wanted to guest and it didn't go that well. The amp wasn't turned on. But he wanted to play with us so we recorded with him after that."

John Krautner: "The whole thing was very innocent. One year at The Blowout, Jack was playing with The Go, Two Star Tabernacle and The White Stripes. Him and Matt Smith were in three bands each that night. I was trying to shuttle everyone around. That was a fun year."

PLUGGED IN...

The saga continues for gritty as they are glam outfit **The Go.** It's out with the old and in with the new as yet another change in lineup spares founding members **Bobby, John,** and **Mark**, while guitarist **Jack White** gets kicked to the curb; devoted friend and (now ex-bassist) **Dave Buick** takes a hike close behind. One could theorize that the grounds for White's dismissal had more to do with the bands resentment over his stake in the spotlight than any lack in the musical department. Shame on you, Bobby and John. Didn't your mother's teach you to share (the limelight, that is?) What's a band to do when faced with the debacle of losing both halves of its star power all in one day? Take on members of the **Wildbunch,** of course! It's not certain whether **Anthony the Rock 'N' Roll Indian** and **Steve the Mojo Frezzato** will remain on the cast of what's quickly morphing from a rock band into a soap opera, but I'd guess that nobody's getting too comfy. As for the the one's who got away, Jack White will continue with **The White Stripes** along with now ex-girlfriend **Meg** and is rumored to be considering a side project with pop hero and proprietor of **Flying Dutchman** kicks, **Brendan Benson.** The buzz on Buick reports that he may be joining the lazy whispering harmony of **Slumber Party,** whose new demo floating around somewhere near you is both gorgeous and surreal and in the hands of **Sub Pop's Dan Trager.**

Who in the hell is **Intercourse**? An ensemble we'll all be hearing a lot of in the near future. The dynamic agro-rock gentry has come out of the cracks after eluding even home-town recog-

nition to sudden airplay on L.A.'s **K-Rock**, an impossible feat for a band sans major label contract. The sudden leap to multiple spins on the most powerful station in the world has alledgedly attracted the attention of record weasels across the map, including scouts from **Epic Maveric, Island/Def Jam, and EMI Publishing**. The shuffle of hanger-on-er's would begin any minute, if anyone could figure who these guys are...

Congratulations to **Outrageous Cherry,** who've made the leap from **Third Gear Records** to the Los Angeles-based **Del-FI** label, original home to **Richie Valens** and **Bobbi Fuller.** What began as a simple one record off-shoot with the West Coast's equivilent to **Motown** has manifested into a three album deal with tour support. The only quandry facing the band now is drummer **Deb Agoli's** June wedding and **Chad Gilchrist's** scholarly pursuits including an imminent math degree. If tour van A leaves at four o'clock going 68 mph and tour van B leaves at six, will anyone in Outrageous Cherry mind two honeymooners in the backseat?

-Jake Stone

A few months after Jack joined The Go, the band signed to Sub Pop—the Seattle label who about a decade before had signed Nirvana and Mudhoney, and who'd spent most of the following 10 years in denial that grunge ever happened. It was going through one of its periodic "rock moments", signing bands like Zen Guerilla, Sweden's Hellacopters and Nebula[xii]. The insurrectionary glam garage grunge of The Go seemed—on the surface—to fit in.

John Krautner: "We're multifaceted. For the past 30 years, the golden oldies have been a big influence on The Go. We're a band that likes the hook of a song. The more hooks the better."

There was a worry that the contract that Sub Pop had lined up for The Go was going to be exclusive, meaning it would give the label the rights to White Stripes material as well. Jack decided against signing it. The Go's debut album, *Whatcha Doin'*—eventually released after Jack left the band, in September 1999—was recorded and mixed at Jim Diamond's Ghetto

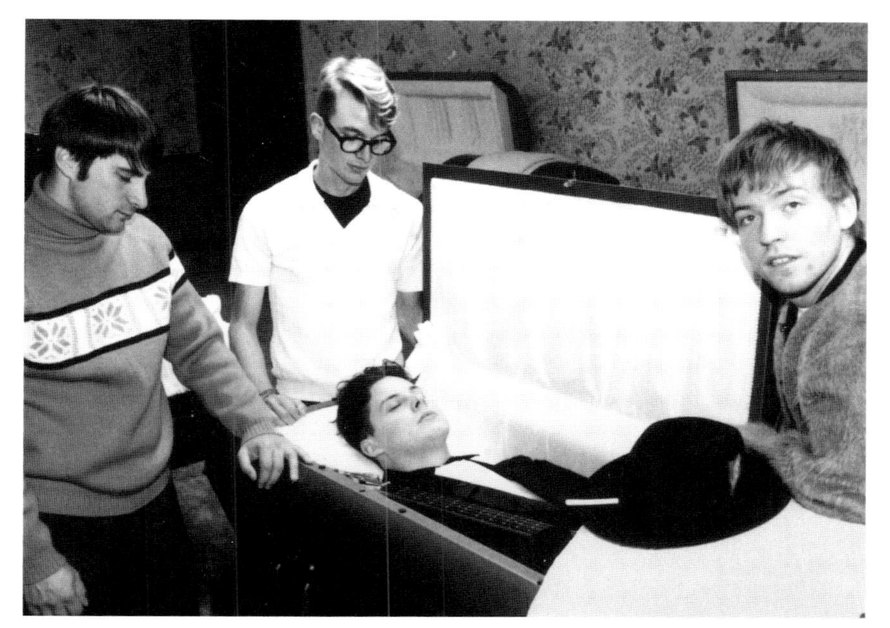

Left: Soledad Brothers. (Pat Pantano)

Above: Real Detroit, May 20, 1998

Below: The Hentchmen bury Jack White. (Rex Features)

x Kim's *Michigan Babylon* CD, co-produced and directed by Kim and Matt, appears on the Detroit Electric label, financed by Car City records.

xi British invasion group originating from Sydney, Australia. Their 'Friday On My Mind' was one of the great pop singles of the Sixties. It reached Number Six in 1966.

xii A fine grungy outfit, their long hair and greasy riffs reminiscent of old school Mudhoney. The other two are bogstandard rock bands.

THE SIGHTS

Eddie Baranek

"I grew up on the east side of Detroit: Car City Records was only four blocks away. I used to spend my Saturday nights walking to the record store, getting a piece of pizza and then going home. There aren't a lot of clubs for kids round here. I went to a private Catholic all-boys school, like the one Ben [Blackwell] went to. We wore a uniform, we grew our hair in front of our ears and they didn't get it. Then around 15, my friends and I formed The Sights. We played the local coffee house for kids and we'd cover 'Trash' by The New York Dolls, 'Strange Town' by The Jam, 'Have You Seen Your Mother Baby Standing In The Shadows' [Rolling Stones]. The other mall punk brats didn't know what we were doing. That quickly progressed to us playing bars at 16, with The Hentchmen and The Detroit Cobras, getting wasted with hot 15-year-old chicks.

"When I was 16, I was into The Creation and The Jam, Mod, The Birds with Ronnie Wood—there was a BBC sessions by The Move that really caught our eye. We looked at the bands that were playing the music and we started smoking a lot of grass and the hair got a little longer, so did the jams, and the smoke got thicker and it turned into more of a Small Faces/Humble Pie thing. Now our sound is as schizophrenic as hell.

"Try being a Mod in Detroit when you're 17 at high school... you get called TC—Tight Clothes, cos everyone else wears baggy clothes. That was fun. Saving up to buy a scooter that I never bought. I remember getting Fred Perry catalogues—that's how I met Ko. She was a bartender at The Garden Bowl. She has a scooter tattoo with the target. There was a scooter rally at The Magic Stick in '98. There were 12 scooters there. I couldn't even go cos it was 21 and older.

"Why form a band? Free beer, you get into shows for free, girls talk to you and you don't have to get a real job. We were like 16, playing Detroit bars and having to go to school the next day. I'd have three hours of sleep and the kids in the class were into sports and jock shit, and they'd have no idea I'd just played a show with The Clone Defects. It was the time of my life. It never mattered whether we got paid.

"In '98, you had the Cobras, Bantam Rooster, Doll Rods—The Stooges route had pretty much been done round here. We still partied with those bands, but who wants to see the same 'Kick Out The Jams' riff one more time? Right away we steered clear of some of that stuff which I still love. I was still going to school. How could I sing the blues?

"I had nothing to compare what was going on to—only to the year before when I couldn't do shit, except sneak beer from my parents. All of a sudden, this whole crazy ass underworld opened up. It was insane: bars every night and older girls. My best friend got cut up and turned into a crack addict by the age of 18. I was seeing shows, four nights a week. I played about 40 shows in The Garden Bowl, on the couches in the bowling alley. You'd walk in on a Sunday, bring a PA and say you were going to play—instant party. I felt like I was a little brother to all these people."

Recorders, with Matt Smith producing—although some of the tracks were remixed demos.

"We recorded a demo with Jack in his living room," states Matt, "using his broken eight-track machine and broken mics. We sent it to Kim Fowley, and Kim sent it out to some Hollywood people who were working on this movie *Detroit Rock City*. They didn't want it, so Sub Pop picked up on it. After we recorded the album, I decided I wanted to use some of the songs from the original demo."

So Jack had to leave because of that Sub Pop contract?

"No," the producer replies. "Jack wanted to make a go of The Go, but he was used to being in control. He'd never been in a band where he just had a role that was defined for him. Also, he was real excited about The White Stripes. But in the middle of The Go record he started acting erratically, because his wife was leaving him. He started getting upset with things I'd do. I put synthesiser on one song and he threw a tantrum, and I was like, 'Take it to your band and if you guys come to a consensus then fine, otherwise I'm sending it off'. It wasn't an ELO record, it was like a Little Richard record, and if anything, we removed tracks that were too slick—but he kept acting like I was over-producing it, so we had some conflict[xiii]. There was one time when he wanted to redo all his guitar solos. I think we ended up fixing one solo."

"We recorded The Go record three weeks before Jack and Meg recorded the first White Stripes album—and," Dave Buick comments dryly, "there were some clashes between Matt Smith and Jack during that time."

"People either loved or hated that record," Matt says. "They were either like, 'This record has changed my life and made me believe in rock'n'roll', or 'These guys are horrible degenerates'. There was some sexual element to The Go that had been missing from 10 years of indie rock, and it freaked people out. In 20 years of playing gigs in Detroit, I still haven't seen another band like it."

Whatever the reason, Jack left The Go shortly after the album was released. Dave Buick followed. The Go went on to record a second album, with Dion on guitar, for Sub Pop. The label rejected it, and The Go's career got stuck in the deep-freeze for a couple of years, despite their storming live shows.

Dion: "A lot of people will tell you that Jack left because he was too busy, but it was also because he had really strong opinions. Jack probably wanted to get more ideas in there than they wanted to do."

Left: The Sights.
(Doug Coombe)

Right: The White Stripes at the Blowout 3/99
(Doug Coombe)

xiii Ben Blackwell: "What Matt Smith fails to mention is that he spent all the recording budget doing numerous mixes of the record."

THE THIRD WHITE STRIPE ?

Johnny Walker: I'd been trying to get into med school for three or four years, working in the emergency room and everything. When I finally got accepted, I called Jack up from Toledo, and he was like, 'Oh, that's cool'. I was like, "Aren't you happy?" And he was like, "Oh, I was going to ask you to join The White Stripes..."

Ben Blackwell: Bullshit!

Johnny: What you going to do? I was a day late and a dollar short, and it would have totally thrown a spanner in the works. I'm not sure I would've joined even if, because it was such a fucking good thing—so simple and so perfect. You don't believe that story...?

Ben: No!

Johnny: Call up Jack and ask him! It was funny cos Ben was bugging me to ask Jack to join Soledad Brothers right after The Go fall-out. It would have been cool, cos he's super-talented, but it didn't necessarily feel right.

Jack White at the Gold Dollar.
(Doug Coombe)

The White Stripes at the Brixton Academy, 11/04/03. (Debbie Smyth/Retna)

(George Campos/LFI)

Meg at Wolverhampton civic hall 4/03
(Angela Lubrano)

27/ 04/ 03
(George Campos/LFI)

Meg at BBC Radio 1 Big Weekend,
Heaton Park, Manchester 04/05/03
(Mark Campbell/Rex features)

(Martin Philbey/Redferns)

Jack White at The Orpheum Theater 20/04/03 (Steven Tackeff/WireImage)

(Courtesy of Steve Gullick CTCL Archive)

Silk, Satin And Suede

"My biggest problem when people talk about bands signing to independent labels," begins Ben Blackwell, "is that no one ever signs anything. Not for 90 per cent of these bands. The way The White Stripes got to put out their first album on Sympathy For The Record Industry was that Steve Shaw [original Detroit Cobra] and Jeff Evans[i] had both really talked up the band to Long Gone John [Sympathy boss]. I remember being excited, like this was it! 'Wow! Sympathy For The Record Industry'...it was a name that you knew of but didn't know why. What else was on it apart from The Detroit Cobras and the first Hole single?"

Long before The White Stripes formed, Sympathy had carved out a reputation for itself among music fans: sweet packaging and a preference for raw, female rock released on seven-inch meant that the LA label (operated from Long Gone's apartment) always had something interesting up its sleeve—be it The Child Molesters' deliberately provocative sleeves, Johnny Legend's demented 'House Of Frankenstein' or the abrasive all-female trio Calamity Jane. Sympathy's reputation spread by word-of-mouth in a pre-Internet age[ii].

"I had no intention of starting a label," Long Gone told Johnny Pontiac in an interview conducted in 1998 to celebrate SFTRI's 10th anniversary. "I was just doing it as a favour to the band [Lazy Cowgirls, SFTRI 001]. I have varied interests, musically speaking. I like rock'n'roll and most of its mutant offspring. I like girl vocalists a lot. I like the hybrid/fucked-up blues. I like pop music. I like just about it all except for rap and anything resembling hardcore."

Shortly before being turned onto 'Let's Shake Hands' by Evans, Sympathy For The Record Industry released the debut Cobras album, 1998's awesome *Mink, Rat Or Rabbit*—thus beginning a relationship that has lasted through all of Steve Shaw's disparate, female-led bands, the Cobras, The Breakdowns[iii] (and thus Ko And The Knockouts[iv]) and, most recently, The Fondas[v].

"Long Gone has a predisposition for bands with girls," confirms Ben. "That's common knowledge. It wasn't like anybody else was asking. There was a verbal agreement that once he recouped his money, he and the band would split everything 50/50."

It wasn't a surprise to Ben that The White Stripes switched labels from Italy: there were no contracts after all, just enthusiasts, and Sympathy could afford to pay for the recording, something beyond Italy's financial scope. [Italy has only released one 12-inch—The Hentchmen mini-LP—and it still has a fair few copies left of that.]

Shortly before the release of the album, a seven-inch single appeared in April 1999, 'The Big Three Killed My Baby' b/w 'Red Bowling Ball Ruth' (Sympathy For The Record Industry SFTRI 578). Initial quantities were pressed in red vinyl. The front cover boasts a flame-scorched photograph, taken by Ko Melina (née Shih), of Jack and Meg standing in front of a giant poster

Left: Jack White at The Gold Dollar. (Doug Coombe)

i Vocalist with blues rockers, '68 Comeback—a group formed out the remnants of Ohio psychobilly cats The Gibson Brothers, and The Gories (Peggy O'Neill originally played drums).

ii Hey! This was the man that *discovered* Courtney Love (singer with Hole), for Chrissakes.

iii Released one Nancy Sinatra-esque seven-inch, 'This Gun Don't Care Who It Shoots' (kill rock stars)—band featured Jeff Meier (Rocket 455, The Detroit Cobras).

iv Singer Ko was a bartender at The Magic Stick, and had previously played bass in The Come-Ons and The Breakdowns. Ko And The Knockouts' self-titled, Jim Diamond-assisted, debut album (2002) is a snotty, brash, Mod, powerpop gem.

v Detroit Cobras-style soul-punk band, starring Julie Benjamin (Slumber Party) on sultry, styled vocals and also featuring Mark Niemenski from Eighties garage revivalists, The Hysteric Narcotics. Sadly, their 2003 Sympathy debut *Coming Now!* suffers from flat production.

IN THE STUDIO

Ben Blackwell: Tell me what you can remember about recording the first White Stripes record.

Jim Diamond: It took a while because they were just a beginning band and they had one of those Sympathy For The Record Industry deals where I think they got $2,500 or $3,000. Meg had barely been playing the drums. We had to do a lot of takes because she'd fuck up... I set her up in one corner of the room with an amp and a mic, to get a big sound. Jack played through an old guitar amp to make it sound dirty. Dirtier than it really was.

BB: Did you save every take or would you reuse tape?

JD: We couldn't afford to keep going through reels of two-inch tape. That would've used up their whole budget.

BB: This was January/February of 1999?

JD: Was it? Or was it '98?

BB: So, the geek stuff: what kind of mixing board did you use and what tape machine?

JD: Well, I hate talking about this shit because all you fuckers are gonna go try and buy one of these mixing boards but they're mine. If you see one, sell it to me, at a decent price. They have this mixing board called an Electrodyne. They were made in LA in the late Sixties and early Seventies and they're totally awesome.

BB: How did that become yours? Did you search out a bunch of different mixing boards or what?

JD: I got it by accident. I bought a 16-track tape recorder from this music school in northern Michigan called Interlochen and they said, "Hey, you want this old mixing board?" I said "Yeah" and I got there and it was huge and ridiculous and it weighed 500 pound. It was made of wood and half-inch aircraft aluminium and stuff, and big VU meters and knobs, and I'm like "Wow, this thing is incredible!" So I plugged it in and it worked—it'd been sitting in a barn since 1980. And I got it in '98. Hmm... So I kinda lucked out.

BB: At that time, was Jack just using his red hollowbody...?

JD: Yeah, his red hollowbody...

BB: ...or did he use any of the guitars you had lying around the studio?

JD: Mick [Collins] had a 100-watt Silvertone that he bought with Dirtbombs' money way back that he embezzled from us... You can print that, too. So Mick embezzled money from the band, Jack used his 100-watt head through a cabinet, through, like, a 15-inch Electrovoice speaker in that cabinet and I mic-ed it with two Shure SM-57's.

BB: And Jack, for singing, wouldn't he just sing through a guitar amp?

JD: Yeah, because I'd go, "Hey Jack, try this mic", and he'd be like, "It sounds like we're in a studio". He was very self-conscious of having it sound polished like he's in a studio. But I said, "You ARE in a studio, if you want to make a field recording, dig up Alan Lomax[i] and have him go hook up his Ampex".

BB: What were they drinking?

JD: I think Meg drank tea, because she was cold.

BB: Do you remember anything that they recorded that didn't make it on the album? Do you remember them doing 'My Little Red Book' and 'Let's Build A Home'?

JD: Yeah, they did do that stuff... I forgot about that. I guess I've got copies of that somewhere.

BB: Or maybe you don't.

JD: I have the DAT... I'm sure I've got the DAT.

BB: I shouldn't have told you that then, because you would've forgot.

JD: Oh my god... it's going up on e-Bay!

BB: Do you get sick of people going up to you, saying, "Oh, you recorded the first White Stripes album, you must be rich".

JD: Yeah, I don't like that at all. I made $2,000 on the damn thing. No, probably two reels of two-inch, that was $150, so I only made $1,700 off the thing. When I handed them the studio bill, Jack said, "Oh my God. This is the biggest cheque I've ever written." It would have cost a lot less if we hadn't had to do all those multiple takes, either... But I've gotten good props out of it. People go, "Cool man, you did that record", and I go, "Yeah, I did 50 others too, you wanna hear those?"

BB: Well, it's the idea that one of them is going to stick out more than the others...

JD: Obviously.

BB: What do you think when Jack has said in interviews that the first album is his favourite—that he doesn't think they'll ever top it?

JD: I don't know... everyone's first record is usually really good because they've had a while to get ready for it. And then, for the other ones, they're pressured to repeat, or do better. So the first one rocks the hardest out of all of them. It's tough sounding.

i Legendary mid-20th Century compiler of field recordings from blues artists like Leadbelly, Woody Guthrie and Muddy Waters.

of a mechanical sculpture created from bottles and iron, backed by a red and white flag. The back contains diagrams/blueprints for the Tucker automobile—the Sympathy label design is based on the Tucker crest.

The A-side is the same song Jack tried to convince Andre Williams to cover: a rare foray into contemporary issues, it takes a pop at the Detroit motor industry for polluting the city and laying off workers. Musically, it's sheer staccato energy; Jack's voice a squeal of indignation. It was described at the time as "chugging like a combustion engine ready to overheat". ["The single was billed as the 'anti-automobile 45,'" recalls Blackwell, "and the B-side was originally meant to be 'Stop Breaking Down'."] In Benjamin Hernandez' *Detroit Rock Movie*[vi] (a rare lo-fi feast, filmed in 1999, some considerable time before the city attracted attention, and featuring cameos from The White Stripes, Two Star Tabernacle, Soledad Brothers, The Go and Brendan Benson[vii]), Jack talks jokingly about how a Ford worker got pissed off at the song.

"All anybody does is spend their money on the car companies," the singer complained. "It seems to be this thing that everybody accepts, like that's the way it's gonna be, and nobody complains about it. I don't understand it."

The B-side is another punk abrasion—Johnny Walker's comment about Jack *wanting* to play the blues but not quite understanding *how to* seems particularly applicable here: it's a mess, a clatter of percussion and overwrought vocals—likeable, but throwaway. The song hasn't resurfaced since.

vi "Within six months of the movie being shot, half of the bands broke up," Benjamin told www.triple-tremelo.com. "The movie actually contains what was then some last show footage from The Hentchmen, The Wildbunch, Two Star Tabernacle and even The White Stripes—most of whom came back together, obviously! The Dirtbombs were broken up and non-existent at the time that the movie was made, as were The Detroit Cobras. The Von Bondies, The Come-Ons and Ko And The Knockouts and just about every other band now charting didn't exist yet. It was a strange time. Fun, exciting, all of those things you would want from a home-grown rock scene."

vii Michigan-born powerpop singer. His bittersweet jangling melodies recall Matthew Sweet, or Fountains Of Wayne (but not quite *so* kooky).

Work on *The White Stripes* began at Ghetto Recorders in January 1999: Jim Diamond co-produced with Jack White.

Below: Meg White hands out flowers to the audience after a performance by The White Stripes at the Bowery Ballroom, NYC, April 8th 2002. (J. Scott Wynn/Retna)

BB: "Do you remember the two original ideas you had for titles of the first album?"

JW: "*Silk, Satin And Suede*. I can't remember the other."

BB: "It was *None Dare Call It Conspiracy*. What was that from?"

JW: "It's an old anti-communist book from the Fifties, from the John Birch Society. There were two books, *None Dare Call It Treason* and *None Dare Call It Conspiracy*. But then I thought it'd be best if our first album was self-titled, to put us on the level with everybody else. It's just a chunk of us to start out with."

Ben Blackwell: "The first title was a play on the debut Cobras album—somewhere there's a picture of Jack and Meg in front of a building that says 'Silk, Satin And Suede'. I don't even know where the building was—probably Detroit. I had a copy of that John Birch book in my car. I'd bought all this weird red baiting literature from the used book fair that's held every year down the road at the church. He put his guitar in the trunk and saw it there. Maybe it will be the title of the fifth record."

Like all the best blues and punk, *The White Stripes* is raw, tuneful and primarily concerned with feeling and texture, not commerciality. The emphasis is on starkness, the silences that linger ominously in the gaps between vocals and drums or guitar on songs like the Robert Johnson cover, 'Stop Breaking Down' and slide-textured 'Suzy Lee'. Sometimes it feels like an elementary glam stomp—Slade, T Rex, the other glitter-bedecked UK outfits from the Seventies—especially when Meg's beats get really ponderous and slow ('The Big Three...'). Above all else,

MEG WHITE: AN APPRECIATION

Ko Shih: Meg has a commanding stage presence because she is a woman, beautiful and graceful, but very powerful. She'll hit a cymbal and there's so much force. A lot of drummers are just drummers, they're sat at the back and you don't notice them. Even if she were in a band with a 100 other people you'd notice her. Meg appeals to so many different facets of your emotions. I've seen little girls after shows, and they all want to be her because she embodies everything I think women should be—talented, graceful and tough. It's not rough and tumble. It's all these contradictory terms that mix together and become one. I think I'd think that even more if I didn't know her. She's glue. She holds it together. She's also one of the kindest, most caring persons I've met.

Dan Kroha: When I first met them, they were married. He seemed to direct her on stage, which I think some women found distasteful. To her credit, I'd say that she took it really well. You could see there's real love there. I totally agree that that band would be nothing without Meg. Meg has a glow. She shines onstage. I call her the baby Bonham, because she does these super stripped-down Led Zeppelin beats.

Greg Baise: Did you see that new Jack Black movie [*School Of Rock*]? There's one scene where this drummer boy and a girl are engaged in conversation. He goes, "Name me two great chick drummers", and she says, "Shiela E and... Meg White". Of course she can play the drums. She's self-taught. It's so intuitive.

Meg White: Maybe Mo Tucker[i] was the first girl musician to inspire me... I don't know... I'm inspired by music, but I don't think of it in male/female terms. I like country singers like Loretta Lynn and Emmylou Harris. I didn't start playing drums until I was 21. I listened to a lot of music before then but I wasn't playing. I was into glam, country and really old rock. I like Art Blakey and Ringo Starr, but songwriters are more influential on me than drummers: strong women who manage to retain their femininity and stay very much women, like Dusty Springfield. I don't know why more women aren't involved in playing music. Ever since we started the band I've always been around guys.

The Wildbunch

Steve Nawara: She's really stepped up to the plate. She's done good.

Surge Joebot: She's got a real bottom thing going on.

Rock And Roll Indian: It goes in and out still, but it's good.

Joe: She's one of the sweetest people in this whole city.

Steve: And she drinks Jack Daniels.

Where is she? Let's bring her out.

Steve: Straight bourbon, too.

i Unsophisticated drummer with The Velvet Underground. Some people argue that—in the same way that Meg is the light of The White Stripes—the Velvets would've been nothing without Mo.

THE GARDEN BOWL

Marcie Bolen (The Von Bondies): All the rockers used to be in a bowling league. Tom, Jack, The Hentchmen, Maxine, Doug... One time, Jack's bowling ball split in half and he got a strike. It was his favourite—the red one.

Ko Shih (Ko And The Knockouts): I was jobless and I walked into The Magic Stick one day, and Ginger asked me if I wanted to bartend days. I'd never bartended before. I was, "Sure, why not?" My first night shift was Sunday. It's a horrible night cos no one goes out then. That's when you stay in and watch *The Simpsons*. The first thing I did was ask Jack to play Bob Dylan's *Nashville Skyline* in its entirety. He said no, but instead he came in and played something acoustic. Other musicians followed, and that's how I got acquainted with everyone. It was well before anyone did anything outside Detroit, so everyone was always home. I paid bands with a fifth of whiskey. The other bartender Andy said it'd be fine, but he never really cleared it with our boss. So we kept it a secret, and it was fine for the first month and a half...

Johnny Walker (Soledad Brothers): You'd get a few people together, and run through some songs—the one time I did it, Ben [Swank] and Jack played with the drummer from The Greenhornes, Meg did a song, Dave Buick played bass, and Tim from The Clone Defects started singing and dancing. There was John Hentch, Marc from The Go... it was basically Johnny Walker and the All Stars. Jack played the one-year anniversary show in November 1999, and he had three different line-ups. Ben and I played a couple of Gun Club songs. Jack's dad came up and did a little soft shoe routine, 'Fly Me To The Moon', that sort of thing. And Dean from The Waxwings came up. It was really good fun, but things came to a crashing halt—literally—when Johnny Hentch got drunk and fell onto a girl and then into a cigarette machine and had to go to hospital. They kept him in for a good while because he was still legally drunk... The idea of police showing up and this fifth being passed around was not a good idea. Also, if you go to the emergency room stinking drunk, they often won't treat you till you've sobered up. I can speak from experience.

Ben Blackwell: Jack did a handful of acoustic sets at The Garden Bowl—three, I can think of. The first one would've been November '98. There's a great bootleg from one of his shows there in June 2001, right before *White Blood Cells* was released. If you listen closely, you can hear me yell out for 'Hypnotized'. That's confused some collectors, wondering how someone knew about the song two years before it was released.

Above: Meg White with Ko Shih at The Garden Bowl, 1998. (Courtesy of Dave Buick)

it's simple: like laughter, or childhood, or the sound a train makes at it passes by the bottom of your garden. Indeed, the theme of childhood is central to this record—and I'm not just talking about Meg's tentative, rudimentary beats that help shape and colour The White Stripes' music.

The mark of a good song or poem or piece of artwork is that you can understand its intent. Solo artist, Nottingham UK's Scout Niblett—who rattles a drumkit and shouts pleas against loneliness dedicated to eternal *Peanuts* misfit Linus—once stated that her ambition was to write a song as clear as a kid's playground chant. Likewise, everything about *The White Stripes* is concerned with stripping away artifice and confusion.

"The past is another country," LP Hartley states in the opening sentence to *The Go-Between*, his powerful tale of convoluted Edwardian morals as seen through the eyes of a child, "They do things differently there."

The sleeve is a strip of photographs taken by Ko of Jack and Meg standing with a peppermint candy in front of what looks like a red panelled garage, Meg's bare legs shockingly white and schoolgirl-ish. It's limited to three colours: red, white and black. On the inside, the pair pose outside a red and white house (wrongly rumoured to be theirs), with typewritten lyrics spread among the photos, plus some text written by Jack relating back to the way children first see the world when they come into contact with others.

Telling, it includes the phrase, "It was easier when you were a child and everything that is happy and fun now is an attempt at recreating your backyard when you first saw others and dreamt that with them you could be happier than you were alone..."

This theme of trying to recapture the innocence and wonder of childhood is one that Jack returns to on numerous occasions in songs and interviews.

"When we started, our objective was to be as simple as possible," the singer told Norene Cashen of *Detroit Metro Times* in May 1999, a month before the release of the album. "Meg's sound is like a little girl trying to play the drums and doing the best she can. Her playing on 'The Big Three Killed My Baby' is the epitome of what I like about her drumming. It's just hits over and over again. It's not even a drumbeat—it's just accents.

"'The Big Three Killed My Baby' is composed of three chords and three verses, and threes are accentuated throughout the song. It was a number I always thought of as perfect," Jack continued, "or our attempt at being perfect. Like on a traffic light, you couldn't just have a red and a green."

Sure, you can hear traces of The Gories' beautiful, brutal minimalism and their beloved Chess blues, also of Led Zeppelin's high-strung power in tracks like 'Cannon' and 'Astro'. There are vestiges of the Doll Rods' early records: as nasty and unrefined and glorious as anything. There are older influences, too: the album is dedicated to bluesman Son House, and Bob Dylan's 'One More Cup Of Coffee' is served up, ragged and torn.

The record starts with 'Jimmy The Exploder'—just a plain drumbeat before the guitar comes rattling in and Jack wails like a Delta bluesman. There's no bass? It doesn't notice: what's more overwhelming is the bleak force of the guitar, the playful thud-thud-thud of percussion.

Left, and below: Jack receives the first White Stripes fan letter in the mail, 1999. ("The first fan letter came in 1998," comments Ben Blackwell. "It's kinda strange that they got a photo of it. How would you know when fan mail was coming? I smell a hoax.") (Courtesy of Dave Buick)

On the Robert Johnson cover, the guitar becomes a clarion call: a summons to revel in the music's power.

This wasn't simple revivalist fare. Too many musicians fail to understand that the lessons to be drawn from old blues singers like Johnson and Leadbelly, and primitive Sixties garage bands like Alarm Clocks, Novas[viii] and early Troggs, aren't musical, necessarily. It's not about recreating old favourites note-for-note. No, what matters is the spirit—the energy, the verve, the *life* behind the performances. The piano-led cover of jazzman Cab Calloway's cartoon-ish 'St James Infirmary', which closes off the album with 'I Fought Piranhas', works precisely because it finds a new twist to an old story—the piano sounding so barstool *piano-like* you wonder whether Jack and Jim stripped the instrument bare so it was just jangling wires and ivory. It's theatrical and playful, sure: but the *Broadway* burlesque adds another welcome layer to The White Stripes' oeuvre. The fiery 'Piranhas', meanwhile, boasts a guest slot from Soledad Brothers' Johnny Walker.

"I was in med school," the guitarist recalls, "and Jack called me up and asked me if I wanted to lay some slide tracks down—they were the first recordings we'd done at a proper studio, so it was kind of intimidating, but Jim's laidback so it was cool. I was kind of going in cold on 'Suzy Lee', but we'd recorded 'I Fought Piranhas' before in Jack's living room…I don't think he'd even played with Meg at that point. There's a ton of takes of it: we were writing it as we went along. *'I fought the boar'* was the original lyric, then I showed him a tattoo of a boar on my arm—it's like my family crest—and I think that caused him to change the lyrics later on."

It's a thin line that separates The Detroit Cobras from one more *Commitments*-style bar band or The White Stripes from The Black Keys[ix], but the line certainly exists. Without it, The Dirtbombs would simply be Lenny Kravitz with less money. Without it, one could feasibly claim that The Vines[x] are exciting. But they're not, and why not? They haven't learnt from the past—they've copied it.

"I remember Jack playing the first album and thinking it sounded so perfect for them," says Dan Miller. "Another piece of the puzzle fitted just right. I'm sure Jack had aspirations to take it further than The Gories had been—and they were such a great band—or even Demolition Doll Rods, cos their first album[xi] had just come out. I remember thinking it'd be so great to have this stripped-down raw music with really emotional, poetic, sophisticated lyrics."

Perhaps the album's stand out is 'Sugar Never Tasted So Good', an acoustic lament with its killer pay-off line *"I felt just like a baby until I held a baby"*, and odd percussive effect on the guitar

viii Minneapolis four-piece with a 13-year-old drummer, best known for their 1964 cut, 'The Crusher'—later immortalised by The Cramps.

ix One authentic blues-rock two-piece too many. This Akron, Ohio group are unflaggingly faithful to their source. Music that sucks the energy out of youth.

x Corporate Australian band, actually based in LA, rather laughingly referred to as "garage", even though it seemed to take six months to record their debut album. Hmm. Just like their heroes (and obvious source) Nirvana—not!

xi And a right rare raw garage-fest it is too!

The White Stripes at Paychecks in Hamtramck, 3/99. (Doug Coombe)

soundboard at the end of each chorus so that it sounds like someone knocking at the door. It's all the more beautiful because it contains so little.

The laidback 'Wasting My Time', meanwhile, is a stone-cold groove—the sort of song Van Morrison might once have delighted to sing, back in the Sixties with his exhilarating attitudinal hybrid blues rock band, Them. The lyric deals with the eternal dilemma of lovers—when to wait, why wait—and could be applied to the break-up of a relationship. But then, so could pretty much all of the blues.

The album took around five or six days to complete: that sounds fast in comparison to most chart records, but in fact is relatively standard for any rock band recording their debut, no matter how many songs (17, in this case). And anyway, The White Stripes only had a couple of instruments: Jim Diamond's great trick as a producer is to duplicate the sound of a band in rehearsal, and that's precisely how *The White Stripes* sounds. And there's nothing wrong with that. If it was good enough for early Beatles, Nirvana (their first album, *Bleach*, cost even less money to record, $606 to be precise) and The Gories, it's good enough for you.

You hear stories of artists taking years and spending millions of dollars to make an album—now what does that really indicate? That the band was razor-sharp, teeming with ideas and songs? Or the precise opposite: that they spent too much time smoking pot and playing pool instead of recording, showed up late, and without a single idea when they first checked in?

Maybe it just comes down to personal preference—but hell. It would've been a shock if the first Stripes record had taken any longer. Just listen to it! Does it sound over-polished?

"The first White Stripes album was the first record I heard that Jim Diamond had recorded," comments Marco Delicato (Rocket 455). "I was struck by the solidity of it. Jim Diamond's presence solidified a lot of the bands. There was finally a common place in Detroit where people were comfortable with exposing themselves, coupled with a high level of production, by our standards."

'Broken Bricks' is a song rooted in the post-riot desolation of Detroit: the harsh nostalgic imagery of the torn-down buildings and police ("caution") tape, the "rust-coloured rain", all

THE GREENHORNES

Ben Blackwell
"The Greenhornes might as well be considered a Detroit band[i]. I think they played in The Garden Bowl more than any local band. They've mellowed out now, but back in '98 and '99, Craig Fox (lead singer) would freak out once in a while. They were supposed to play the '98 Gutterfest at The Gold Dollar, but their van broke down and so they played between bands for the next two nights at The Magic Stick instead, those nights being part of the festival. For their last song, they burst into [Iggy Pop's all-time garage classic] 'I Wanna Be Your Dog'—a ballsy move in Detroit. But they slowed it down, made it more of a blues. Craig threw his guitar down and started screaming. Either way, it was amazing.

"Probably my favourite Greenhornes show was when they played on the lanes of The Garden Bowl, July 9th, 1999. For most of the shows there, the bands would play in the lounge... This is the only show I know of where the bands set up on the bowling alley. It was a double birthday party, for Jack White and Brian Olive [The Greenhornes]. The Jack White Solo Band (me on drums, Kevin Peyok of Waxwings on bass, Brendan Benson on guitar and Jack singing/guitar) opened the show, doing some covers and some songs that would eventually become White Stripes standards. Then The Greenhornes came on and just tore shit up. Craig's guitar was constantly feeding back, so he stopped playing and only sang. It was seeming a little half-assed when the bass and drums went into the beginning of 'Monkey Island' by the 13th Floor Elevators[ii] and Craig gripped the mic in his hands, fell hard to his knees and let out this guttural scream of *'I'M LIVIN' ON MONKEY ISLAND!!!!!'*

"That shit stays with me to this day."

i They're actually from Cincinnati, originally a five-piece, now whittled down to three, operating in similar sphere to The Hentchmen.
ii Fronted by Roky Erickson, one of the original acid-punk Sixties bands: their demented bitter break-up song, 'You're Gonna Miss Me', is one of the most vibrant blasts of rock'n'roll ever.

Above: The Greenhornes. (Tony Fletcher)

underpins a sensitive depiction of early love. 'When I Hear My Name' is more straightforward—over a John Lee Hooker-style blues riff, Jack wails the standard teenage cry of *"I want to disappear"*, echoes of Kurt Cobain in the chorus of alienation. Another stand out is the self-regarding confusion of "Do", a slow burner of a lament, Jack sometimes soliloquising over silence, the guitar and drums a gentle bluesy burr in the background, the mood all down and worried. He howls further in "Screwdriver", eyes screwed up tight, trying to shut out the surrounding world as the guitar spits venom at intruders.

"When people think of Detroit they think of The Stooges, the MC5, and even lately The Gories," comments Ben Blackwell, "but that record is definitely The White Stripes at their most primitive and their rawest, and they'll never capture that again. A lot of people argue that a band's first record is the best—everything leads up to the first album. For raw rock'n'roll that's often true. I'm more into bands evolving, though—I like mid-period Sonic Youth, 1990 stuff.

"The dynamics was pretty much doing takes until it sounded right," the drummer adds. "Jack directed Meg. Essentially he told her what to play until she was able to come up with her own things. He didn't record the drums himself—why not? It wouldn't have been a band. That's what evil people do. All of the stuff is recorded live: drums and guitar together, a lot of the time vocals live, and maybe overdub a solo. The first White Stripes record didn't get its due. It was three years before people took any notice of it—OK, less time than it took The Stooges and The Gories to get noticed, but still three years too long."

About a month after The White Stripes finished recording the album, Jack and Meg stopped living together and began divorce proceedings. On the surface, it seems strange the band didn't split when the marriage broke down but... well, what are you going to do?[xii] Jack created The White Stripes around Meg and her style of drumming—the band couldn't have existed without her. And certainly the band couldn't have existed without him. It was clear to both the couple and people around them that The White Stripes were developing into something special.

"I love Meg's innocence and her childishness," Jack told *The Onion*. "And whether that's a feminine characteristic that's disregarded or degraded or whatever... Or maybe it's not even a feminine characteristic at all. Maybe I could be that way just as easily. But I love that, and I think that's the most important part of the band. Almost everything we do is based around her. It wouldn't be The White Stripes without her. If it were some guy in the band, it wouldn't work. I just love that. I don't know if [the criticism of Meg's drumming] is sexist. Charlie Watts and Ringo, those guys got ribbed all the time because they weren't doing drum fills

xii Other bands facing similar dilemmas in the past include Hole, Fleetwood Mac and Abba.

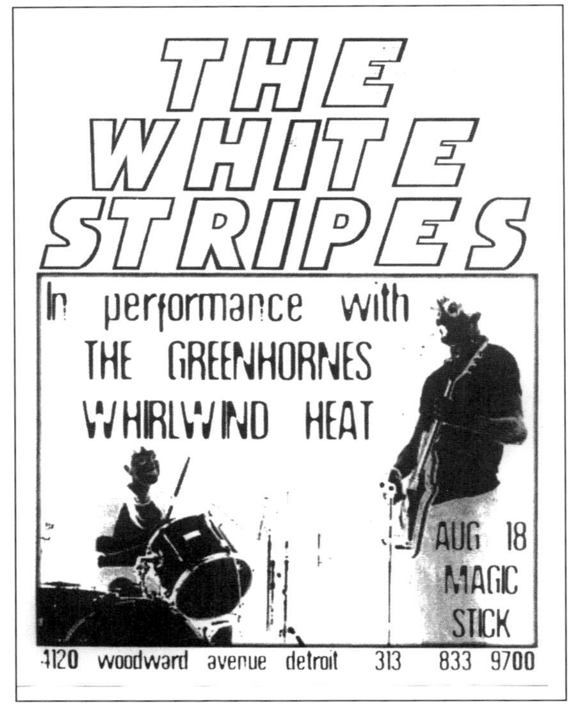

White Stripes poster circa August 1999. Right: August 18, 2000 show, the first of many times Whirlwind Heat would open for The White Stripes.

every two seconds. It's kind of stupid, especially once you realise how great Ringo and Charlie were and still are."

The couple eventually divorced in March 2000, according to the Oakland County Circuit Court records.

"I guess he was a little bummed about it," commented Andy from Flying Bomb. "We had to go through the pictures on the record sleeve artwork to take out the wedding rings. That was kind of entertaining."

There was a moment or two, particularly around the 1999 Blowout Festival in Hamtramck, organised by local free paper *Detroit Metro Times*, when it seemed the band might break up. By all accounts, the resulting sold-out show at Paycheck's was very special.

Ben Blackwell: "They had people we didn't know singing along. It was the whole crowd too, really overwhelming. Jack was totally caught off guard. He stopped singing and started laughing."

Dave Buick: "I was kind of hoping The White Stripes weren't going to play, cos me, Jack and Ben Blackwell were going do a covers band at that place, but Meg called at the last minute, and she was like, 'Well, we can work stuff out, let's just play the show tonight'. During 'Sugar Never Tasted So Good', which is on the second single I put out, the whole crowd was singing along. At that point in time I still had at least 800 copies in my closet. I was like, 'Holy fuck, Jesus'. It was nuts. It was supposed to be the last Hentchmen show and Johnny's organ was falling apart and he was pulling the keys out...It was a bittersweet night."

Rich Hansen: "They played 'Not The Marrying Kind' and the energy in the room was electric."

A knock-on effect from the split was that Meg got a lot more confident as a drummer, doubtless feeling she shouldn't need to take orders from her ex-husband anymore. Before, she did what Jack asked. Afterwards, she had more input.

"Jack's really upset when I gain any kind of skill," Meg told *Rolling Stone*. "He liked it better the first time I played."

"Was I surprised that Jack wanted Meg to continue playing in the band after they split?" asks Johnny Hentch. "No. I was more surprised that Meg wanted to stay in The White Stripes."

In autumn 1999, with a buzz starting to build around Detroit—thanks to The Go, and The Detroit Cobras and The Dirtbombs, and also reports filtering through of The White Stripes—Jack and Meg were asked to play three dates supporting Pavement[xiii].

Ben: "I have a great soundboard tape of a show with Pavement in September 1999. There were 800 people there, by far the biggest crowd they'd ever played to. They were supposed to play for 30 minutes, but they were so nervous they played in 20. Jack did an amazing solo on 'Let's Shake Hands'."

The band had played Toronto and Chicago before, but never more than as one-off shows.

Ben: "The first time they played Chicago was at The Lounge Ax, with The Waco Brothers and The Sadies[xiv]. It was the first of three shows there. I don't think anyone was really into it. We stayed overnight and they even got a hotel, so I'm sure it lost money. It was just me, Jack and Meg in the van—Jack drove. I was still only 16. The van had two seats up front. It was a cargo van essentially. I sat on a beanbag and all the gear was packed as far away from the beanbag as possible, and there were tons of blankets because there was no heat. We probably just ate gas station food—Doritos and a Coca-Cola, maybe a Snickers or a Twix. We had a boom box but the batteries ran out after the first hour. The first time they realised it was a bigger thing was at The Cactus Club, Milwaukee. I can remember Jack saying he wanted to cancel the show because it was too far to drive, but people were singing along and that's special when it's not people you know."

There were plenty of opportunities to play shows back home, too.

Johnny Walker: "Me, Ben [Blackwell] and Jack played as The White Walker Trio in August '99 at The Gold Dollar. We played almost all of The Gun Club album, *Fire Of Love*—it was The Come-Ons[xv] first show in Detroit and they didn't want to headline. We practised just once but word got out that we'd practised twice and people thought it would be really good. Every time someone yelled for a Gun Club song we'd play another."

Dan Miller: "As they got more and more popular, people would say, 'Let's get The White Stripes to open up for us because they're a two-piece'. Jack was getting real frustrated. Even after the first album, he was like, 'When will we be the headline band instead of the stepsister band that people throw a little bone to?' Also, there was the typical thing of people saying, 'They need a bass player, the whole bottom end isn't there'...those people probably still don't like them. I went out to California to visit my sister, and called up college radio stations to request songs. No one knew about them. I remember thinking if something happened and they split up no one would know about this. I was so happy when the guy from Sympathy From The Record Industry agreed that *White Blood Cells* should be sent out to the radio and the press cos he didn't usually do that."

xiii Articulate post-Fall band briefly seen as the inheritors of Nirvana's mantle—but way too smart to be trapped like that. At one point in the mid-Nineties, Steve Malkmus' Pavement *ruled* America's Pop Underground, the same way Sonic Youth did a few years before. 1992's *Slanted And Enchanted* (Matador) is the album to buy.

xiv Damn fine indie country band from Toronto, featuring Neko Case.

xv Starring ex-Gore Gore Girl Deanne Iovan and Dirtbombs drummer Patrick Pantano: play a vigorous, organ-drenched funky R&B take on old Sixties standards. Jim Diamond's production on their 2001 Sympathy album, *Hip Check!* struts.

The Detroit Cobras

I met Detroit's finest soul band—bar none (alright, maybe The Dirtbombs)—in April 2003 when the five-piece were over in the UK to promote their Seven Easy Pieces *EP (Rough Trade). Like their peers back home, the Cobras line-up has been fluid: most importantly, the first line-up and debut album included Steve Shaw and Jeff Meier—the men behind much of the great music in town.*

Left: The Detroit Cobras singer Rachel Nagy.
(Courtesy of Steve Gullick CTCL Archive)

Dancing leads to fucking.

"Yeah," laughs Mary Restrepo, guitarist with The Detroit Cobras. "Rachel was in New Orleans, shouting 'Dancing leads to fucking' everywhere she went. John Sinclair [MC5; White Panthers] was like, 'I love Rachel and her Detroit talk—let's all have a revolution: dancing and fucking on the street!'"

I hear so much great music. Music that inspires me, music that makes me wanna slip off my boots and into my dancing shoes, cutting a swathe across the world's dance floors like it's 2002 again. Man, I hear so much great music, teenage crushworthy stuff: Yeah Yeah Yeahs, Irma Thomas, Timi Yuro, Billy Childish, The Gossip[i], The Dirtbombs, The Detroit Cobras...Names that might mean shit to you, but names that give me a thrill each time I see them written down or shouted in the street. Forget names. Listen to the music.

Slip on *Seven Easy Pieces* or *Myrmidons Of Melodrama* (ace Shangri-La's compilation) or 'Swallow My Pride' (Ramones), and nestle up cosy and warm next to their gentler moments, the raucous gospel groove. How the fuck do you avoid moving your arms round in great arcs, singing along with every half-deciphered lyric? It's great to laugh and giggle and act dumb-ass n' all, but when it comes down to it, there ain't nothing that can beat the thrill of the dance...

I'd be dancing even if I was immobilised—perhaps even more so. Inside my head, I'd be swirling round and jiving, hidden smile slipping into place, useless spine tingling with pleasure every time I heard the sweet soul caress of The Detroit Cobras. Am I sensual? This musical valley is a plethora of earthly delights. Dance! Dance! Dance!

"Dancing is pure and it feels good," explains Rachel Nagy, The Detroit Cobras singer. "Our bodies are supposed to be mobilised. We sit at work. We drive everywhere. Friday and Saturday night are for dancing. You guys are stupid! Look at these girls. They're dancing. You guys wondering why you don't get laid? You're not dancing with the pretty girls. People of my parents' generation, that's how they fell in love! Dancing was their first physical contact. 'Honey, I know your father is a brute, but you've got to understand...he used to be such a dancer!'

"It's part of the mating ritual," she continues. "Unfortunately, the mating ritual now is meeting for coffee and talking on the Internet. There's no glory in that. No wonder all these guys

i Three-piece Riot Grrrl band from Olympia—their singer belts the blues like Bessie Smith, while the remaining guitar and drums play oblique, jagged indie shapes. 2002's five-track 'Arkansas Heat' EP (kill rock stars) is the one.

STEVE SHAW

"I grew up on the West Side of Detroit—the MC5 were from just south of there. It was '65, '66. I was five, six years old. Walking home from school you'd see bands playing in garages. St Christopher's used to have a lot of Motown bands play their joints: kids there used to throw candy bars at Stevie Wonder cos they didn't believe he was blind. That's the kind of neighbourhood I grew up in. I was a big fan of The Who. One of my favourite songs was 'Call Me Lightning'. I only saw the Sixties bands play at the state fair or outdoors shows. I saw The Supremes play with The Mamas And The Papas and Gary Lewis And The Playboys. I saw James Brown. Parliament and Funkadelic played our grade school dances.

"I remember the first guy in the neighbourhood who had long hair. The greasers beat him to death. The greasers listened to soul music, black music. Not the British Invasion shit, that was frat stuff. They were into James Brown, even The Temptations. Those same juvenile delinquents ended up as bikers, five or six years on. A kid on my baseball team, his brother was in a motorcycle gang, and at the championship game all the bikers showed up. They had some sort of portable radio, and they were playing The Doors.

"My older sister had a guitar. I didn't take it very seriously, even though all of my friends were in bands. But later on I did...

"I lived in New Orleans, then I went to San Francisco, and it was expensive. I told my roommate, Mary [Restrepo], that the only reason I'd think about coming back was if I started a band. So she suggested we start a band together. I'd seen her play in a bunch of bands, and I knew what she would sound good doing. She liked R&B, and she wasn't doing that with her band, Fresh Hell. They were whacked out, kind of punk with some crazy chicks.

"We started The Detroit Cobras in '93 in the basement of Jeff Meier's house on the east side. I wanted to do R&B. That went haywire pretty quickly once we started. We were doing 'Testify' by The Parliaments, other oddball soul songs. We were doing The Olympics song that they do now. Then we started doing country, stuff like that. The next thing you know, we're doing Bill Munro songs and gospel: The Staples Singers. I just wanted to be a rock'n'roll band and figured the easiest way would be to do a bunch of cool covers. Jeff was really good at figuring out songs. We had that sorted out before Rachel came in. I gave her a tape with 15 songs on, and we started playing soon after that. I had always assumed we would go on to write our own material, but we never did. That would've been the logical next step. I wanted to bring horns in, too."

are emaciated, effeminate, fucking little dorks. No wonder I don't have sex with anyone. I'd fucking break them."

"You break them," sneers her guitarist, "and next thing you know, they wanna be your boyfriend."

"Exactly," states her singer. "There's no testosterone in these men."

I'm nervous meeting The Detroit Cobras. Not only do they capture the spirit of rock'n'roll but I've heard stories. Many stories. Bumped into that guy Steve from Electric Six a few weeks before (he also plays guitar in the Cobras) and he proudly pointed to his chin: "Rachel bit me there once. Kicked me there plenty of times, too." (Electric Six, you understand, being the *personification* of rock'n'roll.) He told me that Rachel would pick fights with audiences, fired up on alcohol, disgust and adrenalin, how she was an ex-stripper and butcher. I'm not nervous about that. I dig crazy chicks. They're usually more fun to hang with. I'm nervous cos I rate this band so highly.

I don't expect secrets from them. There are no secrets in rock'n'roll—you either have the feeling or you don't. It's just that I'm in awe of such talent.

"Music just wasn't the same after the age of three," sighs Rachel. "Or four, or five..."

The three Detroit Cobras albums—1998's butt-shaking *Mink, Rat, Or Rabbit* with the lasciviously naked dancing lady on the front; 2001's unimpeachable *Love, Life And Leaving*, with its nicotine-drenched soul; this year's *Seven Easy Pieces* with its Frazetta-style cover painting of Rachel, bare-assed—are so damn great, it's painful to think no one's managed this before. (Well, perhaps The Saints[ii] and Jesse Garon And The Desperadoes[iii].) It's so obvious! Find an American chick with the voice (and, more importantly, soul) of Irma Thomas and match her to some abrasive garage guitars that sometimes seem to be the sole province of Motor City USA, Detroit. And that's it.

"We have stumbled on something that is mind-blowing," agrees Mary. "Before that, we'd have to listen to the records everybody else had in town. Now we get to listen to the stuff everybody round the world listens to. We're meeting a lot of Everetts ..."

"There are no other Everetts," Rachel cuts in. "You're special."

Mary laughs.

Time for a little history: The Detroit Cobras were formed in...yada yada yada. Bollocks to that. It's all there in the songs. Listen to them, scroll through the credits and chase up the originals. That's the tradition The Detroit Cobras are from: women with voices to break and mend your hearts. Sure, there are also some blokes in the band.

We meet several of them, drinking all night in the Columbia Hotel when, at four in the morning, some idiot gets fed up with waiting for a drink and starts a fire in the corner of the lounge. Cue strapping firemen. But before that, the Rock And Roll Indian from Electric Six comes down in his polka-dot silk boxer shorts and black ankle socks, and off we go in search of the "fire".

"D'ya reckon it's behind here?" he asks me, pointing to a locked door.

Sure. Why not? But it's locked.

"Not any more it isn't," he replies, giving the wood such a bare-footed blast, the handle pops off.

The following afternoon, as we sit nursing our heads, the concierge shouts over to the guitarist, "Was that you who started the fire last night, Mary?"

He obviously knows her well.

"Honey," Mary sweetly replies. "If I'd started that fire you wouldn't of had a fucking hotel to come back to."

So, anyway: the blokes.

First, there's Kenny Tudrick, ex-Rocket 455 (drums).

"He's like a sultan," explains Rachel. "Women are falling all over him, even in his sleep. Funny thing is, he thinks he's no good with the ladies."

Next, there's Steve Nawara,

"Elvis in his later years," comments Rachel. "We used to call him Barbie, then he became a man, put on weight and became smarter with every pound."

And finally, there's Matt O'Brien—former bassist with Sub Pop's own early Nineties Detroit soul/rock band Big Chief, and contributor to droll US magazine *Motorbooty*. The previous night, Matt buys the largest round of whiskies seen by these eyes since David Yow's[iv] birthday in '96 in a Chicago bar when I asked him what kind of whisky he fancied and he went, "I have no idea", so I buy him, me and photographer Steve Gullick a shot from every bottle behind the bar, 17 in total...

"He thinks he's a changed man," comments Mary.

THE COME-ONS

Deanne Iovan

"My sister married a guy that played in a glam rock band called Cobalt Blue. She divorced him after two years, but before that he sold his bass to my mother. My brother and his friends would play David Bowie and Rolling Stones songs in the basement, so I'd plug the bass in and play along. And it was all because of the men with the glitter-blue platform boots.

"I started The Come-Ons seven years ago with Patrick [Pantano, The Dirtbombs]. Patrick and I both loved these old soul and R&B records and we felt there needed to be a band on the scene that could play music people could dance to, not just a loud rock band. We wanted to do this full-on soul band—and then it became just keyboards, bass and drums.

"I'm a singer by default. I also drum in The Sirens, Detroit's only all-female glam rock band. I didn't want to be the singer of the band. I listened to a lot of Billie Holiday, but I don't sound anything like her. I love all the Motown singers, Aretha Franklin, the usual. I love Frank Sinatra, Brenda Lee and Dusty Springfield.

"I always had a musical inclination. But when you date somebody that's a great fucking drummer, and you're a young girl in your early twenties, you're very intimidated by that. I got the strength to put my cards on the table by breaking up with him. Because then I thought, 'Fuck it, I've got nothing to lose now'. And it turned out that he responded really well, so it worked out for everybody. And we're still playing together. Isn't that beautiful? You can't replace either of us. Getting another drummer to fill in would be like getting another singer in The Rolling Stones. It doesn't make sense."

Left: Steve Shaw.
(David Atlas/Retna)
Above: The Come-Ons singer Deanne Iovan.
(Pat Pantano)

ii The Australian band's 1977 debut *(I'm) Stranded* remains one of the definitive punk documents—as raw, fuzzed-out and blistering as anything this side of early Ramones.

iii Underrated jangling Scots pop group from the Eighties: their music veered between indie trauma and oddly soulful blues.

KO AND THE KNOCKOUTS

Ko Shih

"I played piano from the time I was three till I was 18. One of my teachers used to slam the cover down on my hands if I looked down at them while I was sight-reading. To this day, I still can't look at my hands when I play bass.

"I didn't ever want to sing with a band. I didn't want to play at all. Steve Shaw was trying to get together a band together, post-Detroit Cobras, and he wanted me to play bass. I couldn't play, so Steve Nawara came over twice and gave me lessons. Steve Shaw wanted me to do back-up vocals as well, and I told him I couldn't sing and play... but then I did. When The Breakdowns split up, Long John [Sympathy For The Record Industry] called up and asked me to do a record. He knew what my voice was like because he'd heard The Breakdowns cover Mary Wells' 'Bye Bye Baby' with me on lead vocals. I was like, I don't have a band, I can't sing, I don't have songs, what do you want me to do?' He was like, 'Whatever you want?'

"That was right when Jack was putting together *Sympathetic Sounds Of Detroit*. Long Gone suggested he should ask me. Jack said, 'You've got two days'. So I got Steve Nawara and Jeff Klein together, and the next day we went to Jack's attic to record. When Jack asked whether we wanted to record the vocals or the guitar next, I said guitar, because we had no vocals at that point. I went downstairs, and there was an episode of *The X-Files* on the TV. So I sat there, trying to rhyme something with 'voodoo curse'.

"Both Eddie [Baranek, The Sights—guitarist/vocalist on Ko And The Knockouts' album] and I were really into the whole Mod scene, and there was none in Detroit. He was 16, and I was 24. I have two scooters, but they're in the garage wasting away right now. At first, it was for the music—and the look is great, too. Mick Collins has much the same roots. I really like the sound of the Hammond B3 organ, and it wasn't on anything else back then. You can play one note on that and it sounds great.

"Detroit is a good town to go have a party in. I'm always real excited to come home, but once I'm here I can't figure out why. Detroit today is very different to Detroit four years ago—back then, all the bands everyone talks about now were going out every night, partying. Now, everyone's on the road, and once you get home you don't want to go out cos you've been in bars for the last three months."

"Good," remarks Rachel, "Kenny got fed up of the old one."

These are my new gods.

Tell us a story from your childhood.

"You don't want me to do that," warns Rachel. "Let's see. I've been left in a bank, a supermarket and a department store by my mother, where she got in the car and drove away without realising she had left me!"

Tell us a story to make us weep.

"She wasn't even supposed to have me. She had, like, half an ovary. When she got pregnant her doctor was like, 'There's no fucking way you can have this kid, it's either gonna kill you, it'll be dead, you'll both die or it'll be horribly deformed and retarded'. But she fucking had me."

You should tell me about your tattoos.

"No, I shouldn't."

Why?

"They're not fucking show and tell."

"I grew up on R&B and soul," says Mary, "mostly crappy soul, but I wasn't allowed to have white people's music in the house."

What about you, Rachel?

"I was in Australia at an all girl's school between kindergarten and 12th grade," she replies. "I didn't get along with my own age group, I got along with the girls in high school and they were playing original punk, y'know? The Clash, Severed Heads, amazing stuff. Then came New Wave..."

"Metal," corrects Mary.

"No," Rachel shoots back. "Metal was when I was in Junior High."

"When I was young," begins the guitarist, "they made a cake for my birthday, and we went out to a club, and we left cos I wanted to go see The Saints at the Ritz. I was like, I have to go and see this band, and it was so fucking depressing, but I wouldn't give up my dream. I followed them back to the hotel room cos I was determined..."

"Oh no!" exclaims Rachel.

"... it was my dream, my love, y'know," Mary concludes, "and if I couldn't make it work I'd go and throw myself off the balcony...!"

After the tape clicks off, Rachel tells us a tale from when she'd travel up to New Orleans every weekend with her girlfriend. The police busted them on a regular basis: it got to the stage where they didn't even bother coming up with charges, just throw them in the slammer when they saw 'em walking into town. One time, her friend had a sheet of acid on her when the pair got thrown into the meat wagon, and both girls had their hands cuffed, so Rachel leaned over and ate the entire thing. She spent the next four days inside, absolutely freaked out.

"Every morning they would hose the cells out with industrial-strength bleach," she recalls, shuddering. "I'm not saying it was illegal but they never ventilated the place once. I

swear I came out of that place with less brain cells than I went in with. I used to be smart. Now I can barely think."

Left: Ko And The Knockouts singer Ko Shih. (Courtesy of Steve Gullick CTCL Archive)

Above: The Detroit Cobras, Rachel and Mary. (Doug Coombe)

iv (page 85) Singer with Chicago's gonzo grunge band, The Jesus Lizard—arrested once for indecent exposure on stage.

The Detroit Cobras songs sidle up on you: they don't grab you or offer instant gratification, that's not what this is about. First couple of times you hear their recorded stuff—and yes, it is all covers of folk like Willie Dixon, Wilson Pickett, The Drifters, Tina Turner, Otis Blackwell—you think, "so...?" It's only after you catch yourself listening to the record for the 232nd time you think, "Hmm, maybe they do have something special going on here".

Oh, and by the way. The ability to write a crap song does NOT mean you have soul. Soul comes from what you do with the goddamn words and notes you're given, not whether you've strung a few chords together. The Song does not exist until it has The Voice to give it full reign—and The Guitars to give it heart. Man, the Cobras have that.

For years, I've been desperate to see the Cobras live. Rumours came back that they'd been refused visas cos of alcohol-related shit. True? Who knows? Certainly, Rachel was on a self-imposed alcohol ban over here.

We touch down at Gatwick from a weekend break in Dublin the night they headline London. We have under 90 minutes to get across to town with a large suitcase. We arrive at The Garage seconds before the show starts. Fifteen minutes in, we're trying to avoid getting our travelling gear covered in blood: there's a man passed out on the floor in front of us, blood everywhere. A few seconds earlier, he'd climbed up on stage, folded his glasses away and taken a straight 45 degrees

SLUMBER PARTY

"The reason why there are so many good rock bands here is because we've all played with each other forever. If you put together a rock family tree, it would all be one big branch"—Johnny Walker

Sometimes, it seems that all Detroit is connected. Slumber Party drummer Julie Benjamin sings with The Fondas. Guitarist Gretchen Gonzales is one-half of the experimental female art-rock duo, Terror At The Opera. Bassist and former drummer Leigh Sabo dates Mike Walker (ex-Gravitar, Detroit City Council), Julie is engaged to Dave Buick and main songwriter/guitarist Aliccia Berg Bollig dates Dion Fischer (ex-Godzuki, The Go). Dion produced *Slumber Party 3*, while Matt Smith (Outrageous Cherry, The Volebeats) produced the first two albums. Aliccia used to date Matt. Marcie Bolen (The Von Bondies) has also played in the band—and she once dated Jack White. Hmm.

All four members share vocal duties.

friday, january 23rd 9pm
slumber party
with special yeh-yeh guest
april march
the magic stick
4120 woodward, detroit
www.majesticdetroit.com

Why are your songs so melancholy?

Aliccia: "They're not all melancholy."

Yes they are, all of them.

Aliccia: "What makes you say that?"

They're tinged with ennui. You don't think they're melancholy? How would you describe them? They're all about *"That's why I'm not sad"*.

Leigh: "That's why I'm not sad means we're happy."

Aliccia: "Yeah. They're deceiving. There's one song on the album, what is it? We never play it live, it's called, uh…"

Leigh: "'Never Again'?"

Aliccia: "'Never Again', it's about me trying to quit smoking and everybody thinks it's about a boyfriend."

Two orchids sit on top of the television. I read books about children being cut away from their daemons, and cry. The sweetest two singles I played yesterday were by Kid Koala ('Basin Street Blues', old school jazz, animated like deranged Germans FSK overdosing on poppy-heads and euphonium) and The Barcelona Pavilion ('New Materiology', an old Fall sample sped up among sudden gusts of laughter and frantic percussion). Three Slumber Party albums jostle for position like a bundle of ancient Shop Assistants[i] live tapes cut loose from their pink ribbon, tumbling through the snow: "Slumber Party" with its terribly Gothic cover ("I thought we looked like a Hole cover band"—Gretchen), 2001's sumptuous *Psychodelicate* and the new one, *3* (kill rock stars, 2003), songs coloured in with snatches of merry conversation. Slumber Party aren't from Scotland and don't rock out live as hard as the Shop Assistants, though—they're from Detroit and remind me of the cool blue stillness of Galaxie 500[ii]. Whoa. Now that's some seriously smart references.

Man, Detroit must be a shit place to live in. It has so many cool bands.

Drums peal like distant rolls of thunder: harmonies wistfully drift in and out of focus: a sad, encumbered break-up song turns out to be fake but still poignant: down the front of a NYC kill rock stars showcase, girl fans hug one another as Slumber Party stride the stage with their three-part harmonies and boots ("They sound good and they look good. Pleasing on the ear *and* the eyes"—Maggie Vail, Bangs): phone numbers are scrawled in thick marker pen on arms: lipstick is smeared on lips: a newspaper is put down as banter turns more serious, touching on how it's always the most sensitive and fun people who end up killing themselves because…life is harsh.

"My name's Aliccia. You want me to tell you a story? One morning, my mom put me on the bus. And we went to the grade school. Everything was fine. Then I noticed all these kids are milling about outside the front. And the principle is out there, and he was a scary guy. And they're pointing at this cat, 'Cute cat'. And then I realised it was my cat and it'd followed my bus to school, and I got in trouble cos the principal thought I brought it there."

"I'm Leigh. When I was about seven, I was riding my banana-seat bike—you know, those bikes from the Seventies—up our steep driveway. I thought I was cool because I could ride no handed. And then my bike flipped, and I bit the cement, and that's how I chipped my teeth. Sorry, that's my story. A bit traumatic."

Forget Aliccia's protestations. Slumber Party's music is *drenched* in ennui. It comes suffused with that delicious, Sunday afternoon, childhood feeling—time lingers, you're in reverie, nothing else matters except… Nothing. Nothing matters. I write how my favourite music is either a) Outsider Music, made by those too separate or unable to have any choice in the matter, or b) simultaneously comforts and challenges me: one without the other is too scary and alien, the other too bland—but Slumber Party are exceptional. Their music makes me go weak at the knees. Not an image you'd want to conjure with, I'm sure, but it's the truth. Slumber Party make me *melt*.

Hush now, the ladies are speaking…

"My name is Julie, and I'm not talking about last night's cab ride. When I was little, I wanted to try out for *Annie* and my mom wouldn't let me. It scarred me for life. I used to… I don't know. I'm really sick today."

"First of all, I'm Gretchen."

It was Gretchen's feet that left imprints on my bag last night in the bar: subject of much excited (and ribald) conjecture from friends.

"I was coming home and the highway was closed, so I bypassed the barricade and carried

on down the highway. No cars at all. About a mile up there were more barricades but I could see there was enough space that my car could fit through. I guess that's not the best story…"

Slumber Party formed naturally: Leigh is Aliccia's sister-in-law. Aliccia was bored in her laboratory (she has a degree in molecular biology) so they got together over the kitchen table one day a few years back…she knew Gretchen cos she served her drinks, and… oh yeah, second album bassist Marcie once cut her hair. Gretchen met Julie in an on-line chat room. And that's about all I know. Wouldn't surprise me if the band has a different line-up by now.

The kill rock stars website offers the tantalising information that Gretchen has been in Universal Indians, Titty Sandals and Dr Gretchen's Musical Weightlifting Program; also you can download MP3s of 'Air' from *3*, which—if it's the same song ('White Like Air (Fools)') as listed on the Japanese birthday card Leigh sent me with an advance copy—has some neat, not intrusive, harmonica.

(Quick flashback to the past when I was more coherent than now.)

ET: Do you consider what you do to be naïve pop?

Aliccia: "I think we are all naïve. I guess. But I've been dumped by a boyfriend and robbed this past year so maybe the sound will change?"

ET: Are you punk rock? If so, please explain why.

Aliccia: "I once put a great amount of effort into a thesis explaining why I felt Slumber Party should be considered punk rock. Recently, I've been considering how we relate to Mozart. So I can't remember much about that, although I do remember that at the time I was drunk with conviction and considered it an epiphany of thought—isn't that a little punk rock—so let's make that, Number One: I don't remember much. Number Two: Gretchen wears duct tape tube tops in the summer."

ET: What is your conception of beauty?

Aliccia: "Yikes. I'm thinking about the one philosophy course I had many years ago… I hope you don't want an answer that is thoughtful, articulate and arguable. I think Amelia Earhardt was hot."

I cannot tell you too much about Slumber Party's history, partly because (as we all know) history doesn't exist, partly because all I'm ever interested in is The Moment—and The Moment makes no provision for What Went Before—and partly because the interview tape is confused, crowded, voices submerged under the sound of cutlery clinking and the babble of coffee machines.

Tell me as much as you can about your children's book.

Aliccia: "You think your house may be haunted but it's not, your brother may be playing tricks on you but he's not, that's about it."

Tell me a story about Detroit.

Julie: "One day we were in Young Soul Rebels, and a band was loading in, and there were a bunch of bums around. Dave [Buick] got the megaphone and yelled, 'Hobos, stay away from the emos'!"

Gretchen: "I got banned from Community Games when I was 16. The year before I went out with a friend, stole a car and got so drunk we couldn't even drive home…that's when I met Leigh! The day of the competition, I had to keep having time out to go and throw up. So they had this big committee meeting with representatives from Canada and the US, and they all said I wasn't allowed to compete. I was distraught. I'd competed in table-tennis every year since I was five."

i Eighties band, Shop Assistants were the chirpy, romantic, Ramones-loving kid sisters (and brother) to Jesus And Mary Chain's studied cynicism, as faultless in their fuzzed-out splendour and one album as even The Shangri-La's.
ii Late Eighties/early Nineties NYC band that effortlessly matched the poise of the Velvets to Jonathan Richman's childlike mantras.

Above: Slumber Party
(Doug Coombe)

MARY RESTREPO

"I've been playing in bands for longer than I can remember. In my more 'ho days I probably slept with the whole scene. I made a point to get to know each and every one of my forefathers. I wanted to get deep down to the root of rock

"I adored Rob Tyner cos I thought he was a great human being—but when I met Rob I did not know of the MC5. I met him on stage, and that dude's voice was incredible. My guitar was on 10, and he was still fucking louder than the equipment. He would tell me stories about the MC5, and it meant nothing to me. I was a New York Dolls fan. When I was shown 'Kick Out The Jams' and 'Trash' [The New York Dolls] I chose 'Trash'. All rock'n'roll was the same to me. I grew up around R&B...and that's where Steve Shaw came in. Steve was my teacher. He showed me The Kinks. He showed me a lot of stuff.

"More than playing music, what turns me on is watching music. If I broke my arm and I couldn't play again, that wouldn't bother me as much as if I lost my eyesight and couldn't go see bands play. Every single time I go watch a band, I cannot believe how the same instruments can sound different with five different people playing. It blows me away every time. I cannot get enough of watching live music."

Above: Mary Restrepo. (Courtesy of Steve Gullick CTCL Archive)

dive into oblivion. It took five men to lift him out. The band filmed him passed out in the dressing room.

Sure I was nervous. These assholes are my new heroes.

"When everybody was out of the house," starts Rachel, "I'd crank up Irma Thomas[v]. I'd think I was pretty good until I tried singing the songs without her..."

I've got an autographed Irma Thomas hankie somewhere.

"Holy shit!"

When I went to see her in London, my brother and I were the only two people dancing, so she came down the front and gave us handkerchiefs. Isn't that cool?

"Oh my god," the singer exclaims. "I could fucking kill you, that's so great. Someone gave me an excellent photograph of her, from about 15 years ago. It's on black and white, she's got her arms raised and some nice flab hanging down, and she looks so happy. The first time I understood the Beatlemania thing was when I saw her live. I started crying. Mary was, like, 'Shut up'."

What do you like about her?

Rachel: "Umm, her heart..."

Mary (returning from the bathroom): "You like my heart?"

Rachel: "An old friend of ours took a picture of Mary from the waist down, and her pubic hair was shaped like a heart."

Mary: "You know we don't need to get started on my stories."

Er...Irma Thomas?

"A single note from her can rip your heart out," replies Rachel. "It's so eloquent and simple. Her voice is not perfectly refined, but it's beautiful."

How did someone else discover you could sing?

"The choice wasn't that big," explains Mary. "We had to step over Rachel to go get a beer. 'Hey, you know that white girl can sing?'...You'd step over her and she'd be real nice about it, this clump of blonde hair lying on the floor."

Do you like being on stage?

"It's taken a lot of getting used to," replies Rachel. "I don't need the attention, y'know. My dad may have beat the shit out of me but he also kissed me goodnight. I don't have an empty space in my soul that I need the love of strangers. I'm learning to be gracious. Like when people say 'You've got a great voice', I used to explain to them who was better and why I sucked. You can only be so self-depreciating."

I know what you're saying.

Rachel: "There's a reason why we do these songs the way we do. We would do them like the originals if we had that ability."

I don't believe that for a second.

Rachel: "Hell yeah. I would. It used to be a real letdown, going from singing along to the originals to singing with the band. I would think, 'I could play it so good if I had those musicians'. Just telling the truth! But we've become comfortable with ourselves and let ourselves be what we are, instead of reaching too far like blues scholars."

Mary: "There's a lot more to study than just the notes. There's gotta be a reason why I like those three chords..."

Rachel: "When people go, 'They just do covers', it's like, 'Man, do y'know how hard it is to nail that incredible sound?' One of the reasons people like us so much is that we do get the feel of stuff. Other groups don't understand the intangibles."

Mary: "Drunkards all around the world appreciate us, cos they don't care about the notes and stuff. They just care about feel."

v Irma is the undisputed Soul Queen of New Orleans, best known for incredible Sixties cuts like 'Ruler Of My Heart', 'Time Is On My Side' and 'Wish Someone Would Care', some of which inferior white boy beat groups like The Rolling Stones popularised.

Rachel: "Why deal with more than you have to? It would change the dynamics too much. Either that, or it'd sound like blues scholars bullshit, that fucking blue-eyed soul crap. I don't wanna go there. It's like white harmonica players."

Are there any bands you get compared to that annoy you?

Rachel: "When someone who doesn't know much about this music goes, 'Oh, you're just like Janis', that stops me cold. They realise it when they say it cos they can see the blood pouring out of my fucking eyes! I hate her so much, and I don't think..."

...She could sing?

Rachel: "She could shriek. I sound terrible right now so I do sound like her, but I try to sing not that way. I don't think white women should sing, period. Look at Lilith Fair[vi] and tell me that white women should sing! By the second act you're gonna be fucking jaundiced from your own piss backing up in your system. Someone I do like is Norah Jones. She has a beautiful, uncontrived voice."

What about yourself?

Rachel: "I don't have a pretty voice like Irma Thomas—she can hit one note, one straight note, no bravado, it's the tone, beautiful. I don't have that. I can't just go 'la' and have it be beautiful, whereas someone like Chrissie Hynde could sing out-of-key or screech or wail and her tone would still be beautiful."

Mary: "Some men have the same thing. Marvin Gaye coulda asked me to kiss the floor and I woulda done it cos his tone is so...my god!"

"You know how many girls respect men who dance?" asks Rachel. "Like when you were telling us about how you were the only man dancing to The Dirtbombs in that venue? You might have got rude comments, but in their hearts they were jealous that you could be so free. It doesn't matter if you were good or bad...as long as you weren't doing the chicken."

Damn straight I wasn't doing the chicken.

"Most girls will respect a man who'll dance," she continues, "because they'll know that, either Number One he's gay, or Number Two, he's confident in himself and wants a good time. And confidence is sex."

"Confidence is an aphrodisiac," confirms Mary, "and desperation is the biggest turn off. Don't get on your knees and tell me how much you need me...I need you to make you want me."

"Show it!" exclaims Rachel. "Show me you're a man!"

vi US festival started by folksy singer-songwriter Sarah McLachlan with the laudable intention of promoting women in music. Unfortunately, she filled it with whining, self-regarding performers almost identical to herself—Indigo Girls, Paula Cole, Meredith Brookes, Dido, Liz Phair—thus unintentionally reinforcing several stereotypes.

Let's Build A Home

Ben Blackwell: "I've always been impressed by how ahead of everything you are. Before the first album even came out, you were talking about how the next album was going to be called *De Stijl*; 'We're going to be on the cover with our arms at right angles'. Do you feel prolific like that?"

Jack White: "I don't feel prolific at all. I feel set in my ways. If I write a song, and it's a good song, and it's not the right time to record it, I don't throw it away but save it for another time. We actually recorded 'Dead Leaves' for the first album but it just wasn't ready. By the time we did *White Blood Cells* it was. Same when I come up with the title for the *De Stijl* album. I love that art movement and it just seemed to coincide more with what we were doing on the second album than it did with the first because of its correlation with the idea of the blues breaking songwriting down to its simplest forms. With our second album we were going to multi-track, try piano and violin on different things, and bring up the question of how far we can go. That concept wouldn't have applied to the first album, or to *White Blood Cells*. It didn't matter what songs were going to be on there, it was a matter of the approach of the recording."

Left: Jack White and Meg White. (Kelly Ryerson/Camera Press)

A single preceded The White Stripes' second album in May 2000[1].

'Hello Operator' b/w 'Jolene' (Sympathy For The Record Industry) initially came out on picture disc (a detail from the photo session for *De Stijl*, all block shapes and arms on hips, in white and red: the reissued version pictures a demure Meg seated next to a swirly drumhead). It's an invigorating blast of the punk-blues, Jack's guitar all toxic spleen—the drums alert to every mood change. Jack protests against the dual worries of phone companies and loneliness while Johnny from The Hentchmen blows up a brief storm on harmonica.

"That's a phone company finger-pointing song," Jack revealed to *Live Daily*'s Colin Devenish. "I hate the rip-off company. I know everyone has to have a job, but it's pathetic that the better mousetrap doesn't win out. Meg said she heard one dentist invented a coating to put on teeth so you'd never get cavities ever again, but the government won't let them produce it because it would put all dentists out of business."

The B-side—a cover of the Dolly Parton standard, previously attempted by such unlikely folk as mid-Eighties Northern English band Sisters Of Mercy in all their gothic splendour—is more disposable. Jack's reading of Dolly's heartfelt lyrics somehow turns the song freakish. He refused to change the gender—rendering it somewhat camp. But hell (shrugs): it's fun, and isn't rock'n'roll supposed to be about *entertainment*? It went on to become a live favourite.

1 That itself was preceded in April by a free seven-inch given away with issue 19 of Portland pinball and music fanzine, *Multiball*: 'Handsprings' b/w a Dirtbombs song, 'Cedar Point 76'. Over an AC/DC-style riff complete with "tilt" sound effects, Jack conducts a monologue about he lost his girl to a pinball wizard who plays a machine that plays 'Stand By Your Man', during a trip to the bowling alley. It's a blistering blues, with a pile-driving rhythm.

THE ART MOVEMENT

De Stijl is a deconstructionist art and cultural movement founded in Amsterdam just after the start of the 20th Century. Jack White got into the *Red And Blue Chair* piece by *De Stijl* artist Gerrit Rietveld—loving it for the way it broke objects down into their simplest components. Jack understands the need for restrictions. Work out the parameters of your art first, *then* you can start creating. The album booklet contains the designs and sketches of *De Stijl* artists, Paul Overy, Rietveld, Theo Van Doesburg, Georges Vantongerloo and Vilmos Huszár—very cubist and blocky and simple in red, white and black. The front cover continues the theme of simplicity and the three colours. For it, Jack and Meg were photographed by one-time Dirtbombs and Detroit City Council drummer E Wolf, standing in front of red and white rectangular panels, clothed all in white, with black hair.

"The first time it hit me I was working in an upholstery shop," Jack explained to *The Guardian*'s Keith Cameron in 2003. "There was a piece of fabric over part of a couch. The guy I was working as an apprentice for put three staples in. You couldn't have one or two, but three was the minimum way to upholster something. And it seemed things kept revolving around that. Like you only need to have three legs on a table. After two, three meant many, and that was it, you don't have to go any further than that: the three components of songwriting, the three chords of rock'n'roll or the blues—that always seemed to be the number."

As he explains in *De Stijl*'s sleeve-notes: "Even if the goal of achieving beauty from simplicity is aesthetically less exciting it may force the mind to acknowledge the simple components that make the complicated beautiful."

"Even when you have the ability to do something, let yourself not do it," Jack told Keith. "Like I've made the rule in my life that I'm never going to learn how to play the harmonica. Even though I love the sound of the harmonica. It's good, because it keeps me boxed in: it gives yourself character and meaning. It keeps you centred on what's important. All of this—the band, the aesthetic, revolving around the number three—revolves around the most important thing about art to me, which is knowing when to stop. We set up this box where we created an idea of this band, The White Stripes, we sort of forced ourselves to live inside of it. It was getting in tune with ideals that are heading towards truth and honesty, which in music, to me, is really the blues."

"I love forced creation," Jack revealed in *The Onion*. "I love when artists do something with very little opportunity. I used to own a record by William S Burroughs, called *Break Through In Grey Room*. I always thought that was so great, just him in a room with a recording machine, cutting up the tape. I love that notion, anyone saying, 'I'm going to set up rules for myself and live by them.' It's appealing to know that people had standards. If you were touring the house of some old famous person, and he never liked any lightbulbs in the house, and he only lit the house by candle... People are so enthused by that. It at least symbolises that that person is working toward something. When you see flagrant excess and rule breaking and chaos in songwriting and art, you think that it's not really coming from anything, that they're just getting lucky.

"Eventually the *De Stijl* movement became so simplistic, the artists abandoned it so they could build it up again from nothing. They couldn't get any simpler than primary colours and horizontal and vertical lines. We'd wondered how simple we could get things before we would have to build it back up again. How simple we could get with people still liking what we do. In the same way, we always wear red and white (or black) at our shows. They're like our 'colours'. We always do everything that way to keep order."

"It's like a uniform at school," Meg explained to Keith Cameron. "You can just focus on what you're doing because everybody's wearing the same thing."

"It's another way to keep us together as a band," Jack added, "to keep us solid as a unit."

"We never covered a song because it was cool," Jack explained. "I've always hated the idea of record collectors who are obsessed with how obscure something is. Usually, I just assume something obscure isn't very good because otherwise I'd have heard it already."

In that case, one wonders how Jack would explain why many of the blues guitarists he loves aren't better known. Whatever. To each their own special favourites.

Around this time, other labels started to show an interest in signing The White Stripes—most notably Sub Pop (home of The Go and, more famously, Nirvana), Olympia label kill rock stars (home of Sleater-Kinney[ii] and The Gossip), and also Bobsled from Aurora.

"The most freaked out I got was when I received an email from Calvin Johnson of K Records," recalls Ben Blackwell, who was looking after The White Stripes' mailing list back then. "It was right before *De Stijl* came out, and he wanted to know if the only things Jack had out were the two singles and one album. I just read at the top of the email that it was from him and I screamed—nothing that came before was as extreme as that for me. There are certain similarities between The White Stripes and [Calvin's seminal, minimal, bass-less Eighties band] Beat Happening. I can remember playing *Black Candy* [third Beat Happening album] at the upholstery shop, and The Shaggs record[iii]—and Jack was kind of mad at me for having the Shaggs record, because he didn't. I don't remember him commenting on Beat Happening."

"There was a time when everybody in town was in a band and nobody could do anything except play at a bar," Matt Smith recalls. "Then there was a time when there was nothing large going on, but Jack still had plenty of stuff to say no to. Bobsled had a couple of hit bands like

ii Inspirational three-piece Riot Grrrl band from Olympia, WA—they trace a direct line from trailblazers Bikini Kill but rock hard enough (and conventionally enough) for even mainstream music critics like Greil Marcus to pick up on them.

iii The Shaggs are either the greatest idiot savant garage band ever—these New Hampshire sisters really *couldn't* play their instruments—or impossible to listen to. Their one album *Philosophy Of The World* (Third World, 1969), recorded in one day on the behest of the proud dad, is entirely unique and charming, and one can trace a direct line from it to latter-day naïve Outsider Music stalwarts such as Half-Japanese, Beat Happening and Jonathan Richman.

Stereo Total[iv] and Chamber Strings. Bob Salerno, the guy behind the label, wanted Jack to sign with them—but there was this little green thing on the side of the record that was the Bobsled trademark. So Jack asked him if there was any way they could avoid having that, because his deal was to have everything in red and white and black. And the guy said no. It came down to that, one little icon. History could have been entirely different... For Jack, it was never about getting signed. It was about having creative control."

Where did Jack find that kind of self-belief to hold on? After all, both he and Meg were still working in their regular part-time jobs (as upholsterer and bartender) right up until October 2000. It must have been tempting to take the dollar: especially when there was no guarantee of anything else showing up.

"Maybe it was because when he went to high school he had to leave his neighbourhood friends," Matt answers, "and that prepared him for wanting to do his own thing. He's always had that self-belief. From haircuts to...when they first started playing they had the Silvertone amp on top of a white table. It didn't look good. It didn't add anything, but every show it was there."

PEPPERMINT TRIPLE TREMELO

On the inside of the sleeve to *De Stijl* is a picture of a very classy-looking amplifier: the Peppermint Triple Tremelo, designed and constructed by Jack White, with electrical wiring by Johnny Walker. The sleeve-notes explain, "The cabinet contains three types of Leslie revolving speakers. The peppermint in the viewing window is mounted on a revolving speaker baffle and spins at both slow and fast speeds."

Johnny Walker: Over Christmas break during my second year at med school, I came up and slept on Jack's couch for two weeks. He was working on these Leslie revolving speakers that created a Dopfler-like effect like a vibrator unit on an amplifier, similar to the sound on a Hammond Organ. Jack wanted to put the three speakers together in an X and Y and Z axis in a big red cabinet he'd built. The Leslie speaker in the front was a drum, with a hole in one side that let the sound out, and a speaker that went into it. So he painted peppermint on the top, and I wired up everything. I must have done a horrible job because the speakers kept blowing. The problem we didn't take account of was the weight. It weighed about 350 pounds. It was too fucking heavy to take on tour.

Ben Blackwell: It looked better than it sounded. Jack only played with it live once—but then he carted it out for *The David Letterman Show*. There were three speeds, which meant there were essentially 27 different settings you could have—three times three times three.

Left: (top) (Haags Gemeentemuseum, Netherlands/Bridgeman Art Library), (bottom)(Thomas A. Heinz/Corbis)

Above: Jack with his Peppermint Triple Tremelo amp. (E.Wolf)

DE STIJL

In June 2000, the second White Stripes album, *De Stijl* was released, dedicated to artists Gerrit Rietveld and Blind Willie McTell[v]. It was recorded mostly at Jack's house, with the mixes being conducted at Ghetto Recorders (Jim Diamond was credited with co-producing once again, although it was almost entirely Jack's baby). This decision was made because Jack wanted to take more time over the recording.

"I didn't have too much to do with Meg on this one," Diamond revealed. "It was all Jack—he'd record stuff on his eight-track analogue and bring it over here, where we'd mix it on *my* eight-track analogue. His house was only 10 minutes drive away. I guess he figured he could save money that way. I prefer to be involved from the start, to be honest, not just to do the mixing on what is essentially a home recording. My feeling is the standard isn't quite what it should be. It was not a lengthy project, though—I don't know how long Jack and Meg spent recording at his house, but the mixing bill for that entire record came to about $600."

"We didn't want to make the same album twice," Jack explained to Brian Baker. "So we recorded the whole second album in my living room. There wasn't any studio influence, so we felt comfortable, and Meg felt comfortable."

Later, Jack indicated that he wasn't so sure it was such a good idea to record at Third Man (the name he gave to his home studio) either: "There were too many distractions," he told one UK magazine. "The phone ringing, and all that jazz. And people would knock at the door. We even had one drunk guy wander in the house off the street while we were recording ' Death Letter'..."

Other musicians disagreed with Jim's view of the recording quality.

"With *De Stijl*, you saw better fidelity with the recording," Dan Miller told Brian McCollum in 2003, "I think you saw more of the progression—developing songs and messing with the arrangements more, more of a pop aspect."

"The second album seemed a little more inconsistent as far as the production went," Dan says now, "but the songwriting itself was more poppy. The first album was just the vocals run through a guitar amp, but even then they were doing different stuff—the guitar sound on

iv Playful pan-European New Wave pop group who sing in both French and German.

v Early 20th bluesman who played with an elegant side movement and nimble finger picking style that frequently made his guitar sound like several. Based in Atlanta for most of his life, he began drinking heavily once his 1949 Atlantic recordings failed to sell. Musically, he veered all the way from uptempo ragtime to melancholy blues.

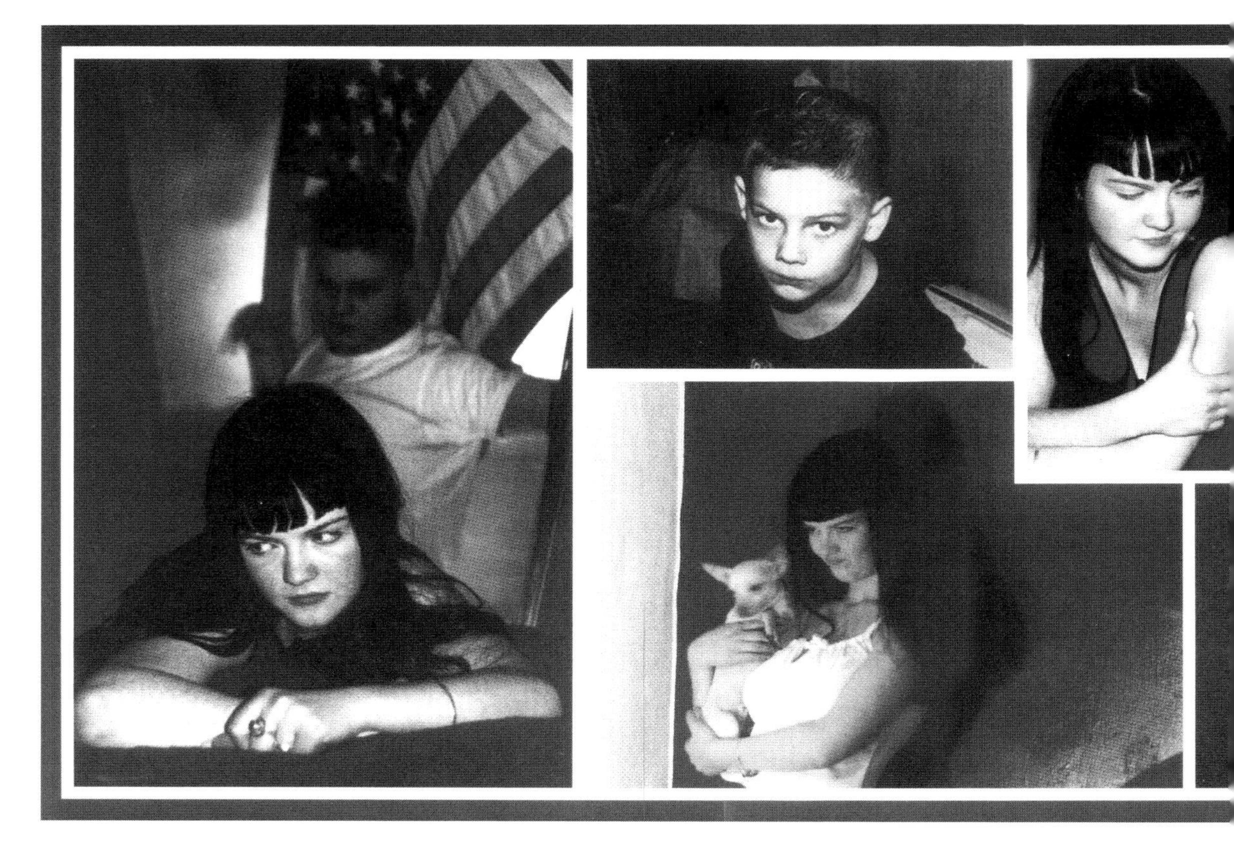

Above: Photo collage on the inside sleeve of the first pressing of 'Lafayette Blues'. (Heather White. Young Jack by Stephen Gillis.)

'Screwdriver', the piano on 'St James Infirmary'—but they still had the genuine emotion. I thought it was the perfect second step."

My feeling is that the second White Stripes album isn't quite as strong as the first. Part of this can be put down to the "disappointing" second album syndrome, whereby groups who've had any amount of time to build up to the first, often rush the second, seeking to capitalise quickly on the impetus they're building up. In The White Stripes' case, it seems that the main trouble is *De Stijl* is basically *The White Stripes* mark two—there's no differentiation. Sure, there are some great songs present—the opening salvo, 'You're Pretty Good Looking' (*"for a girl"*) is a solid caustic blast, and the tumbling piano on the warm 'Apple Blossom' is a real delight, as is the warped bass-y guitar solo; and as for AC/DC-style riffage on the fluent 'Why Can't You Be Nicer To Me?'...well! OK, so maybe it is just as good. It's just the two records are so close in feel that they could be parts one and two.

Or maybe they aren't...

On the second record, Jack loosened the limits of what was and wasn't allowed with his band—going so far as to include guest musicians such as Paul Henry Ossy (who plays violin on 'Why Can't You Be...' and the acoustic 'I'm Bound To Pack It Up', which also includes stand-up bass from Jack) and Johnny Hentch. Indeed, the whole album feels looser than its predecessor—a plus, for sure. It also comes across as more playful and relaxed...

Enough already! I prefer it to the first, OK? It's not as angry, a lot more approachable and with a wider palate of emotion. And, on reflection, 'Jolene' works just fine.

"I loved 'Why Can't You be Nicer To Me'," says Dick Valentine (singer, Electric Six). "I thought the lyrics were hilarious. I remember Joe [Surge Joebot] going, 'See that guy, that guy hates us' and I was like, 'Alright, I guess I won't speak to him'. I was really naïve about a lot of things in the early days. My whole thing was, 'Look at this. What's this? This is interesting.' I can remember being captivated by that song."

Blind Willie McTell features on a sound clip at the album's close, straight after a jovial cover of his 'Your Southern Can Is Mine' boogie, which is also notable for being the first time

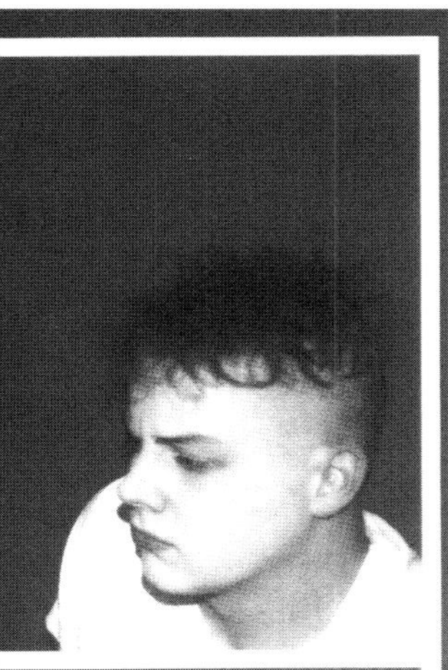

Meg sings back-up on a recorded White Stripes song. ("You keep moving around like you're uncomfortable," his interviewer asks. "What's the matter, Willie?" "Well," the bluesman replies, "I was in an automobile accident, I'm a little shook up...")

The song's lyrics actually tell a story wherein the protagonist beats his woman with a brick. As critic Keith Cameron pointed out in an interview in *The Guardian*, there seems to be a part of Jack White that is so obsessed with the fast lives of the Deep South bluesmen—the Thirties equivalent of rock'n'roll stars—that he sometimes imagines himself to be one.

"I was saying, 'These are my idols'," he defended himself, "yet I probably disagree with their lifestyle a lot: wife-beating, drinking and carousing, sick behaviour like that. I'm respecting the notions they're conveying in their music but I'm not really respecting the people they are. Michaelangelo was probably a complete egomaniac jerk too, y'know? While there wasn't equality between sexes and races at that time, there were a lot of things involving feminine and masculine ideals that were closer to one's own nature. This kind of opinion can be taken as sexist, but it's the same as saying a female can give birth but a male can't. Culture is dying because of mass communication, malls are springing up in third world countries and we're all striving for the same sort of success, but we're missing out on a lot of things about what a family is. What a male is, what a female is."

The child reciting a nursery rhyme at the start of 'Let's Build A Home' is Jack himself, taped by his mum and older brother when he was six or seven: "It was some sort of religious song," the singer told *Mojo*. "I didn't sing it right. It should have been, *'I wish I had a little red box to put the devil in, I'd take him out and punch-punch-punch and put him back again'*."

What's interesting about *De Stijl* is that you can hear far more of The White Stripes' Sixties pop influences—The Kinks, The Beatles, The Easybeats—than on any of their records before or since. "Truth Doesn't Make A Noise" is a real pleasure—the vibrancy of the guitar and the jangling piano keys sound like we're sitting in an old-time bar, whiskies being shot-gunned all around as the pianist rattles out another blues to soothe your heart. Silence is key once again.

These signifiers from the Sixties, as Dan Miller points out, lend the music a tenderness that is lacking in some of their more abrasive earlier outings. Songs like 'You're Pretty Good Looking' have a British Invasion feel to them—with a neat turnaround on the sexist lyrics of such usual "girls, cars and alcohol" songs, Jack croons *"I don't wanna be your toy"* like butter wouldn't melt. In trying to move back to the more innocent, earnest times of early childhood, Jack sometimes forgets to include the mischievousness. Here, the insouciance is captured neatly. On "Sister, Do You Know My Name?" Jack's voice is at its sweetest as he contrasts the feeling of facing up to the first day of school with that of starting a new relationship.

The next two tracks—"Hello Operator" and the worrying control song, "Little Bird" (where Jack talks about his desire to cage his *"little bird"*)—are much more straightforward urban blues. These songs also draw heavily from the primitive Sixties garage feel of The Stooges and The Standells[vi]. And there are traces of Led Zeppelin's Jimmy Page in the lascivious slide on 'Little Bird'.

"When we recorded that song," Jack told *The Detroit News* in March 2001, "We both said, 'People are going to say this sounds like Zeppelin'. But I loved that riff so much, we just had to put it on the record."

'I'm Bound To Pack It Up' is a straightforward broken love song, but none the less affecting for that, Jack's voice all hurt and sensitive, lamenting over Ossy's melody-drenched violin—

vi 'Dirty Water' was their Top 11 hit in 1966—as dirty, mean and lecherous as even the most hardened Rolling Stones fan.

IN THE STUDIO

Ben Blackwell: How would you describe Jack as a producer…after he recorded *De Stijl* and *Sympathetic Sounds* at his house you did the mixing on that, what would you say about his recording technique?

Jim Diamond: He's got some specific ideas on how he likes things to sound, and that's good. Some of it's different from what I would do…he likes things too loud. I'm like, "I cannot sit here anymore" so I hope that boy's ears are working in 10 or 20 years. He's got his own ideas and that's good, because most people have no ideas.

BB: Anything more to say about dealing with *De Stijl* and *Sympathetic Sounds*? Did you have to fix those up or…

JD: No, *De Stijl* was fine. Jack's good at recording his own band—he's not a recording engineer, he's a guitar player and a singer and a songwriter.

BB: Describe Jack White.

JD: I just know Jack from working in the studio, mainly. He's got some talent too, and he knows how to channel it, I think that's why a big part of it is being successful. He and Meg have a good sense of style and fashion, and once you put that together with musical talent and good songwriting, it's a winning combination.

BB: So describe Meg apart from what you already said.

JD: Meg's really sweet. I probably hang out with her more than I do with Jack, just seeing her in a bar or something. She's super down to earth and her drumming has skyrocketed from what it was when I first met her, which is great.

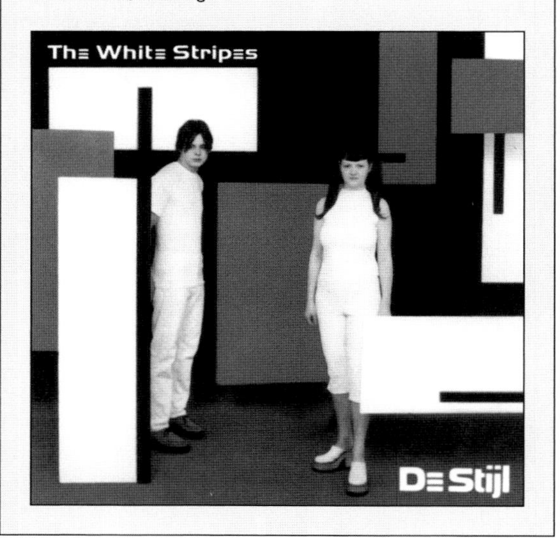

sounding somewhat reminiscent of Paul McCartney, circa *The Beatles* [to give the 1968 White Album its proper title], the acoustic guitar strumming blue sorrow. The Son House cover, 'Death Letter' is a ragged blues: dark and with the storm clouds threatening. The slow-burning 'A Boy's Best Friend', meanwhile, sounds a great deal like Screaming Trees' singer Mark Lanegan's solo work, and that's some compliment.

"Hell, they're a man-woman duo with an aggressively ambiguous relationship," wrote Chris Handyside in his *Detroit Metro Times* review, "a penchant for nursery-rhyme simplicity masking deep, dark secrets, and sporting trademark red-and-white garb and brandishing giant peppermints! Does that sound like garage rock to you!?

"Where the duo's self-titled debut laid out the blueprint of classic rock-via-the-Delta-blues by way of Southwest Detroit," Handyside further commented, "the Whites are now decorating the rooms of their mansion with Dylan-worthy introspection and minimalism, primal howls and cathartic regression (oh yeah, and the occasional 'rock anthem'). Translation? It's fucking brilliant."

Despite the fact The White Stripes didn't have a publicist or manager, the album still managed to get reviewed in a few mainstream publications[vii].

Rolling Stone wrote, "Feisty and clever…Meg White's drumming is so minimal it's almost funny."

The album release party for *De Stijl* was held in June 2000, at The Magic Bag, the same week The White Stripes took off on a West Coast tour. By now the buzz was becoming palpable.

Doug Coombes (photographer): "Lots of people who wouldn't be caught dead at The Gold Dollar were there for that one—the suburbanites."

Ben Blackwell: "The main CDs played in the bus that tour were a lot of Dylan and Captain Beefheart[viii]. Beck's *Midnite Vultures*[ix] was probably hands down the most played CD on any White Stripes tour."

In September, The White Stripes undertook a tour of the Midwest and East Coast, this time supporting Sleater-Kinney for two weeks. It was to prove a crucial turning point in The White Stripes' career.

Mick Collins: "I spoke to Jack right before they went on that tour. I'd never heard of Sleater-Kinney. Then I didn't see him for about four months and when they came back it was all anyone talked about. They were famous and that was it."

"They were just on top of their game," explains Blackwell. "I thought Sleater-Kinney was great but everyone I talked to said The White Stripes blew them off the stage. That's around the time they stopped using set lists, and when I first noticed Jack and Meg having a real strong connection. They had a real flow, going from song to song without a break."

Wendy Case (The Paybacks): "Being a rock journalist [for *The Detroit News*], I was always checking in with Jack, and he'd tell me, 'I don't know what's going on, but people really seem to like us in San Francisco. And I feel really encouraged by the response that we're getting on the West Coast…' There were definitely little pockets that picked up on what they were doing."

Jessica Espeleta (ex-Love As Laughter[x]): "My friend Jared from Karp[xi]/Tight Bros played the first record to me—at the time, we were in a band together, doing a similar thing. I flipped out. I played it to [independent PR] Julie Butterfield and *she* flipped out, and that's how they hooked up with Sleater-Kinney[xii]. I was probably more annoying than anything else, but I

vii You'd think this shouldn't be a big deal, and you're right—it shouldn't. But the larger, music magazines like *NME* and *Rolling Stone* and *Spin* seem to take an almost perverse pride in not knowing what's going on at grassroots level without the assistance of a handily placed PR. It's almost as if music doesn't have any validation without money. Of course, this is more a reflection on the paucity of imagination of your average music critic and editor than on the music itself.

viii The absolute boss of absurd, idiosyncratic blues-jazz-swamp rock-classical-punk: 1969's *Trout Mask Replica* is as seminal as they come.

really did think those first two records were the shit. I played them to everyone. I was a huge Gories fan, as well.

"The first time I saw The White Stripes was at the Sit And Spin in Seattle [June 15, 2000] but the next day was better cos it was an in-store with just 20 people there, at Fall-Out records on Capitol Hill. People were shy whereas the night before everyone was drunk with their mouths wide open. Jack's guitar tone was perfect, before it got too crazy. It was really loose. Nothing was mic-ed or anything, so it was probably the best show I've seen them play. There was lots of improvising. It wasn't as contrived as it is now. It was much more mellow. Later, they toured too much and got too good. I was pretty stoked on 'Jolene' and the slower songs from the second record. Also, they did that Dylan song, 'One More Cup Of Coffee For The Road'. It was great."

Jack White (to *The Detroit News*, 2001): "We went over like gangbusters with that crowd, and it got us a lot of attention and a lot more gigs, so we quit our jobs and devoted ourselves to the music. We're kind of scared about it. We look at other bands we play with, who we love, and we wonder, 'Why us and not them?' And then we think of all the bands that are really fake and lame who get a lot of attention, and we think, 'Are we just like those guys?' We just hope we're getting the attention for the right reasons."

ix Beck is an artful, inventive collector of post-modern junk, lo-fi ephemera and pre-electric folk and blues: confusing, infuriating and inspiring by turns, *Midnite Vultures* (1999) sees the maverick turn his hand to smug Prince-style funk. It may be a White Stripes favourite, but it certainly isn't one of mine.

x Karp were an Olympia WA trio obsessed with the ultra-heavy stoner grooves of (Nirvana favourites) Melvins, with a surreal sense of humour. Tight Bros From Way Back When are similar, but more obsessed with the cock rock strut of AC/DC.

xi Cacophonous, psychedelic and hook-laden punk rock from Olympia.

xii Julie then tells Janet Weiss [drummer with Sleater-Kinney, also in deeply melancholy and melodic Portland duo, Quasi] to check them out. About a week later, Janet—who'd been spending some time in LA—catches The White Stripes' first performance there, at Al's Bar. A couple of days later, The White Stripes support Weezer at Spaceland.

AUSTRALIA

Two notable one-off singles were released around this time.

In October, to coincide with The White Stripes' first tour of Australia, New Zealand and Japan, a red vinyl souvenir tour single came out—'Lord, Send Me An Angel' b/w 'You're Pretty Good Looking'. It was reissued four months later in the USA on Sympathy For The Record Industry. The A-side is a cover of the Blind Willie McTell song, with a tambourine jangling, and the odd thud of a bass drum, Jack's acoustic guitar chirpy throughout, and almost bluegrass, Jack's voice all rootsy and raw. The B-side is a pointless "trendy American remix" of the *De Stijl* track with a crap mock vocoder effect on the voice.

KILL ROCK STARS

Slim Moon (owner)

"I was married to a Detroiter for a while—that's how we met up with Slumber Party. I love The Gories, I love Destroy All Monsters[i], The Witches, Outrageous Cherry and of course The Detroit Cobras—and I'm glad that the Detroit scene is getting some recognition cos there have been great bands there for a while.

"I talked to Jack about signing to kill rock stars between The White Stripes' second and third albums. I was a fan from their first record, and I feel stupid not having approached them immediately following its release. They're working in a genre and a framework that is the kind of music I like a lot, and of course there is a long history with that and Olympia...

"Eighteen years ago when I moved here, a lot of the bands in Olympia had no bass player.[ii] They just had a guitar player and drummer, or singer and drummer, and everywhere they went they got harassed with that concept of not being a real band, or not knowing how to play their instruments. And it was a real big concern to people and bands like that, that they weren't considered legitimate and were made fun of. I know Olympia wasn't the only place like that, but we had such a high percentage of bands without a bassist, and we got a reputation...So when someone says something negative about you, you wear it as a badge of honour: 'Screw you. You don't need a bass to be in a punk rock band.' So whether it's Sleater-Kinney or Jon Spencer Blues Explosion, I've always had a fondness for bands with no bass, and also bands that break that rule of guitar-bass-drums, bands that have a keyboard instead, or three drummers and no melodic instruments. So of course I loved The White Stripes for having the nerve to deny a bass player. Obviously, in the Nineties, a lot of bands with no bass became successful and kids today don't even realise that it was a huge object of ridicule. It may seem really unimportant, but it's one of those examples where my friends and I fought the good fight, and it feels we won. We managed to change the world in some tiny way.

"I like the blues-based garage punk rock The White Stripes play, and for daring to be simple and not showing off their chops all the time. I've always felt that Jack White's talent is much bigger than that. If he'd started a band with two guitars and a bass, it would've been...the true appeal to The White Stripes is not that they keep it simple, or their relationship, or they wear black and red, but that Jack's talent is world-class. He could be writing in any genre, or working with any musicians, and that talent would be insurmountable.

"Also, I feel The White Stripes have some connection with The Gories, and it seems like Jack understands where that connection fits. It's not just about the Delta blues, but also The Gories—and The Gories are one of the greatest bands ever.

"Maybe he was just talking to us to research what a label is supposed to do for you, so he could use it with reference to Sympathy For The Record Industry. Maybe he never had any interest in signing to us. I don't know. The White Stripes played in Olympia after that, at a show Carrie [Brownstein, Sleater-Kinney] and Lois [Maffeo, singer and journalist] promoted. I got to that show and discovered I hadn't gone to an ATM and had no money, and so I waited outside, because I don't believe in people getting in for free because of who they might be. I was lingering in the alley, hoping to find someone who'd loan me the five bucks. It started raining, and the band started playing, and the girl working the door said, 'Oh, come on in, we've already filled the capacity'. It was very crowded, the band played another song, but then Carrie came up and yelled at me for not paying. So I sheepishly left and did not get to speak to Jack or Meg. I just went home and felt sorry for myself."

i Theatrical Seventies pre- (and post-) punk band fronted by ex-model Niagara—her breathy, childish vocals topped a riot of piercing violin and noise. Notoriously signed to Cherry Red without the UK label even hearing a demo, seduced by the inclusion of Stooges guitarist Ron Asheton in the line-up.

ii Notable Olympia-affiliated bands lacking a bassist include Sleater-Kinney, Beat Happening, Mecca Normal, Some Velvet Sidewalk, The Gossip, The Go Team (who once included Kurt Cobain as a guest vocalist), and so on.

Above: Backyard of Raoul Records, St Kilda, Melbourne, Saturday 11/11/00. (Mary Mihelakos) (Mary: "I gave Meg the dress she is wearing—an old checkout chick outfit I had purchased years earlier for $1.")

Australia has always had a proud tradition of supporting garage bands and lo-fi music: right from their earliest punk bands, Radio Birdman and The Saints in 1974, through influential Eighties sounds such as Nick Cave's astonishing Stooges-influenced The Birthday Party and Kim Salmon's abrasive Scientists, through to support for The Gories when no one else was looking and the In The Red/Sympathy-type bands. So it was the perfect place for The White Stripes to play before the big push in the UK the following year—particularly in Melbourne, where the audiences are far more receptive to unpolished music than they are in business-orientated Sydney.

"I saw about six or so shows out of the seven," recollects Australian fan, Bruce Milne (In-Fidelity Records). "My favourite was when they played the BBQ in the back courtyard of the Raoul Record Shop, St Kilda on a Saturday afternoon—and it only held about 20 people. Having enjoyed the records, I liked them so much more live, and also knowing this was a band that was going to become a lot more successful. I was working at EMI at the time, and trying to license their records, but Long Gone John was determined to hold onto them. They played the Empress, the Espy, the 9th Ward and The Tote, and they might have played the Town Hall Hotel.

"The band recorded a single live to acetate at Corduroy[xiii] that they were going to press as a single and sell at the gigs that night," Bruce continues. "They recorded 'I Just Don't Know What To Do With Myself' and a Billy Childish cover[xiv]. However, Jack and the cutting engineer had a falling out, and the record was never released."

"John Baker, their tour manager, is from New Zealand," reveals Mary Mihelakos, music editor at Melbourne's *The Beat*. "I first met him with The D4[xv]. So he got them to Australia via New Zealand. It started small, and grew and grew—the first gig was to 25 people, then 50, then 100, then 200... They were pretty easy-going. The band didn't even bother going to Sydney, so when *White Blood Cells* started to get attention, a lot of the music business people weren't even aware the band had come to Australia previously.

"I interviewed Jack," she adds. "He talked about how he recorded stuff himself, and the black, white and red concept, and the peppermint. And he did refer to Meg as his sister. A friend

xiii A local label whose main business is their pressing plant. Corduroy have done similar tour singles—successfully—with The Dirtbombs and Wayne Hancock, where the artists recorded directly onto acetate and the seven-inch was pressed within 24 hours.

xiv A song he wrote for Thee Headcoatees called 'You're Right, I'm Wrong'. The 'tees version appears on their stellar *Punk Girls* album.

xv Garage-punk band from Auckland.

of Jack's actually told one of my friends he'd been to their wedding—they told me, but I figured it was typical Australian "tall poppy" syndrome. In other words, The White Stripes get their first bit of international success in Melbourne and out come the knives…I felt certain it was jealous gossip, and they really were brother and sister. There's a certain innocence about the band that comes over when you're in contact with them. Meg had a boyfriend at the time, she'd always talk about Mike. Jack seemed like a bit of a control freak over the music. I'd bought a red and white check outfit six years previously, that I couldn't fit into it anymore—so I gave it to Meg and she wore it when they played live the first time. Apparently, she still wears that dress sometimes.

"'Jolene' was pretty great," Mary recalls. "They were incredible live—so simple and magical, and immediate. A lot of people, who don't listen to music anywhere near as much as us, got it immediately. The buzz on the band was incredible when they left. I saw them four months later at South By Southwest in Texas, and I walked around Austin with them for three hours and no one seemed to recognise them."

In December, Sub Pop were scheduled to release 'Party Of Special Things To Do' b/w 'China Pig'/'Ashtray Heart' as part of their one-off Singles Club series[xvi]—plain red cover, limited edition of 1,300 copies pressed in swirly white and red vinyl. All three songs are Captain Beefheart covers: funky, swampy, acoustic blues and swampy. The A-side is as distorted, energetic and oblique as you'd expect a Beefheart song to be: to be frank, nothing out the ordinary, because the Good Captain has such an original sound he's almost impossible to better. Still, Jack throws himself into the song's sentiments, the stream-of-consciousness tale of how *"I met all the cards/The wild cards/Red queen/she turned her head/you know the one I mean/She turned it back and said, 'I've got a brand new game I want to lay on you'/At the party of special things to do."* What's interesting is to note the influence Beefheart's hybrid blues has clearly had on The White Stripes sound—Jack's way of accentuating certain vowels, and the staccato yet fluid rhythms.

Above: The White Stripes live at Cup Day Chaos, Gershwin Room, Esplanade Hotel, St Kilda, Melbourne. PBS radio station benefit, 7/11/00. (Mary Mihelakos)

xvi In true Sub Pop fashion, it actually came out in April 2001.

White Blood Cells

"Listen up, you malingering, bad-teethed, Limey punk asswipes. Your music press sucks the big A, ain't no denying that. All that fucking power, and all they can give you is Coldplay and Stereofuckingphonics. Stereo fucking morons, more like. You'd think that once in Elvis' 'Blue Moon' they'd get it right: law of averages and all that.

"Well listen up: this is the time. But realise this. This shit ain't nuthin to do with dry-humpin' crits and their inability to get it up so they resort to pen-waggling instead: this is the fucken BLUES, fucken classic blues like Kristofferson and Irma Thomas and sweet Simone sang it. It's raw, it's untamed, and your skinny white boy asses deserve this shit about as much as they deserve to be rammed up to the ring with three truckloads of Stax singles. You fuckwads.

"Remember how the Pixies could'a sounded if they hadn't been full of shit. What you do is strip it right down. All you need is a thrift store guitar, a distorted amp and your older sister poking around in the attic, fucking with all your toys. Think you understand punk, punk? You don't understand shit. It's the blues. It's like Dylan could'a been if only he fucking hadn't hired a style consultant in '63. It's like Led Zeppelin if Jimmy Page had ever stopped whining and hired a decent singer. The White Stripes fuckin' rule and they give THIS for your fuckin' fashion! But yes they'll take a cool mill from The Man if he wants to be dumb. Why fuckin' not?

"So there's Jack and there's Meg. Meg is like the Mo Tucker of Detroit. She thumps the drums, and she thumps them good. You don't want to stand in her way, boy, not looking like that. Jack does pretty much everything else: screams, whines, kicks several shades of blue crap outta your moronic ass, rattles a piano, thumps the guitar, produces his own record like Steve Albini[i]...in Albini's panty-wetting dreams!

"I have no fuckin' idea what made you Limeys so retarded, but listen up and listen good. This album is the shit. It's the White Stripes' third, and to my ears it's the fuckin' best, even if 'The Same Boy You've Always Known' does sound like Pink ass Floyd, and there are too many words. Cos, as the man Jack sings, *'I'm not interested in gold mines, oil wells, shipping, or real estate'*. Fucking right, you sing it brother. The Pink Floyd comparison was a joke by the way. LIKE YOU FUCKIN' REALISED. 'Offend In Every Way', my man Jack says, and you know what. He's as sharp as a fuckin' [Jim] Diamond."

—The Incinerator, *Careless Talk Costs Lives*, November 2001

Left: The White Stripes live in London, 2003.
(Courtesy of Steve Gullick CTCL Archive)

i Albini is the Chicago-based producer of Nirvana's *In Utero*, PJ Harvey and...well, pretty much every self-respecting American/UK noise band of the Nineties. Known for capturing the essence of a band's live sound, not fond of frills. Also in Big Black, Rapeman and Shellac—excellent abrasive groups, all.

"It was January 2001," states David Swanson, "when Jack called up and asked if I'd go down and take photos of them recording *White Blood Cells*. I have no idea why he asked. I don't think he'd seen any of my photography, although I did give him a black and white photo when we played together at The Gold Dollar. He's really into black and white stuff. He wanted all the footage to be

ii It was probably a CD copy of The Gossip's debut self-titled seven-inch, released in 1999 on Calvin Johnson's K Records—bluesy and basic. The White Stripes would've only been listening to it cos they'd just been given a copy. In February 2000, The Gossip supported them on a couple of NYC dates, while the *Spinal Tap*-inspired Rye Coalition played in Baltimore. Long Gone John came along for that trip. Singer Chan Marshall's spooked, unnerving Southern drawl has caused many an indie boy to lose his heart.

like that. So we drove down to Memphis in their purple van—me, Jack and Meg. We listened to a lot of Black Sabbath, The Beatles, The Velvet Underground and The Gossip[ii]. Jack and I talked about one another's families. Meg was mostly way in the back of the van, on a bench—she seemed real quiet and sweet. She was really into what she was doing, but she wouldn't over-think it."

Author's note: people close to The White Stripes continually mention how quiet and friendly Meg is—which is true—and how she doesn't like to intellectualise her playing, but the couple of times I hung out with her in Detroit, January 2003, I found her to be a great conversationalist, and also a consummate hostess at five am—frozen pizza? Yes, please! She was funny, bright and could easily keep up with me drinking cheap bourbon (the only kind available in Dave Buick's house that night). Indeed, we were the last two people left awake.

She's articulate and passionate on the subject of drumming, talking about her fear of "freezing up" on stage when her body won't react to mental commands. She recognises her strengths: the fact she's not a conventionally accomplished drummer but that she reacts to the emotion around her, particularly emanating from Jack. She has to feel every beat before she can make it. It's rare that artists are so aware of their own positives and negatives. One other item: she owns a miniature pinscher puppy called Chester that runs over everyone.

"Jack mentioned there was not going to be any covers on the record, no slide guitar, no guest musicians, no blues and no guitar solos," the Whirlwind Heat singer continues. "He likes to set out what they're not going to do. The Memphis studio where they recorded, Easley-McCain Recording, is basically one long, gigantic room with several smaller rooms for overdubs. They

Below: The White Stripes perhaps commenting on the music press' attention span? (Stewart Isbell/Retna)

didn't go into any of those. All the vocal overdubs were done in the main room. Jack had his two amps set up so they were linked together, and he was talking to Stewart [Sikes, sound engineer] about wanting a stereo dual amp sound. He'd face Meg, with a big padded thing in between. For 'We're Going To Be Friends', she'd hit on the ground or a cardboard box. They had the songs pretty well worked out. It took three or four days to record, and a full 15-hour day to mix. Maybe someone else was coming in the next day, I don't know, but we had to finish it all then. Then we drove through the night back to Detroit—it's an eight-hour drive, maybe 10."

Stewart Sikes: "Jack knew what he wanted. Meg kind of thought the songs were too new. She drank a few bourbons and smoked a lot of cigarettes [both musicians smoke]. I think she was a little nervous being in a big studio. Jack talked to me more than once about not making it sound too good. He wanted it as raw as possible."

From these inauspicious, homely circumstances (the mix was completed at a cost of somewhere between $4,000-$6,000) came an album that would propel The White Stripes into the world marketplace. In many respects—the breadth of the material, the radio-friendly production—this was the Detroit duo's own *Nevermind*.

"We ate a lot of Payne's barbecue. It's this legendary barbecue place in Memphis," recalls David. "There was a photo book of everyone who'd recorded there: Cat Power and *What Would The Community Think?*, Sonic Youth and parts of *Washing Machine*—I'm a big fan, and they thanked Payne's Barbecue on the sleeve. I'm guessing we had some pizza. The first day we got there we grabbed something at Subways. One time we went into KFC and there was nobody in line but they'd run out of chicken. Mainly, we drank coke.

"The photography went pretty well. I shot eight hours of footage, and took maybe eight rolls of film on eight mm video camera and cassette. I still have it all here. I tried to capture each aspect of every song: the two of them playing live together, Jack doing an overdub—which he didn't do too much—vocals, maybe tambourine..."

THIRD MAN STUDIOS

Johnny Walker: His house was L-Shaped. There was a piano in the tall part of the L, going perpendicular across it. So there was always a lot of separation, guitars on the guitar track, drums on the drum track—because the piano blocked the sound out. In the tall part of the L we'd put amps, stuff like that. He had a really nice drop ceiling that absorbed a lot of the high-end stuff. We didn't have any guitar closets or shit like that, or nice mics. I had that silver 54 and we always used that on the kick drum for the low frequencies. We were using a little Teac six-channel mixer, it had very basic controls over frequencies—you could pan stuff and that was about it. And we used a Teac quarter-inch four-track reel-to-reel.

Ben Blackwell: Do you ever see yourself doing a White Stripes box set?

Jack White: Yeah, sure. It would be great to do a Third Man Studio box set, there's so many different bands that I recorded there, things that never got released.

Ben: That's just stuff in his attic—there's a whole reel of Hentchmen and Greenhornes outtakes, Soledad Brothers, this amazing band called The Night Moves. My first band, The Rags, was recorded there. We just did a bunch of Nirvana covers. 'Frances Farmer Will Have Her Revenge On Seattle' was our hit. I was 15, drunk on red wine stolen from work.

BB: You recorded my first band.

JW: That's right.

BB: I don't know if you know the story, but you'd gone out and left me and Nick [Orozco, guitar player in The Rags] at your house. Nick had stolen two bottles of wine from work and he was totally drunk when we were recording. I've still got the master tape hidden in my file cabinet. Do you feel like you want to do more stuff with Third Man records?

JW: I do, but I don't feel I have the time or the intelligence. I don't want to be bothered with running a record label because I'm too busy. I'm scared about that because I like producing other bands, and there's lots of stuff I could release right now, but I don't want people to blame me because something's not happening for them. I'm sure if The Von Bondies had signed with Third Man, which was talked about, they'd be doing nothing but complaining to me right now, for ruining their lives or something...

BB: As opposed to just complaining about the label they're on now.

JW: Exactly.

Ben: He wants to do Third Man but he doesn't have the time. It's essentially just him. He doesn't want to be responsible for some band on his label asking for tour posters to be printed up while he's in Italy for three months. He did some Whirlwind Heat stuff at his house, probably May 2001. Since then, he's been fucking busy. Whirlwind Heat are punk kids from the middle of nowhere in the middle of Michigan who shared a love for Sonic Youth and Braniac [Early Nineties Dayton, Ohio band known for their jerky sound], *and were lucky to find each other and a Moog synthesizer. They're insane now cos they've toured so much—their next record is going to flip people's lids.*

White Blood Cells was released on Sympathy For The Record Industry on June 25, 2001. Inside the 12-page CD booklet, there are photographs of blood cells, red hair, red cloth, a red baby's foot with a needle being stuck into it, and a shot of one of blues legend Robert Johnson's hands, enlarged. It's instantly recognisable, even so distorted, because famously only two photographs were ever taken of the guitarist.

The dark figures on the sleeve surrounding the band include members of The Von Bondies and The Soledad Brothers, photographed by Patrick Pantano. They clearly symbolise the encroaching media. Most musicians that operate within the public sphere past a certain level have an uncomfortable relationship with the media—are they here to help us? Are they here to pick us apart? What do they want from us? Can't they see we just want to be left alone? (But we would still like the publicity, thank you.)

Jack, well versed in the lore of blues and rock, was well aware of the pitfalls of his situation—a band that didn't have a manager or publicity agent was being courted by the music industry anyway. (A PR was finally hired by Sympathy for the release of *White Blood Cells*.)

Indeed, after The White Stripes appeared on their first *NME* cover in August 2001, Jack was furious. He thought that such premature coverage—it happened before the band had a UK

WHIRLWIND HEAT

David Swanson (voice, Moog)

"We've known each other since we were 10. Steve [Damstra, bass] had a older brother who played bass, and Brad [Holland, drums] played guitar, and we all listened to music a lot together when we were 13, 14. We wanted to cover Nirvana songs. I was going to play drums, but I couldn't keep a beat. We started writing our own stuff when we were 16: nonsense, pretty much. I didn't have anything to write about, apart from being bored all the time. We'd write dumb songs and throw parties in our basements, and our friends would come over.

"In 2000, there were a couple of other Grand Rapids[i] bands who wanted to play out of town, so we set up a show at The Gold Dollar, and Dave Buick came along and we talked to him a little bit. He told us that he ran Italy and wanted to do a seven-inch with us, and that he had this friend Jack who recorded the bands for him. We'd never heard of Italy Records or Jack White. Kids back home would say they'd want to release our stuff, so we'd record on four-track and they'd put it on cassette tape for their friends—we figured this thing of Dave's would end up the same way.

"Soon after, we played at The Magic Stick with They Come In Threes[ii]. Dave didn't show up, but Jack came. He was wearing a bright yellow T-shirt, and he was by himself. He seemed pretty excited. He said something about Dave Buick and Italy, and asked us to come over that night and record some songs. We were like 18, 19, doing really shitty jobs at burger joints and had to work the next day, so we couldn't. So we set up a different time to do it. He mentioned his band The White Stripes and we were like, 'Sorry. Never heard of you'.

"The day we recorded our Italy seven-inch [the sparky, abrasive 'Glaxefusion' EP, which sounds far more similar to New York '77 then Detroit '97] was the day Jack got his copies of *De Stijl*. He was like, 'Oh, here's our second record' and gave us copies of the first two. He seemed pretty excited about it. We recorded three songs up in his attic, and it's a real small space. For some of them we used an electronic drum. Jack didn't like that, but we ran them through the Moog, and he was into that. Then we recorded 'Decal: Sticker', and Jack told us he was putting together a compilation [*Sympathetic Sounds*] and that he'd really like that song to be on it, even though we're not from Detroit.

"We'd only released one seven-inch before that [the limited edition, 300 copies, split single on Offsite, 'Spyboys Experiments'—quirky space-age electronica]. We got real excited cos Jack actually had a reel-to-reel eight-track, and an analogue system, and knew about music. He was telling us to check out other Detroit bands, like Soledad Brothers and The Dirtbombs and The Paybacks.

"After that, I kept calling up Jack and we didn't do anything until late 2000 when we did three shows in the Midwest with them. One was at O'Cayz Corral in Madison, Wisconsin. The place burned down a week later. Then there was the Cactus Club in Milwaukee: I remember the big brown hollowbody guitar was having a problem so Jack threw it up against a wall. And there was The Empty Bottle in Chicago, where the crowd was really into it. Every show was packed, about 300-capacity. There was a good sense that something was happening which we'd never seen before. That was right after the Sleater-Kinney dates.

"We're quite a bit different from other bands Jack's worked with. I think it's coming from Grand Rapids rather than Detroit. It's quite a conservative, small city—very clean, with a new church on every block. In Detroit, you have a group of people who are really into music and share each other's ideas, whereas we had just the three of us. We didn't start listening to The Stooges until after we got introduced to the Detroit scene. That comes from isolation—from Nirvana we found out about Sonic Youth, from them, Mudhoney, and then the Melvins and on and on, through Devo..."

i Whirlwind Heat's hometown. Grand Rapids is about two hours west of Detroit in a car.

ii Ben Blackwell: "They Come In Threes will be the great forgotten Detroit band in 15 years, and everyone will be looking for their self-released 45 'Where Rev Lived' and saying it was awesome. Their sound doesn't fit in with the rough garage recordings the city is known for: more along the lines of Television or Yeah Yeah Noh. Halloween, 2000 was The Witches record release for *Universal Mall* and They Came In Threes opened up. For a second, you couldn't tell who it was because the entire band was in full costume. But they came out and did an entire set consisting of nothing but Black Sabbath and Prince covers. Fucking genius."

Above: Whirlwind Heat (Sarah Bowles)

record label—would cause the band's career to be over before it begun. Of course, it had the opposite effect: but artists often don't understand the nature of their relationship with the media. If Jack had really wanted to take things slowly in the UK, he would've only talked to the cool underground publications. Instead, every time a new White Stripes interview appeared, it was *always* in tired, corporate outlets like *Q* and *NME*. Clearly, Jack didn't care that much.

Back then, Jack White couldn't even see The White Stripes changing labels: "No one's telling us what to do, the artwork, what songs go on the album, [Long Gone John] will do any seven-inches we want to do, anything," he told Melissa Giannini of *Detroit Metro Times*. "It's become one of the bigger bands Sympathy's ever had. Why should we leave this label as soon as there's been bigger interest? He's helped us along the way so long. Other labels like Sub Pop or whatever, have gotten success with things, gotten lucky. I don't know if Sympathy's ever had a band that's been really huge or anything. So if it does happen, if it gets bigger, it would be nice to be on a label like that."

The primal tom-driven chant of 'Little Room' directly deals with the dilemma of fame: how success coming in too fast could spoil something as precious as The White Stripes. It's a delicious blues warning of the perils of hitting the big time and losing your muse, Jack howling, *"You might have to think about how you got started/Sitting in your little room"*. The lyrics could also be perceived as returning to the first album's theme of childhood: worrying about stepping out from the little room of childhood into the bigger room of adulthood. But what do you do when the offers start rolling in—as they soon would...

"If someone said, 'We'll give you $100,000 if we use your song in a commercial that's only gonna run for a couple months'," Jack mused to Giannini, "At least you could give that money to charity or something. It seems kind of stupid to turn that down, but who knows? It's never come up. I don't think we're good merchandise-selling songs."

Another song that addresses the same problem is their (as yet unrecorded) heavy-duty cover of Leadbelly's 'Boll Weevil' that The White Stripes sometimes finish their live show with.

BB: "I've thought of that song, at least when you were playing it the other day in Detroit. I took to it as the boll weevil being the media..."

JW: (laughs)

BB: "...boring their way through your hats and your clothes. Talking to you and somewhat being friendly, but at the same time being a pest to you."

Ben: "That's what I thought it was—how the media can be so nice and so inviting and then do such evil things, while always smiling in your face. The boll weevil is an insect more common in the South. It ruins cotton crops and is seen as a nuisance. Jack's looking for a home in every city. He doesn't feel like he's home anywhere."

JW: "The artwork for *White Blood Cells* is like that too, an accidental prophetic thing. I didn't mean to set it up that way."

BB: "There's no way you could expect half..."

JW: "No, I was only thinking in terms of the Detroit garage rock scene, that we were at a level where people cared about us more than everyone else in town. Where it felt bad to us, but it also was our chance to break out of the same 100 fans every night. The front cover was like the bacteria and white blood cells and all that—is having people's attention good or bad? And why don't they pay attention to these other great bands like Rocket 455 and The Greenhornes? Why us?"

BB: "So most of the people as the bacteria were the Detroit garage scene?"

JW: "Yeah, exactly. It's funny... Do they hate us? Are they coming to attack us?"

Ben: "I always get kind of annoyed with Hellacopters or Scandinavian bands that sound like Detroit rock—because we've always had rock bands in Detroit that are ignored. Rocket had an energy that you could trace the lineage in this town to."

White Blood Cells starts off in blistering form, with two songs that would later be released as singles—'Dead Leaves And The Dirty Ground' and the angst-ridden 'Hotel Yorba', named after a notorious Detroit doss house. Whereas the latter song is almost frantic in its acoustic lilt, the way the drums tumble over themselves trying to keep up with the chorus, the former is dark—a welter of guitar riffs and spaced-out drumbeats that references The Doors song, 'Five To One'. Like 'This Protector' and 'I Can Learn', it was written before the first album was released, and serves a timely reminder of The White Stripes' raw blues power right at the start of what would turn out to be easily their most commercial album to date.

The brilliant nursery rhyme-like, theatrical 'I Smell A Rat', meanwhile, appeals to the five-year-old in all of us—and also criticises the way that teenage kids can act like petulant five-year-olds, especially when it comes to treating their parents with respect.

"I love that song," Jack White told Colin Devenish. "We wrote that the day before we left for Memphis. The phrase *'I think I smell a rat'*—there was one day when I was home by myself and I played one chord on the piano, and I kept saying it over and over. I could never think of

anything else to go with it. I loved it because I had this whole thing imagined—that it would go into this swinging finger-snapping thing after that—but I never finished writing it.

"We had this [other] song called 'That's Where It's At', that we didn't put on the first album. [The lyric] was, *'All you people know/Just where it's at now/Walking down the street with a baseball bat now'.* It's about the kids in the neighbourhood. I played that chord, and *'I smell a rat'* popped out again. Meg played it with me, and we said, 'This is perfect'. The catchiest stuff we've written, like 'You're Pretty Good Looking', is just the most natural. I didn't sit down and figure it all out. It can't be faked."

'Hotel Yorba' is totally infectious—childlike in its clatter, but adult in its agoraphobic complaints of the constant hubbub emanating from the outside world. The album's second single, 'Fell In Love With A Girl' is similar, and even knocks the urgency up a notch. Jack's vocals are very reminiscent of Black Francis [Pixies], circa that Boston band's classic Eighties album *Surfer Rosa*, his guitar a frenzy of old school Buzzcocks riffage. Like Buzzcocks, love is bittersweet and frustrating and over in under two minutes. Like Buzzcocks, it's a song to take on the world.

Unlike Buzzcocks, it did.

'I Can't Wait' has shades of 'Heart Shaped Box' from Nirvana's swansong album *In Utero* in its grungy, circular guitar riff and stamping drumbeat—the chorus, meanwhile, harkens back to the classic Seventies mid-American rock of Boston and Wings. Jack's contention that this album wasn't going to contain any blues seems particularly appropriate here. Towards the end, the guitar is unrepentantly full on grungy, in the classic Jack Endino style.

A couple of old favourites are pulled in from Jack's Two Star Tabernacle days: the *Citizen Kane*-referencing 'The Union Forever', and the jaunty, lyrical 'Now Mary'—a plea to The Detroit Cobras guitarist not to be so bloody-minded, perhaps? The latter recalls the plangent, jangling guitars of post-Stone Roses Britpop band, The Bluetones—not an insult by any means.

It was in the middle of 'The Union Forever', after a series of lines flavoured by warm Hammond-style organ, during Jack's inspired soliloquy pulling in old catchphrases from the classic Orson Welles' movie about a megalomaniac newspaper proprietor, that this author suddenly *got* The White Stripes—just the sheer audacity of the references and arrogance of ranting over what amounted to silence made me realise that here was a band special indeed. Sure, it's nice to hear two-minute pop songs—especially ones of the power and passion of 'Hotel Yorba' and 'Fell In Love...' But it's even nicer to hear bands strutting at the height of their power, keeping the music taut and in check.

"There's a song in [*Citizen Kane*] called 'It Can't Be Love, Because There Is No True Love', that plays at this party they have in the Everglades," Jack told *Rolling Stone*. "I could never find what this song was about, if it was a Forties song, some jazz standard. I was trying to play it on guitar, and I said a line from the movie while I was playing the chords. And it was like, 'I wonder if I can rhyme that with something else from the movie?' I had a lot of the lines memorised already, and then I went through the film and started writing down things that might make sense together."

A song that drew criticism was the (apparent) post-Meg break-up number, 'I'm Finding It Harder To Be A Gentleman'. Within the song, the narrator expresses annoyance at having to always reaffirm his love for his partner: *"I feel comfortable so baby. Why don't you feel the same? Come and have a doctor visit us,"* Jack spits, *"And tell us which one is sane."* Some critics saw this as Jack drawing too much of the wrong sort of inspiration from the early 20th Century bluesmen and taking on some of their outdated attitudes towards women. The lines between the two sexes aren't drawn as clearly nowadays as they once used to be, and this is good. But Jack—in his desire for the simpler pleasures and definitions of childhood—sometimes seems to disagree.

Other songs are more straightforward: "'Aluminum' is about the formation of aluminium in a factory," Jack explained to one young fan about the feedback-laden, distorted song (not an instrumental, just sung without words). "That is what the voices are trying to imitate." Final song 'This Protector' sees Jack singing over what sounds like an old barrelhouse piano, rolling chords echoing away into the distance.

'Expecting', too, is a relatively forthright punk/metal grind—Jack's voice all brittle anticipation and hope, but 'The Same Boy You've Always Known' sees him lingering in the shadows of self-doubt again, meshing with Meg's organic drumming, the music never

'SYMPATHETIC SOUNDS OF DETROIT'

"There certainly is a core of people working together—or, at the very least, drinking together a lot," ex-Dirtbombs and Hentchmen drummer Chris Handyside told Paybacks singer Wendy Case (ironically enough) for *The Detroit News*[i]. "It's an incestuous scene, sometimes painfully so."

"When I started playing in The Paybacks," recalls Dave Buick, "Wendy had just started working as a local music reporter. And I think that contributed to the exposure of a lot of bands that you're hearing about today. She would have a weekly 'Band Of The Week' column: bands like Rocket 455, The Go, The White Stripes, the Cobras would all get mentioned. She'd write some drunken story about me every couple of months. My mother would be like, 'Dave, I saw you in the paper again...' 'Ma, I'm sorry. It's not as bad as it sounded. It was just a window. I didn't get hurt. I just got thrown through it, ma."

"We're not the best musicians," laughs Mick Collins, "but we're still pretty good rock bands. I don't see there's a music scene here. A music scene implies there's a focus, some common-based thing people are gathering around. Have you heard the old gag about Detroit bands: 'There's a new band in town.' 'Oh really, what it's like?' 'Somebody you know, somebody you know, somebody you know and a drummer.' I object to the fact people think White Stripes are a gravitating point—that's not a scene to me."

In March 2000, Jack White started working on *Sympathetic Sounds Of Detroit* on Sympathy For The Record Industry's behest: "Jeff Evans [The Gibson Brothers, '68 Comeback] was doing a similar compilation for Memphis, and the label said I should do one for Detroit," Jack explained to London journalist Stevie Chick that month. "I just called around the bands that I like a lot, to see if they wanted to do it, so we started working on it."

The compilation was mastered in the summer of 2000, and eventually released some time around May 2001. In the sleeve-notes Jack wrote, "There is a reason why music coming out of Detroit is so different from the rest of the country. Detroit's musicians don't suffer from the anxiety of not getting signed, or not having a connection to get their music in a film. We know from the beginning that it's never gonna happen. No suit from LA or New York is going to fly to Detroit to check out a band and hand out business cards."

"As absurd as it seems now," says Dan Miller, "I think Jack was sincere when he wrote that. The idea was to get a bunch of these bands that were similar in the way they sounded, and record them all exactly the same. Hopefully it'd be interesting for a few hundred people, and it'd capture a moment in time. And you wouldn't think that a lot of people would care about that."

There had been other Detroit rock anthologies before, most notably 1995's *Detroit Electric*, partly financed by Car City Records, featuring experimental bands like Gravitar, Medusa Cyclone and a pungent Demolition Doll Rods; the two excellent Motor City Brewing Works collections, *Ghettoblaster* Volumes 1 and 2[ii]; also Flying Bomb's *Surprise Packages*; but this was the one that really helped to focus and crystallise the emergent scene in the eyes of the outside world. Long Gone John's insistence that all the bands record in Jack's attic led to a consistency often lacking from such albums.

The timing was perfect: coming hot on the heels of the first Stripes tour of the UK, it meant that fans looking towards Detroit for clues as to where The White Stripes came from were confronted with a fully-formed scene to take to their hearts. Yet the recording wasn't without its problems.

"Bands split up over that," sighs Ben Blackwell. "The Breakdowns had a big fight over it, cos Steve Shaw and Jeff Meier had disagreements over Jack's production style. The Waxwings were under a recording contract with Bobsled who would not let them be on it. The Go wouldn't do it unless Matt Smith was producing—but the essential concept was Long John wanted Jack to produce it. All the songs came in specifically, they weren't thrown together like usually happens with compilations. Everything was recorded using the same amplifiers and same guitars. It probably sold around 20-30,000 copies—that's a low estimate—and it's almost certainly responsible for journalists thinking all Detroit bands sound the same. What they don't understand is that it was all produced through the same Fender Twin amp, recorded by one guy in his attic. Andre Williams nearly made it on there—his version of 'The Big Three Killed My Baby' with Two Star—but Jack figured it would seem like there was too much of himself on it."

Whatever the effect and the reaction, there's no denying that *Sympathetic Sounds* is a great snapshot of a city at a peak of its self-belief. It contains 19 tracks of distinctly MC5-influenced rock'n'roll, from the gritty Keith Richards riffs of The Paybacks' 'Black Girl', through The Dirtbombs' crowd-pleasing 'I'm Through With White Girls' (sung by Jim Diamond), to The Detroit Cobras' riotous Otis Redding cover 'Shout Bama Lama', to The Clone Defects' rampant accord, an electrifying Von Bondies, the full-on noise fest of Bantam Rooster's 'Run Rabbit Run' and The White Stripes themselves ('Red Death At 6:14'—a track only otherwise available as a one-sided, mail order only, red vinyl single from *Mojo*).

There are also several short segments in between most of the songs.

"I had bands play instrumental blues pieces, which we cut in alongside the other tracks," Jack told Stevie. "Anything off the top of their heads. I'd say, 'Just play some blues right now', and those improvisations were what made it to the record."

Stevie: "Are many of the bands into the garage rock sound?"

Jack: "Yeah, that's been a nice thing. A lot of the bands wouldn't probably call themselves that or want to get lumped in with that scene, but that's OK. I don't think it's an evil term."

Stevie: "I think it just suggests the band are honest, have a lot of integrity, and are doing things on their terms."

Jack: "Yeah, it denotes honesty to me."

Stevie: "What are the influences?"

Jack: "I'm sure the MC5 and The Stooges are in everybody's blood, there's no way to get around it, but there's lots of different influences there. There are bands like The Detroit Cobras, who are big record collectors, who do all covers, finding the best things from the past to work with. And then there's a lot of other bands writing totally original songs, drawing on their own influences."

"I'd written a song that afternoon," recalls Bantam Rooster singer Tom Potter, "so we went in, and had overdone the solo when Jack said, 'I don't know if that's working'. I was like, 'What do you mean, dude?' But he was right. I went back in and I was drunk as hell, but Jack was like, 'You still need to do that solo over it', so I grabbed this red national and did it. Jack was like, 'Perfect, that was great'. It's not so much as having a producer as somebody telling me what to do. It's the closest thing to Jim Diamond telling me, 'Dude, I don't think you're drunk enough.'[iii]"

i Wendy quit her job there in 2003 to concentrate on her music full-time.
ii 2002's Volume 2 is particularly fine—starring Ko And The Knockouts, The Dirtbombs, The Volebeats and... OK, all the usual suspects. But this one is a little more comprehensive than *Sympathetic Sounds*: The Witches, They Come In Threes and Bogue also make appearances.
iii The pivotal moment for Jim Diamond at Ghetto Recorders was when he convinced Tom to record Bantam Rooster's first full-length there (*Deal Me In*, 1997).

Above left: Jack 12/02 at a one-off Xmas song at Cpop which featured Ben Swank on drums (Doug Coombe)

Above right: Meg White, around the time of *De Stijl*'s release (Doug Coombe)

iii Ben Blackwell: "The Waxwings are Detroit's hardest working band. They just haven't given up and have gotten the least amount of praise. Their music is along the lines of Beachwood Sparks [Byrds], with amazing three-part harmonies. Kevin Peyok might be the best bassist in town. Songs for people who know music."

wasteful or unnecessary. "We're Going To Be Friends' is a mellow, Beatles-esque delight, a paean to innocent childhood romance, the acoustic guitar threading between wistful voice full of wonderment and the rustle of autumn leaves. It's a seriously sweet, understated moment in the middle of an album that sometimes can taste bitter. Indeed, the very next track, 'Offend Each Way', sees Jack's frustration at his situation brimming over again across a resolute guitar riff.

"Jack has said before that he maybe added too much to the second album in terms of guest musicians," comments Ben, "but the way I look at it it's a progression—a band grows and changes, you can see it between the two albums. You can't say it's for the worse. The part of him being so far ahead of himself means he was prolific as all hell. He wrote songs for Two Star Tabernacle that ended up on *White Blood Cells*, and some that never went further than Two Star. It's a gift he has, he never stops and admires what he's done—he just keeps going."

Somehow, Jack and Meg—with no blues, no guest musicians, no cover songs and no slide guitar—managed to broaden their palette sufficiently to make their third album a classic. They'd learnt enough from *De Stijl* not to mess with the formula too much while still seeking to expand their horizons: more importantly, Jack had proved to himself that he didn't need outside help from other artists, whether it be their songs or their presence. Effortlessly, seamlessly—so seamlessly, in fact that you don't notice any movement—The White Stripes had changed their sound just enough to appeal to a whole range of potential fans: not just the older garage or blues purists from their hometown, but also MTV viewers, always on the look-out for a new Nirvana to pin their hopes on.

The album is dedicated to Loretta Lynn, the quasi-feministic (and soulful) Nashville country singer born into poverty during the Thirties. Her best-known song, 'Coal Miner's Daughter', was also the title of her mid-Seventies autobiography, adapted for film in 1980, starring Sissy Spacek (who won an Oscar for her role). She's released 15 Number One country albums in America.

The White Stripes would later hook up with her.

As soon as the album was recorded, The White Stripes went back on the road. From this point on, almost every time they toured, they'd take Detroit bands with them, from The Waxwings[iii] to The Von Bondies, Whirlwind Heat, The Clone Defects, Soledad Brothers, Blanche and Brendan Benson, and also one-off shows with The Detroit Cobras and The Dirtbombs.

"Whirlwind Heat played a couple more shows with The White Stripes, probably in Detroit," recalls their singer David. "The Gold Dollar show was packed. I used to love that club so much. I did merch on their East Coast tour, with Bob Bert's Knoxville Girls[iv] and The Gossip. That's when I thought it was really going to take off. The day before their sold-out show in the Middle East, Boston, was their first real radio interview, in Cambridge. People were coming up in New Jersey asking if they needed management, and Jack was like, 'I don't think so'. Right around then our Italy seven-inch came out. There weren't any others. I think we ruined them.

"We did five or six shows with The White Stripes—Providence, Boston, New York," says Bob Bert[v]. The bands played two sold out shows at Brooklyn's Bowery Ballroom. "The Middle East show was amazing: the first 12 rows were 14-year-old girls staring up at Jack with their mouths open, singing along to every word. I thought it was funny all these kids were singing along to Forties blues songs. The White Stripes were very considerate. They didn't behave like rock stars at all. They even shared their dressing room."

The East Coast audiences didn't always impress the band: "We played Hoboken before we played New York," Jack said, "which is a lot of people from New York, I guess. That was a horrible show. People had their arms folded, 'OK, we're here, impress us'. It was sold out, but it felt horrible. It was like playing to an audience of critics. That's not enjoying music or experiencing it."

"Later," continues Bob, "I ran into Jack at a Greenhornes show, right when they were about to appear on *Saturday Night Live*. Jack was saying how they were giving him a hard time cos they wanted him to play this one song. It was right after Will Farrell had left the show, and they were threatening they'd only let The White Stripes play one song instead of two if they didn't play ball. Jack was like, 'Who cares, Will Farrell isn't on anymore'—and they got to do their two songs[vi]."

In March, they played at Fat Tuesday's as part of the influential industry bun-feast, South By Southwest, in Austin, Texas. Music critic Stevie Chick, then with *NME*, witnessed the show: "The White Stripes are quite a sight," he wrote. "Decked out in a scarlet pantsuit, bee-stung lips curling snottily towards the microphones, eyes peeping out under his moptop, Jack White drags the guitar-slide along the strings and lets out another guttural yelp. Backed only by sister Meg (in matching crimson duds), laying Bonham-esque barrages at the drumkit beside him, Jack's brutish slashes carve out a rock-stomp that echoes across the languid Austin evening, sounding anything *but* minimal. The White Stripes have polished rock's barest elements till they sound fresh and new again. They can't lose."

Chick picks up the story: "At the start of 2001, Simon from Cargo sent me a big batch of CDs. He'd just received *De Stijl*, so he phoned me up and said, 'There's a great band you're gonna love, they're a brother-sister combo, they sound like a cross between Led Zeppelin and Guided By Voices[vii]'. The package also included Mr Airplane Man[viii], Immortal Lee County Killers[ix] and Bantam Rooster, with a note stating that, '2001 will be the year of the two-piece blues punk band explosion', with eight exclamation marks afterwards cos we both knew how ludicrous that idea was. The minute I played *De Stijl*, I knew it was going to be something really, really special—but having said that, there were lots of things I felt were really, really special at the time and no one ever listened to me about them.

"Shortly afterwards, I got sent to a cold seaside town somewhere up North to cover an alternative dance festival—and as I walked around all weekend that January, friendless and freezing, I played *De Stijl* over and over again. When I got home, I wrote a 220-word album review, emailed the *NME*, and gave it eight out of 10 cos I knew if I gave it more they'd mark it down. Week after week I opened the paper up and the review hadn't run. They'd spiked it.

"A couple of months later, [photographer] Steve Gullick and I were in Austin for South By Southwest. We didn't have a list of stuff we had to cover, so we'd get drunk and flit from venue to venue checking out all these amazing, undiscovered subterranean US underground bands. At

iv Hard-rockin' New York band that infuse their country style with elements of punk and other genres. Also contain Kid "Congo" Powers, ex-Cramps and The Gun Club.

v Bob has drummed with Sonic Youth, Jon Spencer's Pussy Galore, The Chrome Cranks and Bewitched (among others) and edits the very fabulous NYC magazine *BB Gun*. "I have two great stories of playing in Detroit," he recalls, "The first time was the very first Sonic Youth tour, 1982—it might have been Ann Arbor. We were really excited because Ron Asheton was at the show, and he took us back to his basement, and so we got to meet Niagara and Destroy All Monsters. Then, in 1988, Pussy Galore played a triple bill at The Greystone, which was a dilapidated church. It was us, Honeymoon Killers and The Black Snakes [featuring photographer Richard Kern, Darren from Mick Collins' post-Gories band Blacktop, and Matt from Lubricated Goat]. It was a good crowd in a bad part of town, and we slept at the venue. During the night, two crack-heads were screaming at each other saying 'I'm going to kill you'. The next day, the promoter refused to pay us, because he'd spent all his money on drugs, so Richard Kern dumped a pitcher of water of him."

vi Nirvana were another band who famously ran foul of the *Saturday Night Live* producers, changing the song they'd agreed to perform right at the very last minute to an amplifier-destroying version of their second album noise-fest, 'Territorial Pissings'.

vii Former schoolteacher Robert Pollard was about 36, and had self-released around eight albums, when this Dayton, Ohio cult band finally got "discovered". Imagine a lo-fi, drunken, more eclectic version of Cheap Trick. Roughly.

viii Great punk-blues female two-piece from Boston, named after a Howlin' Wolf song. Like The White Stripes, introduced to Sympathy For The Record Industry by Jeff Evans.

ix *Another* great hybrid punk-blues duo—this time from Alabama, and *seriously* distorted.

Above: Meg
(left: Ruvan/Retna, right: Sebastian Arte/Retna)

some point we bumped into a fucked-up Justin [Russo] from Mercury Rev[x]. The whole thing culminated with the three of us deciding we were going to get tattoos. Justin had his, but his blood was very thin and there was blood everywhere. It definitely put me off. Steve was having his done, and I was standing outside trying to figure out a reason not to go in, when I started to hear this slide guitar sound...

"The minute I heard it, I knew it was The White Stripes—and I was desperate to see them. I grabbed Steve, he grabbed his photo bag, we bounced over, and they started playing 'Little Bird'—they were doing most of *De Stijl* that afternoon. At the end of the next song, 'Hello Operator', Steve told me to grab his bag and jumped up on stage and started snapping them. The key moment was the cover of 'Jolene'. I thought it was a really audacious move. Indie bands now cover pop tunes for ironic reasons, but there was no irony in Jack's version. He shaved away all the kitsch of the original and turned it into something visceral and powerful. I thought he must be some kind of genius. My initial reference points were Beck and Jon Spencer. We got back to London shortly afterwards and Steve and I forced the new live editor at *NME* to run pictures of this unknown band from Detroit. A couple of weeks later they finally ran the album review[xi]. Some of the people in the subs department had bought a copy. There was a lot of interest from that point on."

"From June 2000 through June 2001," relates Ben Blackwell, "The White Stripes played around 70 shows. They played a lot of one-off gigs with local bands, went to Canada a handful of times in 2001, and toured America with The Von Bondies in June '01. The same month, they played on the Craig Kilborn show, a national late night talk show, and it was like, 'Wow, it's never going to get crazier than that'. We didn't know anybody who played TV shows. Then they went to England and I remember listening to the Peel sessions on line and thinking, 'Man this is really good'."

When The White Stripes played legendary San Francisco venue, the Fillmore West, the entire place was decked out in red and white. At the same show, Jack was presented with a peppermint crash helmet, and a girl made him and Meg silver pins.

x Killer melodic psychedelic noise band from NYC—similar to Flaming Lips, but far more affecting. (Flaming Lips are now turning into the new R.E.M., not good.)

xi Some of those 220 words ran thus: "The White Stripes are arch de/reconstructors of rock'n'roll's heaving canon, applying merciless Stanley knife slashes to the genre's flabbier excesses. So there's echoes of Delta blues, Zeppelin swagger and even Slade-esque balladry in The White Stripes' din, but any of the indulgences that render them museum pieces are cleanly excised."

Jack live in Wolverhampton 2003. (Steve Gillett)

For the album launch party, The White Stripes decided to play three shows at a variety of Detroit venues, June 7, 8 and 9. The first night was at The Gold Dollar, with Rock*A*Teens and Ko And The Knockouts, the second one was at The Magic Bag with Greg Oblivian [Cartwright][xii] and Reigning Sound, and the final one was at The Magic Stick with The Go and The Insomniacs on June 9.

The original idea was to have the entrance fee as something red-and-white for The Gold Dollar: "Just bring us a red-and-white present," Jack said in *Detroit Metro Times*, "although we haven't talked yet how that will work out. There are other bands on the bill that need to get paid money."

The Gold Dollar night was not without its problems.

"We almost didn't do it," recalls Neil Yee. "There was a little bit of controversy beforehand. I tried to have some level of integrity. I'd already booked Rock*A*Teens, from Atlanta, and I knew they'd get a decent crowd. Then The White Stripes changed their dates, but I didn't want to cancel this show, so it was suggested they play at the same night. Their agent didn't really understand the concept. He was like, 'Next time they're going to be too big to play your next place' and I was like, 'If this is what's going on, they probably already are'. It was a great show, and brought a huge crowd. At the start, Jack said, 'We're going to play the entire album all the way though', and he did. The police showed up for a minute and looked around cos it was so full. We also had a small set-to with the agent over the guest-list, because we had at least 150, 160 people in there already. That was the last time they played at The Gold Dollar because we closed a couple of months later. We closed when it was at its most profitable, in August 2001. I just got bored with it. I was in it for the music exclusively. I wanted to be able to promote things I thought were interesting.

"I'm not a big fan of The White Stripes' recordings," Neil adds. "I actually sold their first single on e-Bay a couple of years ago [in 2001] for $150. I didn't pick up a record that night. It wasn't until a year later I bought it, having heard it on radio first. Then I went back and listened to my live recording of the show. It came out great. The White Stripes could be monumental live. Jack has an intensity. He makes every note count.

xii Greg's the underrated genius behind such underground Memphis garage greats as The Oblivians and Compulsive Gamblers. The Hives have based most of their career on him.

Right: Meg at BBC Radio One's Big Weekend, Heaton Park, Manchester, May 4, 2003 (Mark Campbell/Rex Features)

xiii Mind you, they also once said that I was "The Man That Invented Grunge"—so what do they know?

xiv A "garage" band that was anything but.

Since the demise of the club, certain bands have looked to cash in on its fame—most notoriously, Soledad Brothers. Their *Live* album (Dim Mak, 2003) is meant to've been recorded at The Gold Dollar in June 2000. It wasn't.

"I have some recordings of Soledad Brothers that are far better than that," laughs Neil. "It's funny people think our name is so marketable. I'm working on a *Live At The Gold Dollar* album now. I've transferred most of the analogue stuff onto digital, but I'm in a Volkswagen Van travelling round the country so it's not my highest priority. I'm leaving the finer details to Ben [Blackwell]. I have a feeling we won't be able to use any of The White Stripes stuff."

Even before the release of *White Blood Cells*, The White Stripes were starting to attract wider attention at home and abroad.

Rolling Stone named them as a "band to watch in 2001". *Entertainment Weekly* said the Detroit scene bore some resemblance to Seattle before grunge hit big[xiii], *Time* magazine ran an article, and even Jack White's beloved *Mojo* magazine interviewed the pair: "I'm still really dumbfounded by it all," Jack told Kevin Ransom of *The Detroit News* at the time. "When *Rolling Stone* first called, I thought it was someone joking. But then they called back. Afterward, everyone in the room was stunned. We were like, 'That was *Rolling Stone*!'"

It was around this time that the "Meg and Jack are siblings" story started to unravel, a story in the *Detroit Free Press* on March 30 mentioned that the pair's previous marital status was common knowledge in town—a theme that *Time* later ran with. (Their marriage certificate was eventually posted on the Internet.) It was a shame, somehow—a sweet, innocent half-truth (boyfriends and girlfriends often refer to each other as "brothers" and "sisters") that didn't hurt or harm anyone, just added to the mystique around the band. It was nice to imagine Jack practising his drums upstairs in the attic while his elder sister looked on indulgently and finally decided to help out. To many fans they remain brother and sister: that close.

"There was a lack of information coming from us, but a lot of need for copy," Jack told Keith Cameron from *The Guardian* in 2003. "So a lot of things started arising. The one thing the fucking media hates is not being able to dissect someone so that every little part of their existence can be written as a soundbite in a paragraph. What they want is, 'Jack White, 26 years old, likes race cars and soccer, grew up in the inner city of Detroit and is now top of the world. Can't stand chocolate ice cream...' That's what they want, biographical dissection until there's nothing left for anybody else to know. No, that's not what you need to know about, that's got nothing to do with the music we make. It's the same thing as asking Michaelangelo, 'What kind of shoes do you wear?' It doesn't have anything to do with his painting."

Probably half the reason the media was paying such attention was that the pair had such a strong visual identity, and their almost Luddite approach to music made them seem freakish in comparison to other acts. Maybe red and white is that strong.

"It's the best colour combination of all time," Jack told *Detroit Metro Times*. "For some reason, it makes people think about stuff. It seems to me that if I were wearing green pants, people wouldn't come up and say, 'Wow, those are green pants'. There's nothing special about them. They're just old senior citizen pants. Everybody wears street clothes all the time. Why should we just do that? Blues musicians that are my idols, they wore their nicest suits and nicest hats when they played shows. It's just being polite. It's like going to church. You wouldn't wear your pyjamas to church."

"We don't have cartoons here like The Vines or The Hives[xiv]," stresses The Magic Stick promoter, Greg Baise. "Maybe some of The White Stripes videos are animated or whatever, but they're not cartoons, it isn't caricatured. That means a lot to people in Detroit."

It hardly mattered whether people considered the image or brother-sister story or minimal sound gimmicky or not. The music and songs were clearly strong enough to win through. All it needed was one final push, one last catalytic agent—and where better than the UK? Britain has long had a reputation for picking up on new sounds way before its more conservative cousin across the Atlantic.

On The Road

Bruce Brand (drummer, Thee Headcoats, Holly Golightly)

"Hello, I'm 'Someone Called Bruce'.

"I've played with The Pop Rivets (a punk rock'n'roll group), The Milkshakes (a rock'n'roll group), The Kravin' "A"'s (a beat group), Auntie Vegetable (a psychedelic acid-rock group featuring Sexton Ming[i]), The Len Bright Combo (with Wreckless Eric[ii]), Thee Headcoats (a punk rock'n'roll group), Dutronc (an Anglo-French rock'n'roll group), The Adventures Of Parsley (a Hammond-led TV and film theme band), The Masonics (a punk rock'n'roll group)[iii], and currently Hipbone Slim & The Kneetremblers (a rock'n'roll trio) and Holly Golightly. I've also recorded with Link Wray.

"I started off playing guitar, but somewhere along the line demoted myself to drums. The first group I was ever in was called Bruke Farouk's Jambusters. We played Rolling Stones, Cream, Status Quo and Bachman-Turner Overdrive songs and (mercifully) only ever did one concert, at the Sheppey Little Theatre. I was about 16, still at school and wore my dad's white flat cap—the predecessor to my current black fisherman's cap—and played my then pride and joy, a slightly secondhand Fender Telecaster, which I still have and use today.

"I had a couple of schoolmates who were wizard guitar players, but they were more into the Rory Gallagher/John MacLaughlin end of things. Most of my contemporaries (ie: school friends) were into progressive rock and unnecessary 'head' music in those days.

"I don't know why I first wanted to play rock'n'roll, but I remember seeing The Pretty Things in the 1967 Norman Wisdom film[iv] *What's Good For The Goose* on TV. Norm's character was a departure from his previous 'Pitkin' persona; he played a respectable businessman who was adopted by a couple of dolly-bird swingers and taken to a club called 'The Screaming Apple' (latterly the name of a German record label who released some of our material). Seeing Dick Taylor [Pretty Things] in action, I thought, 'Cor, I wanna play guitar like that'. (I was also quite taken with Twink's top-hat.) Years later I was thrilled to find myself in the enviable position of rattling the traps for a reformed Things at Slim Chance's Wild Western Room in North London's St John's Tavern.

"My formative years were spent during the early Seventies in the little seaside town of Sheerness on the Kent coast (renowned for its extensive inbreeding program). We didn't have a record player until my dad bought a colossal walnut-veneer radiogram off my mad Uncle Jack. Somewhere along the line I blew it up when I experimented trying it out as a possible guitar amplifier. I still have it, and it still doesn't work properly. The first record I bought was Mungo Jerry's 'In The Summertime', but as it was the first 'Maxi-Single' and a stereophonic disc to boot, it wouldn't play on the colossal walnut-veneer radiogram, so I exchanged it for something else. I

Left: Jack at Dingwalls, London, 30/07/01 (Ian Whent/Retna)

i A very eccentric, and fine, London performance artist.

ii The man responsible for one of the finest punk singles ever, the tormented, minimal 'Whole Wide World'.

iii The Masonics play "devilishly stylish garage rock with a lo-fi fixation," according to *In Music We Trust*. Their name is a smart pun on seminal Sixties Seattle garage band, The Sonics. ("Although Micky never realised that at the time"—Bruce)

iv Norman Wisdom. Ever the lovable victim of his own clumsiness.

have since upgraded my apparatus and consequently am able to spin such discs and am happily in possession of a replacement copy of 'In The Summertime'.

"T Rex, Status Quo and Led Zeppelin were my staple musical diet for a while, being the closest I got to 'rock'n'roll', but I remember if I heard anything by Chuck Berry, Elvis or Jerry Lee Lewis *et al* on Radio One, I would start bouncing off the walls. I couldn't quite put my finger on why I liked it so much but I finally worked it out: because it's Rock'N'Roll!

"Stupidly, it never occurred to me these records were still available, but eventually a copy of the 'Jailhouse Rock' EP fell into my hands and a friend played me 'You Really Got Me' [The Kinks] off an old Pye Hits compilation, which rang a big bell from when I was a titch. I never looked back. Or should I say other than back..."

"I knew Detroit existed because of Tamla Motown, the MC5, the race riots in the Sixties and all that malarkey, but it was five years ago, during the last Headcoats tour of America in 1999, when I encountered the music of The White Stripes and discovered it was still there.

"Long Gone John, who runs Sympathy For The Record Industry, was putting John the bass player and myself up. He gave us a copy of their first album and some singles and told us to check them out. Usually, I maybe play stuff once and that's it, but I thought they weren't too bad—they might warrant another spin sometime! When I got home to London, none of my mates had heard of them, and I thought it'd be great if they played over here. I kind of tried to make contact with them through the Internet, but without success.

"A year or so later, our US tour agent contacted me saying The White Stripes were coming to England and would The Masonics like to open for them (and lend them a drumkit, amps and put them up). Obviously, the answer was a resounding 'Yes'. Then I started hearing them on the radio, 'Eh, what's going on? People have heard of them!' I got a call at work asking me to pick them up from Gatwick, so I went down on the train, as the last time I attempted to drive there it took me two hours just to get out of London. Anyhow, there were only two of them...

"They show up with two heavy-duty guitar cases, a snare drum and industrial strength cymbal case, plus John, their tour manager, who had about seven hundredweight of records and assorted merchandise ('Ya gotta have moichadise') precariously tied to a shopping trolley, so they wouldn't have fitted in my miniscule Datsun Hanky anyway. First we got sent to the wrong platform so we were flapping about for a while, but eventually landed at Farringdon Road Station. I hailed a cab within minutes, but the driver took one look at them and bolted. 'Er, welcome to London,' I nervously ventured.

"Then I had to hire the 'tour bus', a not-quite-clapped-out Mercedes Sprinter, and drive them around. There were eight shows, four in the south and four 'oop the north', all sold out, it transpired. I helped carry their luggage and lent them my drum set. (I have pictures of Meg playing it—and it's not even red. Or white!) They bought an amp from my mate Andy in Denmark Street, a Fender Twin Reverb for a good price.

"The first thing they did was a John Peel session, which was my first encounter of them live and I was gobsmacked at how great they were. They set up live with an invited audience in the studio. I listened in the control room and it sounded amazing. I think they deserve everything they've got. I like everything about them—Jack's voice, Jack's guitar playing, Jack's songs and choice of material and Meg's drumming—what else is there to like? Also, there's the passion and telepathy between them. It's raw, exciting and it's honest. Not bad for a couple of spotty American kids—they like pizzas, burgers, fried chicken and Jack Daniel's. Jack a great laugh and likes his funny voices and impersonating people. He aspires to Mr Burns from *The Simpsons*. (Not a lot of people know that.)

"The bands travelled together in the back of the van. After the first date in Bristol we stayed up all night singing and kept them awake."

Bruce's personal diary for 2001

Tuesday 24th July

To Gatwick—got Jack, Meg & John. To mine and Tim's. Work. Got W/S from Tim's. To 'Source' Records & Union Tavern for nosh. Then 'On The Rocks' (bad NY band) & nasty bar. John staying.

Bruce: "Originally, they'd planned to stay at mine but decided not to as they're allergic to cats, and I had two of the buggers at the time, but luckily my pal Tim offered to put them up for a couple of nights. I went back to work after that. (I worked for a printer doing graphics, now I work at home as 'Arthole'.) Source was a label in Farringdon that wanted to sign them. That evening we went on to a club called On The Rocks in Kingsland Road, Shoreditch because they were looking for somewhere to play a secret show at the end of the tour. It used to be great on Sunday nights there when it was the BiG! Club; they'd play old rock'n'roll, R&B and soul records, but it was never more than three-quarters full so there was room to breath (and jitterbug), but that night there was an awful band from NYC called A.R.E. Weapons[v]. It's horrible when it's rammed. I suggested The Boston Arms in London's prestigious Tufnell Park as a better option. John is their tour manager, John Baker from New Zealand, otherwise known as 'Mr Pastry'. We've since become good friends."

v Aw, they're OK. Can't vouch for them live, but their records have an infectious glitter beat.

Wednesday 25th July

Van @ Russell's. (Took Masonics stuff.) Delaware Rd W9. Brilliant John Peel session and dinner. (Rant about -.) W/S (Peel Session).

Bruce: "Russell is Russell Warby from the booking agents. Delaware Road is where the BBC Maida Vale Studios are located. After a soundcheck at the studios, Peely took us to a restaurant round the corner and regaled us with his life story, and then they went back and did the session. Earlier that day I'd got call from a friend who used to be an occasional stylist at a trendy 'lifestyle' magazine, and she said they'd ripped off an idea of hers. She was outraged and consequently so was I; so much so that I went into a rant about it and think I said something like, 'Don't do any interviews with them because they ripped off my friend (...and it's just a trendy, useless "lifestyle" rag etc)'. I suppose I'm in big trouble now, ho-hum."

Thursday 26th July

100 Club—White Stripes—Loaded late, I drove. Set up & s/check. Sold out. W/S 100 Club & Masonics (VG).

Bruce: "That was their first live appearance in England. It was very, very hot—that tour happened during a bit of a 'warm snap'. Every gig was sweltering. But we played, they played, and everyone had a good time. I can even remember someone coming up to us afterwards and saying, 'That was great mate, you were much better than that other lot!'"

Friday 27th July

Moved Jack & Meg to Jacqui's. ToeRag—finished O/D's. Jack & Meg & John to 'lunch' in Leyton w/Liam & I (instead of 'D&C' interview). Buff Medways (B/A).

Bruce: "What happened was they had the Friday off and were supposed to do an interview with the aforementioned London-based media magazine but they said they'd much rather have the day off, so I suggested a trip to Toe-Rag Studios in Hackney and they liked it. We spent a good couple of hours driving around trying to track down pizzas for them, but we ended up in a greasy spoon where they made do with chicken nuggets and chips somewhere in Leyton. The next day I got call from Mr Pastry at work, and he said, 'God, you've created a monster—everyone's really mad at The White Stripes for not turning up to the interview. They think they're flakes!' (It didn't seem to do them much harm though, did it?) That evening they relocated to my friend Jacqui's place for the duration then we went to see Billy Childish's band, The Buff Medways, at the Dirty Water Club behind the Boston Arms and they agreed it would be a good place to do a secret show."

Saturday 28th July

Bristol Louisiana. (Tiny). Stayed in B&B. W/S & Masonics.

Bruce: "It was a tiny club, about as big as my living room. A chap called James from the *NME* was there and hauled Jack off for an interview. 'Don't tell 'em anything, Jeff!' I shouted after them. (By then we were referring to them as 'Jeff' and 'Madge'.) I was frequently asked about their relationship: 'Are they really brother and sister, or divorced?' I always responded with, 'They're ex-brother and sister'. Got to keep the legend alive."

The White Stripes. (Doug Coombe)

Sunday 29th July

Oxford. The (Boiling) Point. Hot hot hot!

Bruce: "It's just called The Point really, but some genius had trashed the air conditioning and there were signs up in the club denying responsibility for any consequences due to extreme heat (including death!). When The Masonics finished our set we nearly collapsed, so I ran out and sat in the van, starker, with the light off (and on my own, unfortunately) trying to cool down for most of the main set. When I went back up to the venue there was this almost solid wall of heat. It was like trying to dig into the centre of the earth. I couldn't get in there."

Monday 30th July

London (Dingwalls). John and W/S got drums from work—set up & s/checked. VG (and v hot!). Had shower—still sweating. Met Steve (Sid).

Bruce: "I have a really annoying habit of making up nicknames for everyone—if I can't remember someone's name I'll invent one for them. Steve is a friend of Jack's from Detroit, in Whirlwind Heat [Steve Damstra, bass]."

Tuesday 31st July

Nottingham. Drove to Nottingham.

Bruce: "I guess that means I drove the van to Nottingham. Hmmm... methinks I missed my vocation as a rock journalist. Waddya rekkin?"

Wednesday August 1st

Manchester Roadhouse. W/S did 'laid-back' set. (Jack got shouted at, which made him mad).

Bruce: "They decided to tone things down a bit that night, concentrating on the more melodic and down-home numbers, which seems to have distressed one member of the audience in particular, who decided to holler his disapproval. Jack leaned out and grabbed him, saying, 'Are you f***ing with me?!' He came over all Travis Bickle for a second. I was dead proud of him."

Thursday August 2nd

Leeds—Cockpit. Saw 'Mr Rumbold' from 'Are You Being Served[vi]'. Slept in van by road.

Bruce: "Mr Pastry (John Baker) spotted a TV star marching past the van while we were loading. That night he was driving and came over a tad weary, so he pulled into a lay-by and we all spent an extremely cosy night in the van."

Friday August 3rd

Glasgow—King Tut's. Russ helped with sound. (+ 'Eska')

Bruce: "Russ Wilkins from The Wildebeests (previously the bassist with The Milkshakes and the Len Bright Combo) came along and helped the sound chap who it seemed didn't really know his onions. There was lots of feedback and the stage was reverberating because it was hollow apparently, so it was hard to get a good sound even with one guitar and drums. I assume 'Eska' refers to the opening band[vii]."

Saturday August 4th

Took W/S to airport for Irish 'Witness' fest. Took Russ home. Saw Saskia & Elsa. Got Polo stuff from Morecambe. Dropped Sid off. Unloaded van @ home.

Bruce: "The White Stripes were booked to play at the Witness Festival in Ireland, so they flew from Glasgow and I drove the van home, via Russ's in Dumfriesshire or somewhere to see his girlfriend's new baby. I also had to collect some stuff from Holly's old car, which had broken down and been deserted in Morecambe at Christmas."

Sunday August 5th

Matt collected van. Probably worked.

Bruce: "Ho-hum…"

Monday August 6th

W/S at On The Rocks (crossed out) Boston Arms.

Bruce: "They wanted to get Billy to open for them. Jack wondered whether it would be better to have The Buff Medways or Billy solo. I suggested Billy's solo act was probably more 'conducive', so he played his blues-based set. Amusing memory: while The White Stripes were mucking about in soundcheck I was standing in the middle of the hall with Billy, and he turned and looked at me and said, 'Uh, they're not very good are they?' 'In what way "not very good"?' I countered. He said, 'Well, you can just tell—they're not very good'. I just bit my lip and walked away to avoid a possible altercation. Presumably he's changed his opinion now. I think I was 'spinning the wax' that evening with Liam [Watson, Toe-Rag], until I got bored and emptied the record box over the table, handed my duties over to my friend Carlo and waltzed to the bar. Ardent pro—that's me. That was the 'night of a thousand stars'. Well, the bloke out of Pulp and that skinny model (all bones and salt-cellars) were there, apparently. About that time, every newspaper including *The Daily Star* were full of articles like 'Ten Things You Didn't Know About The White Stripes', such as: 1) There are two of them, 2) They wear red and white, 3) They are brother and sister, etc… It was White Stripes Mania—fun while it lasted."

vi Popular camp Seventies British sitcom set in a department store, full of double-entendres about how Mrs Slocum's pussy needed stroking.

vii He assumes correctly. Mogwai's Stuart Braithwaite once drummed for them.

Fell In Love With A Band

Left: Meg White at Mizner Park Amphitheatre, Florida, June 19, 2003.
(Larry Marano/LFI)

UK TOUR

It all depends on where you're standing as to who was responsible for the massive amount of attention The White Stripes gained when they came over to the UK in August 2001 for a quick club tour. Some say John Peel. The influential late night Radio One DJ originally came across *The White Stripes* in a record shop in Groningen, Holland and—intrigued by its cover and concept—started playing it on his show. As the man who helped break punk in the UK and virtually every new act worth its guitar strings since 1967, Peel certainly played his part.

"That sort of proper, over-the-top guitar playing has always been something I've enjoyed very much," he explained to Brian McCollum. "It was just good to hear that kind of sound again. [2001] was an extraordinary time. The thing is, it wasn't hype. The *NME* has an obligation to find a new sensation every week, because that's what sells. But I think people were relieved at the simplicity and the directness of The White Stripes, and the fact they were making a noise they could identify with."

Meg White's "terribly strange, white legs" also attracted the DJ. But he saw The White Stripes as being from a long and noble tradition of classic R&B and blues—he even prefers them to The Stooges (who he's old enough to remember first time around). Early on, Peel made a comparison between the spontaneity of the Detroit band and Jimi Hendrix that later excited some of his more staid peers. Again, Peel actually played some shows with Hendrix in '67 and '68, so he's in a good position to comment.

Some say it was the *NME*, a music paper that has looked increasingly desperate as the years roll by. It missed out on grunge and Nirvana, where it was a sad third-, or fourth-, best. It failed to review the debut Stones Roses album (a band whose arrival they later claimed to be akin to the Second Coming of Jesus). Indeed, it's been some two decades since it last led from the front.

For once, with The White Stripes, it pinned its colours to a band that *meant something* at the right moment. Even if it did then try to lump them in with some spurious "New Rock Revolution", featuring a ton of bands that were anathema to The White Stripes and their Detroit brethren's approach of keeping everything stripped back and minimal. I'm talking The Datsuns, The Libertines, The D4, The Vines, The Hives...great for a drunken evening out perhaps, but hardly setting the world aflame with their originality or raw power. This wasn't garage rock as practised by The Hentchmen, The Gories and Rocket 455—this was *haircut rock*, mostly created by trend-chasing musicians seeking the corporate dollar. The Strokes, whom The White Stripes strangely aligned themselves with during 2002, were some of the worst offenders: rich kid New York dilettantes dressing up in daddy's old tie-dyed T-shirts. There was a reason why that music went away in the first place. It was crap.

SIMON KEELER

"I look after mainly the US import labels at Cargo distribution. I've been doing this since the grand old days of Shigaku (What Goes On, etc)... Every week we get offered records and we pre-sale them, send them out to the press if we have promos, try and get them to the right shops and key indie stores. I can remember getting the first White Stripes album in: we took 30 CDs and 20 LPs from Mordam [US distributors]. No one really picked up on it. However, we kind of dug it—we'd always liked working with The Dirtbombs and Demolition Doll Rods, bands formed from the ashes of The Gories.

"It wasn't just The White Stripes I was attracted to. I've always liked raw, gritty, unpolished, heartfelt, soulful rock'n'roll—the real deal basically, and they fitted in with that. There was a whole lot of stuff. The first Detroit Cobras album, the first Dirtbombs album, The Greenhornes... The Dirtbombs album was a total noise-fest and must've sold about 300 copies. Songs like 'Can't Stop Thinking It' are better than anything The Strokes will ever manage. There are still records like that about today—if they're not from Detroit they're from somewhere else in America, or Australia—and they should be selling 5-6,000 not 5-600. There is British stuff as well, but a lot of that leaves me cold.

"As far as reinventing the blues goes... the blues were always there, but The White Stripes allowed people to delve into something that's quite hard to digest in its rawest form. They turn songs like 'Boll Weevil' or even 'Jolene' into their own, but make you want to listen to the original. That's the sign of a truly great artist. They make you want to investigate further.

"I was lucky enough to be invited to the live Peel session—that was pretty special. Two people in a studio environment playing as though they were in front of 300 people, and playing some of the most exciting, live, electric... at that point it was already beginning to snowball, and you could tell it was very special. There's a classic moment where they had dinner with John Peel beforehand and they were talking about Gene Vincent and then they threw in a Gene Vincent cover at the end of their set—that, to me, is proof enough of an artist who cares about their work. Then there were the shows—the 100 Club, a clutch of regional dates, *NME* going on the road—well done, *NME*! Then when they came back and did the tour with The Von Bondies in November, at The Forum and The Astoria, they transferred to the big stage in the easiest of fashions... If The White Stripes have done anything they have made people want to investigate the underground garage and live music scenes again."

The *NME*'s patronage of The White Stripes almost didn't happen, according to the journalist responsible for first writing about the band in the paper, Stevie Chick.

"They played at the 100 Club," Chick recalls, "and I managed to get into the show after buying a ticket from Simon [Keeler, Cargo Records]. I was walking down the staircase when the live editor came up and said, 'I'm supposed to be reviewing this but I'm really fucked off, can you give me 600 words by tomorrow morning?' The show was stuffed full of industry people, but the band were great. I ran home and stayed up till four am writing this 600-word diatribe which I felt would make the perfect argument why people should like the band... Looking back on it now, it's reads kinda histrionic, but it was like all these clichés were being played out for the very first time. I said something like, 'We've seen rock'n'roll reborn'. It felt really fresh. They clearly had a great understanding of rock'n'roll's past."

Some say The White Stripes' success was down to Simon Keeler at Cargo—the distribution company that has given unflagging support to Detroit bands and raw-assed music over the years. Certainly, without Simon's ability to pinpoint influential counter-cultural figures, and his willingness to chase seemingly lost causes, The White Stripes may never been heard of in the UK at all.

"I remember getting the first single from The Detroit Cobras and Henry And June [Ben Swank and Johnny Walker's pre-Soledad Brothers band] on Human Fly," he smiles. "It was exactly what I liked—dirty, scuzzy rock'n'roll. Then we got stuff in like Rocket 455, and the occasional Hentchmen ditty. It was all there. It just needed something to wake up the mainstream UK press, and that's what The White Stripes brought to the party. It was that first swathe of live performances in the summer of 2001, and the live John Peel session, that finally pushed them over the edge—a while after the US and Australian scenes.

"There were three things that made it happen over here," Simon says. "The support of John Peel; and the support of the Rough Trade record shop, which created an A&R vulture fest—people like Nigel at Rough Trade [London] are very, very important. He'd be ordering *De Stijl* left, right and centre and playing it to everyone in the heady days of autumn 2000, and selling tons. Then there was the Radio 4 *Today* programme interview which took it to a totally different level and led on to the tabloid coverage and all that bollocks, not undeserved. *The Sun*[i] would phone up for photos of The White Stripes and to inform me they *had* to be at the show—and to ask which 'cool' stars were going to be there—and the rest is history."

Maybe it was the British tabloids and broadsheets then, desperate for something to fill the pages during the traditional summer silly season—loving the directness of The White Stripes' image, and seemingly incestuous nature of Jack and Meg's relationship. Whatever the reason, music fans knew something was up when the *NME* put them on their August 8 cover.

Stevie Chick picks up the story: "By this point I'd already done a phone interview with Jack for *The Evening Standard* [the London daily], which ran before *NME*'s *On* [new band section] piece. The 100 Club review ran a week later. The day after my review ran, I got a call from another writer, saying they'd been listening to Radio 4 that morning, and it'd done a documentary on The White Stripes saying that John Peel was a huge fan, and that the announcer had read out huge chunks of my live review live on air."

Radio 4 is a respected radio station: not so given to flights of fancy or the "celebrity culture" that's infected most of the remaining media, filled with highbrow talk shows and the odd

i The UK's leading tabloid is best known for its half-naked Page Three girls and lurid headlines like "Freddie Starr Ate My Hamster".

intellectual entertainment programme. The idea of it profiling a raw punk-blues "brother/sister" act from Detroit who thrived on minimal art was unheard-of. Simon is almost certainly right: it was Radio 4 that sparked the feeding frenzy in the mainstream (non-musical) media. This led to ridiculous extremes, such as *The Sun* running a full-page review of the band's live show, several months before creaking old music rag *Q* deigned to even look in The White Stripes' direction. It's nice that the *NME* noticed them and everything—but that's pretty small beer compared to the rest of the media.

"The day after that," Stevie continues, "*The Times* reprinted pretty much the whole review in a feature, and then *The Sun* quoted it—everything got very hysterical and bizarre, but it was still very exciting. The band played a secret gig at the Boston Arms—known as Billy Childish's home from home—in Tufnell Park. I managed to sneak a couple of tickets from Slam City Skates[ii]. It was a surreal experience. Kate Moss[iii] was in the audience and a couple of other celebs. The photographer from *The Sun* took great pleasure in pushing people out of his way, so we took great pleasure in spitting wads of chewing gum into his bag. That was an insanely good show. It was the best I ever saw them."

In between gigs, The White Stripes recorded a live John Peel session: "British bands are so worried about being thought un-cool," Peel told McCollum, "that they have to pretend that they're unaware of any music more than two years old[iv]. So I was amazed when Jack was happy to talk about things from my own childhood. He didn't think it was un-cool to know them. We were talking about one of the great concerts of my life, when I saw Eddie Cochran and Gene Vincent play at the Liverpool Empire, four days before Eddie Cochran was killed in a car crash. When The White Stripes played that night, they ended their set with an Eddie Cochran song and a Gene Vincent song. I thought, what a nice thing to do, but also incredibly cool."

"There are silly seasons," wrote Keith Cameron in *The Guardian Weekend* magazine, in April 2003, "and then there is Radio 4's *Today* programme regaling its listeners with the feedback squalls and impassioned screaming of a band whose music was at that point available only via imported copies from the US. Within the space of a week, and without a record contract, lawyer, manager or publicist, The White Stripes became the world's most sought-after musical commodity. Record companies were all but folding blank cheques into paper planes and throwing them onstage. After existing virtually unnoticed since 1997, no one was more perplexed than they."

"We'd been doing what *we* wanted to do for so long," said Jack. "Because we'd heard that the English press would blow people up to 'saviours of rock'n'roll' level and then throw them away three months later, we thought this is what would happen to us. So we had to decide are we going to let this destroy us or are we going to jump in head on and manipulate it so it works for us? And not let people push us around and destroy what we've been doing. We were forced to do that."

Something had to give. Some time around October 2001, The White Stripes signed to XL Recordings, home of dance noise terrorists The Prodigy, for what was rumoured to be a cool million pounds (but wasn't really anywhere near that amount). Jack was given his own imprint, Third Man Records.

"Let's make that one million pound advance from XL three million," remarks Ben Blackwell caustically. "And Jack's got four toes, not five."

In the US, it was Richard Branson's V2 records that finally prised the band from Long Gone John's tender clutches—not without some problems: Long Gone's compensation is still being discussed in the courts. The V2 contract was unusual, inasmuch as it allowed the band to retain ownership of their recordings.

Andy Gershon (president, V2): "I thought 'Hello Operator' was absolutely brilliant. I found them completely fascinating, both musically and conceptually. I figured it would never get on the radio. But I didn't care about getting hits."

White Blood Cells was reissued and—with the help of MTV and some smart videos—has gone on to sell over one million copies. Shortly, life would never be the same again: for Jack, certainly. Like Kurt Cobain, he's developed an allergy to fame that affects his regular movements. Whereas Meg can still be seen, smiling in a corner of a Detroit bar, Jack doesn't go to his old haunts as much. Maybe that's cos he moves in more rarefied circles: he's the one with a celebrity girlfriend and who's been asked to star in movies. More probably, it's because he's far

ii London skateboard shop above Rough Trade Records in Covent Garden.

iii Waif-like model who smokes cigarettes and is considered "hip", for no apparent reason. She later appeared pole dancing in The White Stripes' black and white video to promote their Burt Bacharach cover, 'I Just Don't Know What To Do With Myself'. And it's their dullest video to date.

iv A trait that publications like *NME* actively encourage.

Right: Live in London, 2002. (Andy Willsher/LFI)

more visible. In the space of a year, Meg and Jack went from having the bare minimum to survive on (Meg even kept hold of her old restaurant uniforms in case it didn't work out) to having enough money that they never need to work again. Assuming they don't squander it all on shoes or old blues records…

In November, The White Stripes played two sets at the mural-festooned Diego Riviera court in the centre of the Detroit Institute Of Arts in front of 3,750 fans, with the city flag behind them. "You could tell they were on their way," Magic Stick promoter Greg Baise comments. "I didn't go, but my *dad* did. He thought they were amazing."

The next day they flew back to the UK.

White Blood Cells was hastily released by XL, and a single pulled off the album to help promote it—'Hotel Yorba' b/w 'Rated X (Live At Hotel Yorba)'/'Hotel Yorba (Live At Hotel Yorba)'. The A-side is a real Pontin's holiday camp singalong of a number, similar to Brain & Michael's classic 'Matchstalk Men And Matchstalk Cats And Dogs' or perhaps Country Joe & The Fish's upbeat anti-Vietnam protest number, 'I Feel Like I'm Fixin' To Die Rag': you can imagine it on *Top Of The Pops* during the Seventies, everyone clapping their hands along during the counting section. Or maybe it recalls the famous video of Bob Dylan's 'Subterranean Homesick Blues' where he's dropping cards on the sidewalk—only with a far less densely packed sound.

The two acoustic songs on the B-side were indeed recorded live in a room at Hotel Yorba. (Meg: "It has urine-soaked carpets and towels that are bar towels.") 'Rated X' is a Loretta Lynn song that Meg used to sing live, sung by Jack on the CD. This one puts one in mind of Kris Kristofferson all soulful and aloof, reluctantly leading the lorry-drivers on their revolt against The Man in *Convoy*, only it's far less heavy. The drumming is exceptional. Meg exhibits a delightful lightness of touch. Jack's voice is high and expressive. The second version of 'Hotel Yorba', with its tambourine jingling, is structurally similar to Don McLean's 'American Pie'.

Much of the video was filmed outside the hotel, although the interior shots were filmed elsewhere. Jack strums a guitar on the bed, Meg bounces up and down and drums on a cardboard box, also strokes a pet rat. There are shots of Jack walking around with a redheaded girl (Tracee Miller, the wife of video director Dan Miller) with Meg walking dissolute behind, tied by a length of rope to Jack.

"I thought it suited the video," Meg told *NME*, "It's like I'm his little sister and when you're a kid, you have to drag your little sister around wherever you go, though you're trying to live your own life."

The single entered the UK charts at No 26.

"I went to Europe with The White Stripes, doing merch," says Ko Shih. "I'd never toured with anybody before besides the basic 'pile in a van, don't soundcheck, get really drunk and fall asleep on a floor'. So it was strange. They were just getting real big. It was scary. People don't realise how much work those guys have to do on tour. It's not just a matter of getting on and off the bus—it's getting up every day and doing hours and hours of interviews, and then getting on the bus. Every day, they faced the same questions—'Are you really brother and sister?' Something else I noticed was that when they played, there'd be a good mix of men and women at Meg's side of the stage. At Jack's, it was just men.

"That whole tour stood out," the Knockouts singer continues. "It was the first time I saw people play enormous audiences. People would crowd-surf to 'Hotel Yorba'. They weren't as big in America as the UK at that point. In the UK, it was 1,000 capacity venues, everyone going nuts. In the US, 100 people would go nuts and the other 200 would stand around cos it was cool to be there."

"There was a moment when they played The Astoria," says Stevie Chick. "There was me, Simon from Cargo, and my friend from *The Standard*. He said, 'If it wasn't for you two it would never have gotten this big'. I don't think that's true. The key is that they're amazingly talented, and their stuff will stand the test of time. At the time of the first explosion, everyone was calling them a hype and it was kind of obvious it's not. A hack at *The Daily Telegraph* interviewed me and misquoted me saying that 'the *NME*'s job is to hype stuff out of all proportion'. That's not the case. If there was any hysteria about those early pieces it's because The White Stripes totally justified it.

Above: The White Stripes live at The Astoria, London, 2002. (Nicky J Sims/Redferns)

v The band's first appearance on the BBC chart show.

vi He plays keyboards on the session version of 'No Sugar Mama'.

"In the interim between their first two tours," Stevie continues, "there was a whole Detroit explosion with The Von Bondies, The Dirtbombs and The Detroit Cobras. The Von Bondies were doing a John Peel session at Maida Vale so we went along to watch that. The session almost didn't happen, cos Marcie had decided to tag along to *TOTP* with Jack because The White Stripes were playing[v], and she was very late cos she'd had an opportunity to meet Paul McCartney. She was like, "You'd stick around to meet Paul McCartney, wouldn't you?' and that seemed very strange. Jack[vi] and Meg were there. Jack seemed really cool, such a genuine person. Especially as Ryan Adams was in the room, desperately trying to get it on with Meg. I've remained a huge fan since, but there's a hysteria that surrounds the band and a starfucker mentality, and I don't want to contribute to that—I don't want to run up to Jack and say, 'I'm the guy who wrote your first review in the *NME*'."

On Tuesday 6th November, the band recorded two songs for *Later With Jools Holland*, a late night TV show. The following day they recorded a Radio 1 Evening Session, and the day after, another John Peel session, this time at his house.

LACK OF COMMUNICATION

In between all the hyperbole and fine music and weight of expectations, Jack was still working at a prolific rate. Not content with taking Whirlwind Heat under his wing, in April 2001 he produced the debut album by Ann Arbor four-piece, The Von Bondies, *Lack Of Communication* (Sympathy For The Record Industry, June, 2001: reissued in the UK on Sweet Nothing, 2002). Imagine the howling wah-wah guitars of Mudhoney crossed with a severe sense of claustrophobia, with a little Detroit garage and a fair smattering of The Gun Club's swampy blues thrown in. Mix with an inclement sense of claustrophobia, and stand well back.

Previously, Jack had produced the band formerly known as The Babykillers' debut 'Nite Train' single (D-wreckEd-hiT, 2000) and 'It Came From Japan' (Sympathy For The Record Industry)—on which he also sings backing vocals. The fact Jack was dating guitarist Marcie Bolen probably helped explain his surge of affection for the band—a feeling he was to later regret, when singer Jason Stollsteimer started to downplay Jack's contribution to The Von Bondies' success, claiming that engineer Jim Diamond (*Lack Of Communication* was recorded at Ghetto) had far more to do with the Bondies' sound than Jack.

This eventually led to a well-publicised punch-up in December 2003 when Jack confronted Jason at The Magic Stick in front of his band-mates Marcie and Carrie [Smith, bass] and beat several shades of blue and purple out of his face. Jason, by all accounts, didn't try to defend himself. By this point Jack was internationally famous. The brawl made it onto CNN Headline News and into the pages of *The Sun*. Both sides seemed equally aggrieved about the fight when I spoke with them about it a few weeks later.

"It was such a quick thing," says Dan Miller. "There were these three 75-year-old musicians playing traditional jazz music between bands. This old drummer guy Joe was playing drums like he was like Buddy Rich, and Jack was in a great mood. I went back to the dressing room, and three minutes later everyone was like, 'Jack and Jason got into a fight'.

"For the next few weeks," he continues, "All you heard was The Von Bondies' side of the story: that Jack walked into the club, walked straight up the stairs, right up to Jason, punched him several times in the face and ran out. But everybody knows what kind of guy Jason is, that he rubs everyone the wrong way. He'd been slagging Jack in the press for a long time, after he'd let them record in his house for free, and after he produced their album for free.

"You can understand Jack being mad about it. No, what happened was they started yelling at each other, and one time Jason grabbed Jack by the hair and pulled him down—and then I guess the real fighting started and Jack won the fight. It was a bar fight. And then all these photos appeared on the Internet! It seems like something that will hopefully be laughed about in years to come."[vii]

ON THE ROAD: PART TWO

Monday Oct 29th
Collected Meg's drumkit from 'Beat On The Bush' & took to Matt Snowball's & got Jack's Fender Twin from Tarmigan. Lunch at Hemingford.

Bruce Brand: A drum set was bought for Meg in a place near Shepherd's Bush that stocks and hires great old gear. It was a signal red Slingerland, and I took it to the storage place. Previously it had been kept at my old place of work, so I indulged in a spot of liquid lunch at the local, which I heartily recommend. I had also been asked to paint the red and white swirly "peppermint" thing on the drumhead for them.

Tuesday Oct 30th
Got W/S drumhead. Got paint & brushes. Took Jack to vets for ears.

Bruce: That'd be about right. I went down my local Leyland's for that. I remember I got it all over my best green check shirt—it's still there. At some point I remember Spider Stacey rang me up and asked if they'd be willing to play with The Pogues or The Popes or whatever band he was playing with at the time, but they couldn't fit it in because the tour was already booked. I don't think "Took Jack to vets for ears" relates to Mr White. I think that probably concerns my dog.

Thursday November 1st
Painted drum skin white.

Friday November 2nd
Painted drum skin red.

Bruce: I think it must have been that night that Jack came running over to mine from the Holiday Inn they were staying at opposite to play me a song he'd just written with a view to recording it at Toe-Rag with Holly to see how it was. I think I must've looked at him funny, as he said, "You don't like it, do you!"

Monday November 5th
Left @ 9 to get gear & see t-shirt printers. To MTV. Interviews @ Solo/Soho(?) lunchtime. Toe-Rag—Jack, Meg & Holly recorded song.

Bruce: All I can say is the tea was never better that day! [Bruce is indeed the same Bruce that Holly Golightly instructs to get a *"Cup of tea then, Bruce—let's celebrate"* at the very end of The White Stripes' fourth album, *Elephant*.]

Jim Diamond was phlegmatic when asked his opinion of Jason earlier in December: "Jason, you know..." he laughed. "He and I have had fine times together in the studio. Sometimes he can talk some shit, but he's always done right by me, so I never have anything bad to say about him. He's using the garage rock thing right now to his advantage, which is great, so we'll see how their record goes...

"I can say this for Jason," Jim added. "Out of any of the people who have gone on to the major labels he is the only one who has seen to it that I get points, and that we have our legal paperwork in order. None of the other 'biggies' in town I have worked with have acknowledged my prior work with them legally or financially; maybe the Electric Six [Jim recorded and played sax on their Number 2 UK hit 'Danger! High Voltage!'] but I did have to threaten to sue!"

Marcie (earlier in December): "So what do you think of The Von Bondies?"

Dave Buick: "I don't know a band called The Von Bondies. You mean The Babykillers?"

Dion Fischer: "I'd almost say I liked them better when they were The Babykillers. I still love them but The Babykillers were just so much more messed up."

The Babykillers is a better name.

Dion Fischer: "You've got my vote. But they got a hard time about that name, that's why they changed it."

Tom Potter: "The Von Bondies got the same treatment as The White Stripes, where you can talk about a band that nobody was going to see for a while. They were like the first band at every show at The Gold Dollar, and no one would be there."

vii In March 2004, Jack was ordered by a Detroit court to attend anger-management training and pay a $650 fine, plus $325 in costs. "I regret allowing myself to be provoked to getting into a fistfight," the singer commented afterwards.

Meg White at a RRR rooftop gig, Melbourne, Australia, 30/1/02 (Martin Philbey)

viii Jack had wanted the Buff Medways/Thee Headcoats singer, Billy Childish, to appear alongside The White Stripes, with his oils and easel, creating a picture. The show's producers refused to let him. So Jack wrote his name on his arm as a protest, Riot Grrrl-style.

Dave Buick: "The first show where I remember myself paying attention was when they were still The Babykillers. Jason had cut his strumming finger really bad at work or something, and he had to have stitches. He took a whole bunch of pain med and was really out of it. It was a great show."

FAME

At the start of 2002, The White Stripes returned to Australia and New Zealand, to play the travelling Big Day Out festival, where they played on the second stage.

"Jack White and Shirley Manson [singer, Garbage] were hanging out round each other's trailers," recalls Mary Mihelakos. "He was still really nice. Meg was doing lots of shopping, and he was the one doing the technical stuff. They sold a surprising amount of merch. I got The White Stripes clock and The White Stripes slip mat, and the 'I Love Jack' and 'I Love Meg' badges. It was gimmicky, but it was good fun. I still wasn't expecting it to explode the way it did a couple of months later. When I went to America in March 2002, the 'Fell In Love With The Girl' video was on MTV constantly. That's when I knew they'd gone from being a huge pocket like Jon Spencer or The Dirtbombs to something quite bigger. They'd become a MTV generation act."

The second UK single, 'Fell In Love With A Girl', was released in February 2002. It was backed by a multi-format single (two CDs, and a seven-inch) and an innovative, commercial video that depicted the band as moving Lego Bricks. Following a second *Top Of The Pops* appearance[viii], it reached Number 21 in the UK. But it was the video that shot the band over the edge, especially in the States—directed by Michael Gondry (Bjork, Radiohead), it's a riot of primary colour and real and computer-generated Lego. The band race along a Lego landscape, bricks piling on top of bricks. It's cutesy, memorable and quirky. Everything an MTV addict could ask for.

"That video was probably the most calculated thing they ever did," comments Neil Yee. "But I'm sure they didn't realise it would cause them to explode the way they did."

Above: Jack with Julian Casablancas (lead singer, The Strokes), Bowery Ballroom, 08/04/02 (J. Scott Wynn/Retna)

The A-side is as close to the Pixies as Jack has ever sounded—it even has a Spanish feel and strangulated vocals like the Boston band's earliest work—but, crucially, it's *good* Pixies. People forget that the Pixies turned really bad—like a lame surf parody of themselves—before they split in the early Nineties. Also, the single is much rawer than anything Black Francis' band ever released.

One B-side gave the new White Stripes fans a chance to rediscover the first two A-sides, 'Let's Shake Hands' and 'Lafayette Blues'. The other one contains a chilling version of Dylan's 'Lovesick' recorded live at The Forum, Kentish Town during the second UK tour on December 6th, 2001. It starts off quiet and then explodes, Jack's voice all pent-up, worried and warbling. Plenty of modern-day rock bands cover Dylan, and claim to be fans—but Jack revealed himself to be a die-hard, by pulling in a song from a 1997 album.

The second song is even finer: a stripped-back version of the song made famous by Dusty Springfield 'I Just Don't Know What To Do With Myself', taken from the Radio One Evening Session in November 2001. It was so good, in fact, it turned up again in 2003 as both a single and a track on *Elephant.*

The day after the single's release, the band played a show at the tiny 93 Feet East in East London, and then flew off to mainland Europe to play more dates, before returning to the States for another tour.

On March 18, the band appeared on the prestigious late-night US chat show, *The David Letterman Show.*

"Every show seemed so great," says Dan Miller. "There were three shows in a row in LA, June 2002, that were amazing, where they were making the biggest strides in terms of being played on the radio and everything else. All three nights felt really different. One of the great things about The White Stripes is how they feed off the crowd."

In May, The White Stripes played a sold-out date at the Royal Oak Music Theatre where, in front of a suburban crowd, Jack White dropped to his knees during the opening guitar solo on 'Dead Leaves', and greeted the crowd with a, "Good evening, children. My name is Jack White and this is my big sister, Meg, on drums."

THE VON BONDIES

Jason (guitar/voice): When I was about four, I was friends with this little kid who lived on my block. We were real smart kids. We have nothing to do so we decide to toss around a brick. So we throw the brick in the air, catch it, throw the brick in the air, catch it, throw the brick in the air...and it smashes his head open. I start crying. I thought I'd killed him. Our moms came out and tell my six-year-old brother, "You watch Jason". They go off to the hospital and we go inside. I'm shaking—I've just killed my best friend!

So my brother sits me down at this huge barstool and gives me a glass of pop. But I'm a little kid, and the glass slips out of my hand cos I'm so shook up. It hits against the table, and engages itself right in my knee. It's stuck in between bones, right in the joint. I can't move. I'm silent. My brother looks down to see blood everywhere, pouring out, and I remember I've just killed my best friend, and my brother gets scared and thinks that he's gonna get in trouble so he gives me a wash cloth and turns off all the lights, locks all the doors and goes and hides upstairs. I'm sitting there in the chair in the fucking dark for a long time.

My mom comes home and doesn't have her keys on her cos she'd rushed off to the hospital. She can't get in, all the lights are off, I can't get up, and my brother's scared shitless. I'm sitting on the barstool, crying. My mom eventually gets in through the garage, and she's like, "Hello?" She turns on the light, sees me sitting there and asks what's wrong. I don't say anything. She sees my knee, with this huge coke glass stuck in it... "Oh my God!" So she rushes me back to the hospital and I wave to my friend, who's not awake, but at least there's no white sheet covering him!

Carrie (bass): I fell out of a two-storey window when I was five. I was all right! My mom had flown away to see her family, and my dad was playing monsters with me and my sister, he was chasing us around. It was in California, so it was nice out, right? We had a couch that was pushed against the wall and there was a row of windows right behind it, open. I was screaming at the top of my lungs, and I climbed up on the back of the couch and leaned on the screen. The screen popped out and I fell out the window! Two-storeys. I didn't bounce, there was a wooden bench underneath, and I fell onto it. I sometimes have flashbacks while I'm playing bass.

Marcie (guitar): When I was little, I wanted to be in [Eighties cartoon] *Gem And The Holograms* . Actually, I wanted to be the singer in The Misfits, the bad band. We used to get all dressed up. We cut guitar shapes out of cardboard and painted them.

Don (drums): When I learnt how to play the drums I would get my dad to play with me on his old, beat-up acoustic guitar. He was a born-again Christian, so he'd write these Christian songs. And I'd put all these horrible punk rock beats behind them. So we'd sit in the basement and play this really weird music. And my brother would play the trumpet. But, uh...we recorded it.

Jason Stollsteimer

What's your motivation for making music?

"Depression, I guess. Even our catchiest song has the most depressing lyrics. When I started making music, I'd never played guitar, I'd never sung in a band. I was going through a bad time and it was better than what I was doing. I was drinking Nite Train [title of The Von Bondies' debut single]. I was making my problems disappear through drink. I had some bad days when I didn't think I was going to have another day. A lot of corporate bands, they write a song to get a single. We write songs that deal with shit."

What made you turn to music?

"I couldn't paint. If I would've been able to paint, I'd be painting right now."

What was it about rock music that appealed to you?

"Otis Redding. He didn't have the best voice, but you could hear every emotion he had. It wasn't The Stooges. It wasn't MC5. I didn't get into that till this year. That's very new to me, 'the rock thing'. I was never a Led Zeppelin fan. I wasn't a Beatles or a Rolling Stones fan. I probably heard about eight different records, and that was it. Public Enemy had aggression. It's not about selling lots of records. Tom Waits is my rock'n'roll icon."

What made you want to sing?

"I got forced into it. Marcie and I were in a band called The Babykillers, with a female singer who played keyboard. It was like The Gossip or Bikini Kill. I played guitar. It was horrible. We kicked her out, and Marcie kept telling me, 'You should try singing.' It wasn't planned out. I wasn't confident. This is a five-year process, becoming a rock band. I get a little more confident each show. We've done 200 shows, easily. My singing voice doesn't sound anything like the way I talk. I sing very aggressively. I'm can't paint a picture. I can't even draw a circle. My brain doesn't work for a lot of things, but I can write a song. Even my favourite musicians don't know what they do. One day I'd like to call myself a songwriter. Whatever the hell that means."

What's your motivation now?

"The new record [*Pawn Shoppe Heart*, Sire, 2004] is about things that happened when I was 23, and I wasn't dealing with it very well, being in the spotlight and losing friends because of it. Dealing with people listening to rumours and lies—in papers or on message boards. There's one song that Carrie sings that goes *'I'm not that social, just a good drinker'*. Two of the songs I sing are about a girl, and the rest of them are about what happened when the band started touring and how people reacted.

"The first record was about a girl. I had a rough girlfriend for a while. She was an S&M girlfriend, but I wasn't into S&M. She'd be running down the street, drunk, in her underwear. There are some frat houses near Wayne State, downtown Detroit, near where I used to live, and she was screaming, 'Help me!' All these frat guys thought I was raping her. I was like, 'No, I didn't do anything! That's my girlfriend'."

Marcie Bolen

"I moved down river. I started playing when I was 16, and didn't know what else I wanted to do. I was into art. I was not very social. I'm more mechanical. I like facts and mathematical skills. I met a guy in high school and he bought me a crappy guitar, and taught me Beatles and Allman Brothers songs, and Black Sabbath. When I met Jason we started practising once or twice a week, to get out of the everyday thing of going to school and going to work. I'd drive my crappy car out to Ann Arbor, much to my parents' dismay. Eventually we got something going, and started playing house parties and stuff. That was The Babykillers. It was like monster-y punk rock."

What made you want to play guitar?

"I already had some musical skill in playing trumpet, and... There's nothing going on down river. It's like a wasteland. It is gruesome. I wanted to do something different. I wasn't on the same wavelength as most people. I didn't know how to communicate with them. I was into fashion and no one else cared. My sister and I would put on stupid little shows for our parents. That's something that's always made me happy, expressing myself that way, to whoever would listen instead of trying to hang out with people I didn't have anything in common with."

Left: Everett True with The Von Bondies.
(Sarah Bowles)

The same month, the band played another couple of dates in the UK, including a rather risible "new to *Q*" show (a fact blazed triumphantly on video screens either side of the stage) at Shepherd's Bush Empire with The Dirtbombs and The Von Bondies in support. New?! They'd been trailed all over the tabloids about eight months before!

On June 6th, they played the MTV Movie Awards. The White Stripes started to perform 'Fell In Love With A Girl', stopped, and went into medley of 'Dead Leaves And The Dirty Ground' and 'I Think I Smell A Rat'. Before the show, a message was sent out through The White Stripes website asking for people to get on stage with them for the performance, so there were about 100 or so fans present, dancing in red and white in front of the red and white banners overhanging Meg and Jack. It was a fine sight.

In the middle of the media frenzy—a frenzy that was only heightened when the first two albums were reissued—offers started to come in from corporations keen to associate themselves with the duo. The Gap clothing chain was rumoured to have offered them a million dollars.

"It wasn't a million dollars," Jack laughed, "but we did turn down a Gap ad. I think a couple of them. There were so many insane offers like that. There still are. I'm sure that any band that gets that kind of attention, that kind of buzz, gets stupid offers from people trying to leech off them. We still haven't done anything like a commercial, but I'm not really against it. You start to think, 'Man, I might really want that money 50 years from now'."

"Everyone said, 'why not?' the singer commented elsewhere. "It's almost as if, if people are willing to give you that much money, you are insulting everyone you know by turning it down—people's opinions about selling out seem to have changed over the years."

In August, came perhaps the year's most prestigious shows—four co-headlining dates with The Strokes in Detroit and New York and an afternoon appearance at the 60,000-strong Reading Festival in England. The two bands split the headline slot between their respective home cities: The White Stripes went on last at Detroit's 6,000-capacity amphitheatre Chene Park (August 9), and also Clutch Cargo's (August 8). The Strokes headlined NYC's Irving Plaza (August 14) and Radio City Music Hall (August 15). For the encore at Radio City, Jack White joined The Strokes on stage for a version of their 'New York City Cops', with Strokes' singer Julian Casablancas still on crutches after having sprained his knee, or some-such injury, a few days before. The two bands chatted to fans out of their second floor dressing room windows and threw T-shirts into the crowd.

"At the Radio City show," recalls Ben Blackwell, "The White Stripes got to soundcheck for literally 40 seconds because of union regulations—at what was, at that point, the biggest, most important show of their career. Of course the show went great."

"Jack had to alternate between doing those shows and producing our album," says Whirlwind Heat's David Swanson. "I really liked the Clutch Cargo's one, cos it was a lot smaller, and had a lot of energy. 'Fell In Love...' was happening, but it still wasn't at the Grammy level, so the excitement of everything being new was there... The Strokes were happening, too. I was doing the guitar tech stuff on the side of the stage. Jack uses three guitars—the Airline, the main one, and the red hollowbody that he used on the self-titled album, and then he had the brown Kay. That's the one he uses for all slides, all open tunes."

What's the rider like?

"Now, it's a six-pack of beer, some whiskey, their tour manager likes soy milk, chips and salsa, and that's pretty much it. They've cut it down. They used to get a deli platter or a vegetarian platter but no one ever ate it, cos there's always catering. Sometimes Meg does her hair up high, in the old style. For the Australian dates, Jack had huge [Melvins singer] Buzz Osborne hair. They both have a last cigarette before they go out. It's usually pretty consistent. It's not like they have a prayer or huddle. They don't have any set-lists. They go right up on stage and however it comes out, it comes out. Some of it is planned, what song they start with—but that changes all the time. Sometimes they'll play a bunch of stuff they haven't played before on the whole tour. They have such a wide range of songs and so many covers—you never know what may happen...

At Reading, Stevie Chick, now writing in *Kerrang!*, said, "The White Stripes' set is an unfettered thrill. Jack'n'Meg sweat pure passion and wit, their cluster bomb of blues'n'punk as sonically revolutionary as it is lovingly reverent. Jack's guitar virtuosity is never vainly flash,

Above: Jack at the Hudson River Rocks Concert, Pier 54, NYC 08/16/01 (Edward Dougherty/Retna)

ix It was actually 'For The Love Of Ivy'.

alternating walls of gritty fuzz (like antique shellac blues records shattering in a hurricane) with the kind of crazed bottlenecked soloing that'd give Jimmy Page pause. Beyond the music, there's their stagecraft. This petite duo aren't once swamped by the expansive stage, moments of high drama including a searing cover of The Gun Club's 'Elvis From Hell'[ix], Jack'n'Meg near-canoodling on her drum stool, and Jack throwing his sodden crimson T into the crowd, by way of a finale. This Motor City inferno burns a million times hotter than the traditional Reading cider-bottle cookout."

Much to the delight of the capacity crowd, Jack later came out onto the main stage to encore once more with headliners The Strokes on 'New York City Cops'.

A third single was released from the album to tie in with the festival season, August's 'Dead Leaves And the Dirty Ground', backed with 'Suzy Lee' and 'Stop Breaking Down'. The two songs on the B-side were tracks from the debut album, rerecorded at the same Radio One Evening Session as the Bacharach cover. The A-side is brutal, with some fine melancholy fuzz and hammerhead drums. The B-side is *fine*, especially the strung-out reading of the Robert Johnson song.

The single reached No 25.

In the video, directed by Michael Gondry again, Jack comes home to find that his house has been destroyed by a group of uninvited party animals. Jack donned a bowler hat remarkably similar to that of the "droogs" (gang members) in Stanley Kubrick's startling dissemination of future society, 1971's *A Clockwork Orange*. The film is a cult favourite among musicians, to such an extent that it's almost become a cliché to reference it. That didn't stop Jack from sporting the hat to many award ceremonies in the months that followed. The video was also available as a DVD single alongside a clip of the band getting an ear bashing from manager Arthur P Dottweiler for turning down The Gap commercial.

Other perks of fame included appearing with Beck in August and joining The Yardbirds' guitarist Jeff Beck (no relation) on stage at London's Royal Festival Hall on September 13 and 14. For the performance with the younger Beck, three songs were chosen: '99' (from a seven-inch by

The White Stripes perform at the Z Tour, Union Square Park, NYC, October 1, 2002 (Dimitrios Kambouris/WireImage)

Barbara Feldon of the theme to *Get Smart*, released on Melbourne's Au-Go-Go label), Beck's own 'Cold Brains' [from 1998's *Mutations*, his downbeat collection of folksy, post-fame songs] and Robert Johnson's 'Last Fair Deal Going Down'.

For the performance with the older Beck, Jack and Meg played the entire Yardbirds part of the show: 'You're A Better Man Than I', 'Heart Full Of Soul', 'Lost Woman', an instrumental 'Train Kept A-Rollin'', 'I Ain't Got You'...

"Can you imagine?" Jack asked. "It was unbelievable. It was the most fantastic thing I have done. I really love that he is still that guy who just doesn't care about anything, who wants only to play guitar and nothing else. We would take cues from him and I stood and watched when he first plugged in his guitar. He played a chord and slashed his way with several overtones, and it was so awesome. No effects pedal, just from the fingers, straight through the amplifier."

On October 16 and 20, The White Stripes supported The Rolling Stones in Toronto and Columbus respectively – a slot traditionally given to up-and-coming media favourites, as the creaking rockers desperately try to pretend that what they do has any relevance or verve whatsoever.

Jack was impressed anyway.

"Meeting the Stones was one of the year's absolute highlights," he said. "And to be suddenly standing in a room, chatting with the Stones, was bizarre. They even thanked us for supporting during their own shows. And we later understood from their roadies that they never watch the support band and they never thank anyone for anything, especially not from the stage. So we must have done something to impress."

In between the two dates, on October 19, they slotted in a performance on *Saturday Night Live*. The same month they played a free show in Union Square, NYC, backed by car giant Nissan. After a fair barrage of criticism in the press, Jack chose to open the show with the band's third single, the anti-corporate car company blast of 'The Big Three Killed My Baby'. The band were supposed to play for an hour, no longer, but at the end of the show when the plugs got pulled, Jack sang an a cappella version of 'Boll Weevil' without a microphone at all.

Above: Jack in *Cold Mountain*. (Courtesy of Miramax/Everett/ Rex Features)

Right: The White Stripes (Nicky J. Sims/Redferns)

x Rootsy Texas singer-songwriter who's perhaps better known as producer of artists like Elvis Costello, Sam Phillips and the truly horrible Counting Crows. He's also played guitar with Bob Dylan and country sweetheart Emmylou Harris.

COLD MOUNTAIN

In November, Jack found time to start filming his role as deserting soldier turned travelling troubadour alongside future girlfriend Renée Zellweger in the epic, Oscar-tipped, film based around the American Civil War, *Cold Mountain*. The film was released Christmas 2003.

"That was scary," Jack told Andrew Male, for *Mojo*. "You have 200 people around you and they call 'Action!' I've been in front of 60,000 people on stage but never felt pressure like that. (Then) I went down to Nashville, and met all these amazing bluegrass people. I wanted to start crying, I thought they'd picked the wrong guy."

The White Stripes even played a show on November 23, in Transylvania where the movie was being filmed: "It was surreal," Jack explained to *The Onion*, "Very odd. There was this Romanian dance troupe, and they'd rehearsed a couple of numbers, 'Fell In Love With A Girl' and 'I Think I Smell A Rat', to dance with us when we played behind them. So there were these very clumsy Romanian dancers in these Twenties flapper outfits in this Communist cabaret theatre with Nicole Kidman and Jude Law dancing in front of us."

"It was at a stylish old hotel in Brasov, outside Bucharest," he recalled. "We stood up there and played 'Isis' and 'One More Cup Of Coffee' with T-Bone, who had played both of them with Dylan on the Rolling Thunder Revue tour [1975]. That was definitely the high point of the film project for me."

Jack performs five numbers on the soundtrack, including a mournful version of 'Wayfaring Stranger', played on mandolin. His voice is almost unrecognisable, it sounds so rural. Jack attributed his screen debut to the fact T-Bone Burnett[x] was in charge of the music.

"I was flattered that T-Bone Burnett knew that I had this love of American folk music, enough to recommend me," Jack told London writer Keith Cameron. "And of course the songs in the film like 'Wayfaring Stranger' and 'Sittin' On Top Of The World' are songs I *love*. 'Sittin' On Top Of The World' is the first blues song I learned how to play. So I just felt this huge calling—that this part was for me. The funniest part was, we were recording *White Blood Cells* in Memphis, long before any mainstream success, and listening to the *O Brother, Where Art Thou?*

soundtrack, which T-Bone Burnett did. And I remember saying to Meg, it would be so cool if we had gotten famous and this movie had come out a year from now and maybe we could have gotten on the soundtrack somehow. And a year later that's exactly what happened! It was a lot of work. I don't think I could ever be a full-time actor. I don't know how those people do it."

The year ended with the release of the fan club seven-inch single, 'Merry Christmas From…The White Stripes'—a reissue of 'Candy Cane Children' from the Flying Bomb 'Surprise Package EP' backed with two slightly weirder tracks, 'A Reading Of The Story Of The Magi' and 'The Singing Of Silent Night'.

The A-side is a flash of casual genius, mostly carried through the ricochet drumbeats and Jack's enthusiastic vocals about *"How nobody knows how to talk to children"*. The song also boasts a playful mock ending. The B-side is in the grand tradition of the early Beatles fan club singles, earnest but silly. The titles are literal: Jack reads out a passage from St Matthew's account of the Three Wise Men's visit to King Herod, while Meg attempts her first recorded solo vocal on a sweet, breathy rendition of 'Silent Night' that unfortunately gets somewhat messed up halfway through, over confusion over the lyrics.

It was a lovely way to finish the year.

TWO'S COMPANY

Why do you think it was The White Stripes that got big?

Matt Smith: Name me one other band from Detroit that hasn't been plagued with personnel changes and record company hassles for the last two years. The Electric Six were breaking up every other week. The bass player from Outrageous Cherry would decide he couldn't play on anything released on CD because they're bad for the environment. People were leaving and joining The Go all the time. Every band was like a revolving door of people. Detroit likes its authentic music, but on another level, all these bands are one step away from 1910 Fruitgum Company[i] and The Ohio Express[ii].

Dave Buick: Do you remember when Steve Nawara was in The White Stripes? He played bass for them on one show at The Gold Dollar.

Chris Handyside: It's true. Until recently even The Wildbunch (née Electric Six) were consistent. The Hentchmen have been consistent. They've had the same line-up since I wasn't in them.

Dave: I think all the bands have at least two original members. Except The Dirtbombs.

John: It's difficult for any band to hold on to four or five members for any period of time. If you take the band seriously you have to make sacrifices. Some people work, some people can't, some people chose not to. It's not always easy for people to make that commitment.

i Anonymous studio band, manufactured adroitly. Their upbeat 1968 bubblegum smash '1-2-3 Red Light' soundtracked one of the most painful episodes of my life…but let's not go there.

ii The Ohio Express were put together by the same producers as 1910 Fruitgum Company: Jeff Katz and Jerry Kasenetz—their big 1968 hits were the even more saccharine 'Yummy Yummy Yummy' and 'Chewy Chewy'.

3

Death Of The Sweetheart

ELEPHANT

In early 2002, at the height of the media feeding frenzy, The White Stripes started writing songs for their fourth album—the sprawling exorcism of *Elephant*.

Elephant was recorded in East London's Toe-Rag studios between April 24th and May 13th. Arch garage fiend Liam Watson engineered and Jack produced. Toe-Rag isn't Ghetto Recorders, but it ain't exactly Olympic Studios[i] or Abbey Road either. It's situated in a narrow alley between two semi-detached houses in the rather dingy suburb of Homerton, North London. No fancy swimming pools or cafeterias—this is a studio crammed with an electric array of old and new equipment, with the emphasis on old: a studio for *musicians*. Toe-Rag had been associated with the raw three-chord splendour of Billy Childish[ii] and associates for years now.

The album ended up sounding very different to the record Jack and Meg had originally envisioned for their first post-fame outing—metamorphosing from what was meant to be a gentle, reflective album into a howling metal monster, complete with guitar solos to equal even the excesses of Queen or Big Brother And The Holding Company[iii]. It was centred round the twin themes of corruption and the elephant: the further the outside world encroaches upon the individual, the more wrong it will do them.

Clearly, it's an album very influenced by the situation the band found itself in, one that Jack felt they hadn't sought.

"This album is dedicated to, and is for, and about the death of the sweetheart," wrote the singer in the CD booklet, sounding uncharacteristically weary. "We mourn the sweetheart's loss in a disgusting world of opportunistic, lottery ticket holders caring about nothing that is long term, only the cheap thrill, the kick, the for the moment pleasure, the easy way out, the bragging rights and trophy holding."

I think I smell a rat, indeed!

"It wasn't a political statement so much as a social idea about the attitude," Jack tried to explain to *The Onion*. "Teenage girls with tattoos and body piercing, and the white boy from the suburbs who adopts a ghetto accent. There's this whole attitude that you have to be hard, right out of the gate. And the sweetness and gentlemanly ideas are really going away. I've gotten the feeling that parenting and the way people are brought up now is getting away from these natural ideas and natural instincts in the male or female personalities. They're being sacrificed for the idea of equality or good parenting."

"The main reason we named the album *Elephant*," Jack told *Mojo* critic Andrew Male, "is the idea of one creature representing both Meg's and my own personalities, whether onstage *or*

Left: Jack and Meg at the Roosevelt Hotel in Hollywood, 02/06/02. (Robert Gauthier/Retna)

i The Spice Girls danced round their handbags there: Hole wasted several hundred thousand pounds there: Led Zeppelin and The Rolling Stones rocked the joint.

ii Childish adheres to the Stuckist Art Manifesto and its quest for authenticity. Point five: art that has to be in a gallery to be art isn't art.

iii They were the back-up band for the overwrought, sometimes gut-churning, screaming of hippie icon Janis Joplin—proof to some (not Rachel of The Detroit Cobras) that white girls can indeed sing the blues.

Above: The White Stripes at the Ferdinand house, in between *White Blood Cells* and *Elephant*. (Pat Pantano)

in real life: power, subtlety, anger, innocence, clumsiness, stability. Another reason was the way elephants relate to death. When a group of elephants come upon the dead remains of another elephant they become very emotional and try to bury the bones, which directly relates to 'The death of the sweetheart'. It's no longer the quiet version of *Elephant* we planned. It's heavy duty."

In an attempt to distance himself from what Jack perceived to be false modern-day values (particularly when it came to the use of Pro-Tools in cleaning up recorded sound) the new record was recorded on eight-track reel-to-reel. The sleeve boasted that, "No computers were used during the writing, recording, mixing or mastering of this record".

"If we can't produce something that sounds good under those conditions, then it's not real to begin with," he explained to *The Guardian*'s Keith Cameron. "Getting involved with computers is getting involved with excess, especially when you start changing drumbeats to make them perfect or making the vocal melody completely in tune with some programme, it's so far away from honesty. How can you be proud of it if it's not even you doing it?"

"Digital recording devices are the devil's handiwork," Jack told *Sonic* magazine. "They hollow out the talent of people and make them sound like mumbling robots. Kills their creativity. It makes the recordings totally lifeless, without soul. Jennifer Lopez's latest hit single was written by 12 people and recorded by five producers and it consists of only Pro-Tools and machines and those things have nothing to do with making music. That is not music, that is a

TRACK BY TRACK

Reprinted with the kind permission of Andrew Male, *Mojo*

'Seven Nation Army'
Following a brooding bass and tribal drum intro, Jack White announces that, *"I'm gonna fight 'em off/A seven nation army couldn't hold me back"*. A dark, paranoid intro, followed by a most metal James Bond guitar break, it touches on themes of homelessness, exorcism, and escape.

Jack White: That's not a bass at the start but my guitar with an octave pedal. The song's about gossip. It's about me, Meg, and the people we're dating. The world constantly tries to dissect people, chew them up and spit them out. We get that all the time, people wanting our songs for commercials, wanting to know what the inside of Meg's bathroom looks like."

'Black Math'
Driving, grubby, over-literate garage metal about bad teachers. It rocks.

JW: I was thinking about a time in high school when I turned my books in to the maths teachers and said I refuse to learn from you any more. The song's about asking questions. A lot of people are taught just to regurgitate information. People don't care if you *learn* any more. Opinion gets trampled on.

'There's No Home For You Here'
'Dead Leaves And the Dirty Ground' reworked as an eight-track 'Bohemian Rhapsody', about kicking bad people—*"drinking soda, taking pictures"*—out of your hometown.

JW: I just said, Let's just open this song up. I layered vocals over vocals, like 12 different voices of myself all up the scale, all done with splicing tapes. It's anti-anything we've ever done.

'I Just Don't Know What To Do With Myself'
A heartfelt, squalling cover of the Dusty Springfield/Bacharach & David classic.

JW: This was Meg's baby. Definitely Dusty's version. I think it's one of the best recordings we've made. I like my singing on this. It's mellowed.

'In The Cold, Cold Night'
Meg's song. An eerie little beauty, underscored by a light organ hum. Initially believed to be a cover of some lost Peggy Lee or Mo Tucker song.

JW: I wrote that specifically for Meg. I wanted it to be half Mazzy Star and half Peggy Lee. I played it for her in my attic. Meg laughed. She liked it. That organ sound was from me lying down on the studio floor pressing the organ pedals. If you listen close you hear wood popping on the piano pedal. Toe-Rag's scary to a lot of people. They don't want to be confined. But the limitations make you work.

'I Wanna Be The Boy To Warm Your Mother's Heart'/'You've Got Her In Your Pocket'
Companion songs, both beautifully reminiscent of *No. 1 Record*-era Big Star and Seventies-era McCartney. 'I Wanna Be The Boy' is the sweet song of tentative, unrequited love while 'Pocket' is its dark side, about tricking a woman into a possessive relationship.

JW: 'I Wanna Be The Boy' is the ultimate sweetheart part of the record. When we went to Toe-Rag the first time we recorded [final track] 'It's True That We Love One Another' with [The Headcoatees singer] Holly Golightly. Afterwards I played 'Pocket' and put everybody in a bad mood. It's Meg's favourite.

'Ball And Biscuit'
Seven minutes of prowling, bragging electric blues. A tale of mean sex and meagre confectionary reward taking its cue from an ancient "ball and biscuit" microphone at Toe-Rag.

JW: I love the imagery. A biscuit is such a cheap treat. I hate that people in America are gonna think it means buttermilk biscuit and not cookie. I would never talk up a girl like that. My whole vision of the song was a girl passing by and me thinking these things.

'The Hardest Button To Button'
Nervy, screwed-up Iggy-meets-Bobbie Gentry tale of screaming babies, voodoo, bad family members and things buried in the garden.

JW: There's a button at the top of my navy pea coat, and it's the hardest button to button. I thought that was a great metaphor for the odd man out in the family. It also comes from sayings of my father, like, "My uncle Harold had a 10-button vest but he could only fasten eight".

'Little Acorns'
After what sounds like an American preacher telling the inspirational tale of a squirrel collecting nuts for winter comes the pounding, wailing fuzz-toned White Stripes version. Altogether now—*"Be like the squirrel, girl/Be like the squirrel!"*

JW: My brother, who works at a radio commercial distribution place, had been bringing around tapes for me to record on. I was recording a piano melody and when I played it back it had this guy speaking on the other track. Totally accidental. I based a song around his story. He's actually a famous news anchorman in Detroit, Mort Crim. I thought he'd hate it. He loved it.

'Hypnotize'
Under two minutes of punk love, hand-holding and caveman drumming. Perfect.

JW: I wrote that song for [Detroit rock'n'roll purists] The Hentchmen and they never used it. It doesn't need to be any longer. That's the rock'n'roll length.

'The Air Near My Fingers'
A Troggs-esque picaresque about life on the road and the love of a good mother. Not Jack's favourite.

JW: I almost took it off. The lyrics don't really mean anything. The only thing I liked about it was where I talk about mothers, cos mothers come up a lot in the album. And there's a bridge in there I like. Everything else I hated.

'Girl, You Have No Faith in Medicine'
Another mean, mercurial Stripes monster, this time about a woman's irrational fear of over-the-counter headache remedies. No, really.

JW: "It came from a discussion between me and other guys about when girlfriends have headaches and won't take certain medicines cos it has 'something in it'. Guys will swallow anything. It was supposed to go on *White Blood Cells*. It was no fun at all to sing. Meg had a lot of problems with it. I actually took a lyric out because I thought it was too harsh—*'I don't have the patience to watch you battle with every minuscule disease'*."

'It's True That We Love One Another'
The perfect outro. Jack and Meg join Holly Golightly in a gentle country strum about whether Jack really loves Holly, or Holly really loves Jack. Meg doesn't care, *"cos Jack really bores me"*. Ends with much clapping, and Holly calling for tea all round.

JW: "It's supposed to be about ourselves, like The Mamas And The Papas' 'Creeque Alley'. It was the first song I ever wrote, recorded and mixed in the same day. It forced me to work. On the next album I'll have a lot of people I respect write down a song topic and write a song about it. I'll be confined with having to come up with something.

TOE-RAG

Liam Watson (engineer)

"The White Stripes first heard about the studio through The Hentchmen—John [Hentch] did a session here one time he was in London for a week. They liked the sound of all our old gear. The studio is built up to be a studio like it used to be. It's not true that we have no equipment made after 1963, like some press release said. That really pissed me off! When Jack saw the place, he thought it was excellent. He was like, 'Wow, there's nothing like this in Detroit'.

"I like to record a band for as long as it takes. Most of the bands I'd been recording till a couple of years ago never really had a budget. That's where I learnt to be fast. I can understand if it takes longer, but I prefer it this way. Also, when we did *Elephant*, we were using an eight-track machine. If you're recording on 24-track, it takes longer. With eight-track, you can do a lot of the things they do on 24, but you have to mix them down.

"It was easy working with them. Jack was very polite and good mannered. He got on with the job, very efficient. Every now and then we'd stop for a cup of tea. A few times he was still writing lyrics in the evenings.

"We basically mixed it in a day. I always enjoyed doing 'I Want To Be The Boy To Warm Your Mother's Heart'—I liked the slide on that. There wasn't anything I didn't like. I enjoyed doing the Queen bit on 'There's No Room For You Here', cos Jack had no idea how I was doing it on an eight-track. People don't have any real comprehension how you can endlessly overdub. I've got my tricks! When The Beatles were doing their famous stuff, there were four of them recording at the same time, so it was all on one track, bouncing between two tape machines. This was more extreme. Not quite as tasteful as George Martin.

"Meg's very sweet, very quiet, good fun. There's a lot of pressure on her—if the drums are right, everything else sits on top. She's a good drummer, she's not flashy or anything, but once she's got the beat she's very solid. We didn't have to do many retakes on the drums. Once she'd done her part she didn't hang around unnecessarily. She'd come up to say hello while we were doing overdubs in the afternoon.

"The Pizza-Go-Go in Hackney was delivering almost every day, and every now and then we'd have a Vietnamese or Chinese. No alcohol was consumed. Meg might have had a glass of whiskey when she came in the evening. Jack was drinking a lot of soft drinks and teas—not very healthy.

"He was pretty aware of who we are. When we met up he was asking me about a lot of records—he's a big fan of Billy Childish, Thee Headcoats and Thee Headcoatees. The Holly Golightly track was the first thing that was done for the album. We did the one song, 'We Love One Another', and tried a couple of others—Jack singing with acoustic guitar, one with drums on. I've worked with Holly on numerous occasions: 90 per cent of her work has been done here."

Above: Toe Rag Studios.
(Lee Powers/Camera Press, London)

fuckin' computer programme. It's a bunch of scientists trying to create something to make us feel good, they could just as well be making drugs or a computer game or..."

Although *Elephant* doesn't feel too different from the previous three albums—*De Stijl* was recorded mostly in Jack's front room, remember[iv]—what's immediately apparent is the maturity of the band's sound, developed from the numerous, spontaneous live shows. No more adolescent Geddy Lee/Robert Plant shrillness for Jack: his voice has become much warmer and more expressive over the years. It's now one of the finest voices in contemporary rock, bar none. There's a sophistication to the innocence: it's not clatter-and-hope anymore.

The album was released on April 7, 2003[v]. Advance copies were sent out to journalists as double-LPs in a plain red sleeve—one more attempt by Jack to reinstate some of the old values he felt should never have been allowed to slip. (Pretty much all music fans know by now that CDs have a far more sterile sound than vinyl.) Some critics boasted rather foolishly of having to "dust off their old record players" so they could hear it.

They shouldn't have ever allowed the dust to settle in the first place.

BB: "You were saying earlier that you never throw away a song... I know some songs on *Elephant*, like 'You Got Her In Your Pocket', you were playing as early as 1999, and 'Hypnotize' you originally wrote for The Hentchmen and they couldn't do it... I could mention 30 songs that you've got lying around."

JW: "Yeah, there's a bunch of them. I haven't rethought about them in a while. We did a lot of that on *Elephant*. I'll work 'em up once it's time to do another album."

BB: "So you will draw...?"

JW: "I just don't like to throw those things away. There's a time and place for them to hang around. Sometimes they just sit there and it's time to do them, I guess."

Ben: "He never throws away a song, because he writes good songs. He knows how to put things together—whether it's words or sounds or objects, he's a very good constructor. The man never forgets a song, much like an elephant. Giving songs to other bands, that was his idea of everyone

iv Third Man studios alternated between Jack's attic and the front room.

v And no, the date wasn't pulled forward by a month to combat potential Internet bootleggers, as was erroneously reported.

being friends in Detroit—he hoped everyone would write songs for each other. If it doesn't work for your own band, maybe it'll work for another. But I guess he was about the only one to ever do it."

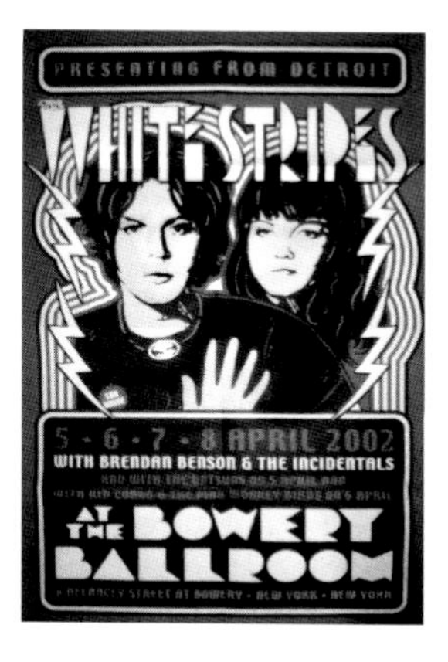

Having proved to himself that he could work within severe restrictions on *White Blood Cells*, Jack promptly relaxed some of them for *Elephant*. Most notably, he allowed guest musicians back onto a White Stripes album.

The lure of working with Holly Golightly—former singer with Billy Childish spin-off group Thee Headcoatees, and a lady with several charming solo albums to her credit—was clearly too great. The resulting acoustic country duet with South London's Queen of Late Night Garage that closes off the album, 'Well It's True That We Love One Another' is utterly irresistible. Holly and Jack trade lines back and forth in best Lee Hazlewood/Nancy Sinatra tradition, while Meg chips in a handful of disinterested suggestions. It's a quaint, enjoyable way to finish off what is easily the darkest White Stripes album to date. Even if the lyrics seem to exist only to bolster Jack's ego: *"Why don't you go off and love yourself?" "If I did that, Holly, there wouldn't be anything left for anybody else."*

"Jack was staying at the Holiday Inn round the corner from me," Holly's drummer Bruce Brand recalls. "He came crashing round one night, and he was like, 'I've written a song that me and Holly can sing'. So he went down to the studio the next day with a glorified, clapped-out, acoustic guitar, and put one mic on it, sitting in a line, recorded live. Then he put a big piano on it. We might all have done a little finger clicking. Right at the end of the song, Holly, in truly Holly style, demanded I put the kettle on—and so I'll forever be known as that 'someone known as Bruce'."

Jack also did away with the rule regarding guitar solos (one could argue that this one never got enforced anyway). Certainly, the epic and frankly lewd "Ball And Biscuit" (one critic likened it to an elongated wank-fest) boasts several screaming guitar lines that wouldn't have been out-of-place at a Jimi Hendrix show. This isn't a criticism, more an observation—indeed, when The White Stripes played the song live at the massive Alexandra Palace in North London, January 2004, it was stunning to see Jack handle the solos, one-handed. The guitar crackles with electric static: Jack's voice is all hoary, world-weary and—it must be said—macho.

He is indeed the seventh son.

"I don't really know what happened," Jack explained. "We were about to record 'Ball And Biscuit'. All was peaceful and calm when, suddenly, it was as if the devil got into me and I could not hear anything except guitars. Fat, dirty, ear-destroying guitar sounds. It was as if some higher power said to me that now, Jack White, is the time to start playing guitar solos."

Ha!

If there is one way *Elephant* differs from its predecessors it's that it's a very *male* album. There again, the blues—almost without exception, and meaning no disrespect to such fine singers as Etta James[vi] and Bessie Smith[vii]—is a very male form of expression. The rather dubious sentiments of the ferocious, theatrical 'Girl, You Have No Faith In Medicine', picking up where 'I'm Finding It Hard To Be A Gentleman' left off on the previous album, help give credence to this theory.

"It's about the irritation I was constantly getting with females arguing about headache medicine," Jack told Keith Cameron. "Like, 'Oh, I can't take Tylenol, it doesn't work'. Whereas a guy would just take anything, he doesn't even think about it. It seemed like this tiny thing was a big, telling sign of feminine behaviour. In my eyes. A guy can just put his coat on and run out the door, but a girl has to take 25 minutes waddling around looking for her purse or whatever. Not that one's better than the other, but they're different."

Not even Meg could remain mute in the face of this (Keith wrote): "I don't know about that song," she sighed. "Makes me wanna smack him. A lot."

"But is it true?!" Jack asked.

"I don't know, Jack. Maybe you're just hanging around with the wrong women."

"You might be right about that, Meg," Jack laughed.

BB: "Are you finding it harder to be a gentleman?"

JW: *(laughs)* "Yeah."

vi Ballsy blues/Southern soul singer, best known for the chilling, searing 'I'd Rather Go Blind', and the rampant 'Tell Mama'—rock'n'roll like it should be played.

vii The Empress Of The Blues.

Right: Jack after his performance with Beck, Ann Arbor, 8/02 (Doug Coombe)

Left: Jack with Sting. (Lester Cohen/Wireimage)

viii He's in love with the modern world—and rock'n'roll!

Ben: "I always thought that song nailed it, a feeling, the Jonathan Richman type point-of-view. The guy standing in the corner with his hands in his pockets, but... I just thought of 'Hospital', the feelings and the way it's put together. Jack would listen to the first Modern Lovers album[viii] *a lot—him and Meg were really into that. That was the only time I ever saw it manifesting itself in The White Stripes."*

JW: "Lately, people have been hitting us that we're being too conservative or too old-fashioned. I'm not trying to preach to people, I'm just throwing the idea out to see what the reaction is. It's so funny to shock people with a conservative idea. It's shocking you should be nice to each other, to be sweet... whatever. It's scary to see things have gone so far that people would think that. Because I'm not a conservative person, I'm not a Republican or anything. I don't think that way at all. It's just because of the lifestyle rock'n'roll bands have, it's very hard... we're all polite to each other, but why are we polite to each other? What's the moral grounding for everything? Just society in general: what's the norm? Like, 'Oh yeah, you don't usually walk into a room full of people naked'. Well, why not? 'Well, I don't know.' You just don't do it. 'Well then, why do you do anything?'"

BB: "Well, that goes all into Freud and everything like that."

JW: "I guess so."

Ben: "That's Jack getting psychological. If you hold a door open for a girl it's because you like and respect her, not because you want to get laid. You're totally killing it for anyone who truly believes in their actions. I argued with him about the lyrics to 'I'm Finding It Harder To Be A Gentleman'. I thought he was saying, 'If I hold the door open for you it wouldn't make your day'—that was totally how I felt about girls at the time. He wasn't in a similar state of mind, or relationship. He was like, 'No, it would make your day'. To me, interpreting it that way, it got through much more."

Despite these criticisms, *Elephant* is a brilliant album: with the expectations of the music industry upon them, Jack and Meg effortlessly came up with 14 songs that further expanded their template and threw the challenge straight back. 'There's No Home For You Here'—with its overwrought, *Rocky Horror*-style opening, the multi-tracked harmonies and frantic lyrics that tumble out of Jack's mouth like lies from a tabloid writer's pen—is one song that clearly addresses the situation. Jack's voice drops to a quietened whisper, until suddenly bursting worth over a welter of feedback into a chorus to crush all detractors.

"Just go away," he yells, dismissively. *"Just go away."*

An old tape of Detroit TV announcer Mort Crim introduces 'Little Acorns' offering advice on how to deal with sorrow[ix]. Jack then launches into a scathing retort, countering the woolly sentiments with a quick reality check. The song also gives a nod to the vocal mannerisms of doomed T Rex singer Marc Bolan (as does the vengeful 'Black Math')—the glamour continues, and is even knocked up a notch on the inspired Bacharach cover, 'I Don't Know What To Do With Myself' [the only song not recorded at Toe-Rag, but taken from the 2001 Evening Session recordings]. Jack doesn't even to pretend to hold back as he throws himself full-pelt into the lyrics—swelling guitar chords and drums alert to every minutiae of emotion. Three-quarters through, the Sixties lament is turned into a roaring metal attack as Jack claims the song entirely for himself, without detracting from the desirability of the original—now that's the mark of a great artist.

Meg's first solo vocal follows—on the slinky, mischievous 'In The Cold, Cold Night'—and it's a real treasure, the early parallels with Mo Tucker even more applicable, for the way both musicians sound so coyly hesitant when they sing.

MARCIE ON JACK

What's Jack like as a person?

Marcie Bolen (The Von Bondies): He's never sacrificed his integrity for anything. He does what he believes. He's not gonna take anything less from anything or anyone. He's a very strongly opinionated person. He's sometimes hard to get along with because he'll have an idea and if you don't believe in that he's not gonna listen to you. I haven't talked to him much lately. We had a falling out a while ago just because of our differences. He's a person of very good character. He's never done drugs. He doesn't really drink... He's very different with Meg. I think she goes with his opinions more—not that she doesn't have a mind of her own. He's such a strong person she gets sucked into what he does.

Do you think his family helped shape who he is?

Marcie: Yeah, since there were so many kids in his family, he had to constantly get himself out there, and talk louder than his other brothers. I have just one sister and she's as quiet as I am—I never had to adjust myself with all those other kids around. And, in my band, I guess I don't mind being more in the background.

If you come from a large family, it can go one of two ways.

Marcie: Yeah. Being in my band now is like having a family where you're either gonna project yourself, or say "I'm gonna do my own thing and do it well". I'd rather be the one in the background, holding things up.

Above: (CPS/LFI)

"She doesn't like her own voice at all," Jack told one journalist. "I wrote that song for her to sing specifically. She likes it all right now, but she wouldn't tell you that." In the same interview, Jack rather dismissively suggested that Meg doesn't have "the personality" to be a songwriter: "She's very shy and she's super-polite and she won't speak unless spoken to," he explained. "In songwriting and presenting something that you create to people, you kind of have to have an extroverted attitude."

Noting the almost Rolling Stones 'Under My Thumb'[x] sentiments of the disarmingly gentle solo number 'You've Got Her In Your Pocket', and also the lyrics on 'Hypnotize', one wonders whether this is a case of Jack taking his desire to control all facets of the music too far. It's no secret the singer is a control freak: he insists that travelling members of The White Stripes' touring party wear their stage clothes when out and about, and throws tantrums at fellow musicians and journalists when they have differences of opinion. Maybe Meg's shyness is compounded by Jack's extrovert personality, overshadowed by his desire to both communicate and control.

There's nothing shy about her ferocious, full-on drumming on the album's opening track (and future single) 'Seven Nation Army'—one more acidic retort to the duplicity of the outside world.

"Sometimes it feels that Jack White came along because rock'n'roll was being done *wrong* (both in a practical, and old time morals kinda way)," wrote Stevie Chick in *Careless Talk Costs Lives*. "If you believe in music as something which can 'progress' in any linear fashion, White circumnavigates the dead end rock'n'roll found itself in by eschewing the bad habits it fell into in middle-age: homogeneity, studio sanitation, faked emotion, seeking consensus instead of individuality."

BB: "Do you have the fifth album idea already in your head?"

JW: "Yeah, but I'm not gonna tell you." *(Laughs)*

Ben: "He says he does. I don't know, doing a record on the fucking moon, the guy always surprises me. Whatever the last thing you think it'll be. I was surprised they recorded Elephant *so*

ix His presence on the album came about through chance: Jack found a tape of the monologue in a batch of radio station tapes his brother had given him to record over for home demos.

x A song thoroughly derided by the emergent feminist movement of the late Sixties for being misogynistic—and rightly so. It's repulsive.

HOLLY GOLIGHTLY

Words: Everett True and Jon Slade

JS: The images that come to mind when I hear the words Holly Golightly aren't what they used to be. Obviously, it used to be Audrey Hepburn in *Breakfast At Tiffany's*—elegant American lady, cigarette holder, big hair with the tiara, blah blah. Now it's someone entirely different—elegant Medway lady, constantly smoking Benson & Hedges, hair all different ways, blah blah.

ET: It's weird you say that, cos I'd completely forgotten that Holly Golightly isn't her real name. I guess that means she's two fictional characters. Weird! You've met her, what's she like?

JS: She's very charming, if a little guarded. She seems kind of old—not in years, but like she's from a different age—late Fifties, like in that White Stripes song that involves her from *Elephant* where Jack sings, *"There's just so much I don't know about you"*. It's an odd line, it doesn't scan, but it should be there because it's totally true. Some people says Holly drives a truck for a living, others says she lives on a farm, others say on a boat... All could be true, or none.

ET: Is Holly her real name even?

JS: I think Holly is, but Golightly might not be.

ET: So why do all my friends go crazy over her?

JS: That's hard. She writes some good songs. There's an air of mystery about the whole Holly Golightly/Billy Childish axis. No one really knows what Medway is, or where it is—it's probably close to London but if you did know where it was you'd probably be scared to go there. Also, they play a simple kind of rock'n'roll that I like—Holly is different to the Buff Medways, for instance, she plays a lot of country folk styled stuff, but it's simple. And Bruce Brand is one of the best drummers ever. You know Bruce, right?

ET: No. [Yes.]

JS: I can't even remember what my favourite records of hers are called: they're all seven-inch singles. She was in Thee Headcoatees between '91 and about '98, and probably the first to leave. Why? I can't go into that. It's just gossip anyway. Thee Headcoats used to play, and play, and play, until the little audience that was there would all pretty much be gone home and even the most hardcore fan would be losing interest a little bit, or tired from dancing so much, and then the girls in Thee Headcoatees would come on and the party would start again.

ET: I always got a Sixties girl group feeling off them.

JS: They were a girl group, but man they were tough—they had a raggy old glamour, a motley crew. They looked great. Everyone was in awe of them. They were the kind of girls you thought you could be friends with, but you might not wanna... Also, I liked the fact they covered that Headcoats song, 'Come Into My Life' and changed it round so it was 'Come Into My Mouth'—I don't know if that was their idea or Billy's idea.

ET: They did a lot of covers, didn't they?

JS: They did 'I Gotta Move' by The Kinks, 'Wildman', but I don't know who did that... They all used to sing along at the end of 'Davy Crockett' [Thee Headcoats], 'Have Love Will Travel' by The Sonics...

ET: Is it a Damaged Goods[i] aesthetic, the whole Holly thing?

JS: I guess that's part of it, that simple, cheap, dirty, attitudinal, punk rock, rock'n'roll.

ET: She's very prolific, solo.

JS: That's very true—since leaving Thee Headcoatees, she's had 10 solo albums out. I haven't heard all of them but as far as quality control goes, some are better than others. 2003's *Truly She Is None Other*, is one of the better ones: it's a tad more considered, and more accomplished. She gets better at songwriting all the time.

ET: So, to sum up, Holly's appeal lies in a combination of the simplicity, the mystery, the glamour, the understated Sixties girl group harmonies, the backbeat and the ROCK'N'ROLL.

JS: *(Nods)*

i London purveyor of decent, scuzzy, lo-fi, deranged rock'n'roll.

Above: Holly Golightly (Alison Wonderland)

xi Don't ask. I interviewed the one-time challengers to Happy Mondays' skronk dance throne for their new record in 1991. The album eventually appeared a decade later.

quickly after White Blood Cells, *while the hype was still there. They didn't sit on their asses. It wasn't like some Breeders or Stereo MCs thing[xi], 10 years between records. I bet you he already has the entire next record written, I'd put money on it. He knows what's going on.*

"People compare The White Stripes to Nirvana. The obvious parallel is that both are bands responsible for increased attention on the rest of their city. People have mentioned how Jack doesn't like his celebrity the same way Kurt Cobain didn't. He doesn't do it to be a celebrity. He does it because he loves music. He's not a self-promoter—in this day and age when every celebrity is a self-promoter. That's part of the media insanity—rock stars are so quick to suck a journalist's cock. The fact The White Stripes didn't want to be on the cover of the NME, *I'm sure the people there thought it was totally cool. I honestly think there are parallels between* Elephant *and* In Utero [Nirvana's third album]—In Utero *switches back and forth with* Fun House [The Stooges] *as my favourite album of all time.* In Utero *is nothing like* Nevermind. *It was creepy and kind of dark, very medical, all body parts and diseases.* Elephant *is creepier than any previous White Stripes record and it too came after the praise had been heaped upon them. Everyone waited for* In Utero, *and everyone waited for* Elephant. *And they both cover Leadbelly.*

Dan Miller: "When I first heard Elephant *something sounded wrong with the guitar tones. I guess it's a comfort level thing, that older-sounding, raw garage-y vein of tones. Some of that stuff sounds too Marshall-ish. But Jack was always pushing forward and it definitely grew on me, a little shocking at first—like 'Little Acorns', the sound really put me off but now I love it."*

The sleeve of *Elephant*—photographed by Pat Pantano once again—sees the pair sitting on an old trunk in an empty room, framed in red, lit by a solitary lightbulb. Jack is dressed in red with white frills on his jacket, clutching a cricket bat (a game foreign to America). Meg is wearing a long white dress, dabbing at her eyes, with the rope from the 'Hotel Yorba' video still tied around her ankle (the rat from the same shoot appears on the back sleeve, along with a shot of Meg's black-painted toenails, up high on a stool). Bruce Brand designed the artwork. Clearly, he's a man of many talents.

"I knocked up the sleeve for 'Dead Leaves And The Dirty Ground'," he admits. "Originally, Jack wanted to have a projector on the front, cos they'd just done a video for it with loads of projections in. I couldn't find anything like that, but I had a picture of an old piano and used that instead. I thought that was much more relevant!

"Jack and Meg decided *Elephant* was going to be their English album [hence the cricket bat] so they asked me to do the sleeve. I did all the layouts and typography. He emailed me the back of an old blues cover he wanted the credits to be similar to. Also, I knew they had the fixation with the number three so I reversed all the E's so they became 3's.

"There are six different versions of the sleeve—two for each territory [Asian, European, American: CD and vinyl]. In some, Jack and Meg are wearing white, in some they're wearing red, and so on. Because of the difference in the way monitors display colours and the printing process, the English version of the LP—which was supposed to be ruby red—originally came out as grey. I mucked around until it was close, but it's not as good as it should be. I got it all done in the end.

"The best thing was when Jack asked how it was going. I was like, 'OK, but my computer keeps crashing all over the place'. A few days later there was a knock at the door, and there was a new G4 Apple Mac. I was dancing all over the furniture."

BB:"I heard that you're recording on even more primitive equipment than what Toe-Rag has?"

JW:"I'd like to, yeah. It'd be cool. I got an idea of an album; me and Liam [Watson] are working on it. I don't consider these albums 'concept' albums at all. It's just an approach. The album itself is just song-by-song. Each song is from a different time when I wrote it. I never write a ton of songs at once. It's from all over the place. Force them in that box and make them work."

Ben:"That was an idea I heard being kicked around: it's also to show people that you don't need a billion dollars and Pro-Tools. He did this record on eight-track that everyone loved. Just because certain advancements are made doesn't mean they are needed. The recording equipment from the Sixties still does just fine."

Dan Miller:"Jack has made the point that for the last 30 years or so, with every advance in recording, people say, 'It sounds like a vintage 1964 whatever', because that's the pinnacle of the way things sound. His point about Pro-Tools is that if it's available, producers will start cleaning up everything. But if they're used in moderation and you don't clean up every wrongly played scratch of the plectrum, it can be good."

BB:"Is the first album still your favourite record?"

JW:"I don't think we'll ever top it. *Elephant* is a close second. I love *Elephant*, but we're never gonna capture that Detroit rock'n'roll like we did with the first one. It was good we got that out of the way. If we hadn't, I'd probably still be searching for that. Same with 'Let's Shake Hands', the first 45, we'll never top that, but as long as it's there, I can move on."

BB:"Do you think of yourself as a sweetheart?"

JW:"Yeah *(laughs)*, sometimes. I try to be, but it's very hard to not get involved in that. I'm jealous of people too. I'm jealous of guys who just go out and get drunk and do drugs and have a good time 24 hours a day because I don't. I wish I could. I don't have fun. It's sad, but I don't know what to do about that."

Hypnotized

By the start of 2003, The White Stripes looked unstoppable.

That winter, however, Meg slipped on some ice in New York and fell badly, breaking her wrist in two places—resulting in the drummer walking around with a cast on her arm for six weeks[i]. Obviously all pre-*Elephant* shows were out—but fortunately the band was still able to play a short UK tour in April[ii].

It was their first dates in Britain since Reading Festival the previous year, and White Stripes fever was rampant. It was reported that advance promotional copies of *Elephant* were selling on e-Bay for £125, and that tickets for the live show were selling for up to £80 (the dates sold out within a couple of hours). A vintage Airline guitar, the same model and colour as the one played by Jack White, was put on sale for more than $1,000, with the claim it had been autographed by Jack. According to the band's spokesperson, Jack had only signed a detachable generic scratchboard. The scratchboard was then fixed to the guitar.

"Jack's sound crew went into a guitar store recently," relates Ben Blackwell, "and they had Jack's Airline on the wall for $2,000. It used to be a real cheap guitar. The guy said, 'You know Jack White raised the price on this'. And they were like, 'Jack didn't raise the price on this—you did.'"

The tour included a couple of dates at Brixton Academy on April 11 and 12, with Whirlwind Heat and The Go in support—Jack's red and black trousers tighter than ever. A cartoon of *Felix The Cat* was aired before Meg walked tentatively on stage to tumultuous applause. Jack joined her—cue even more cheering—and the pair launched into an inflammatory reading of 'Black Math'. Meg found the support a little overwhelming.

"I don't like people in the front row being squished," she explained. "Most of the time the kids rush in to get to the front, and wait in the queue and everything, and they end up getting smacked on the head and being pushed forward all the time. It kind of distracts from the whole thing."

The same month, a new single was released to help promote *Elephant*—'Seven Nation Army'[iii], a thunderous declaration of intent, later covered by scourge of lovers of free music everywhere, Metallica[iv]. Jack's guitar was electronically altered so it was pitched an octave lower, sounding like a bass at the start. *Q* magazine wrote that, "Jack plays the role of a brutish egomaniac male trying to overpower a girl with his confidence and balls"—sentiments ironically not far removed from those of his more notorious Detroit peer, Eminem. (Ironically, because such macho bragging is precisely one of the traits Jack professes to despise about rap music.)

On the flipside is a storming rendition of the traditional bluegrass folksong, 'Black Jack Davey'[v]—the guitar aflame, the drums a rumble of malicious thunder—and a Brendan Benson cover, 'Good To Me'.

Left: Jack and Meg (with broken wrist)
(Eric McNatt/Retna)

i No promotional work was postponed. If you look closely at the 'Seven Nation Army' video you'll notice her left hand is not shown throughout the whole clip.

ii This tour was preceded by a short, five-song set at the Electric Cinema, west London on February 7, 2003: Jack teased the select crowd with a mix of the old and the new: covers of Led Zeppelin's 'In My Time Of Dying' and 'Black Jack Davey'; two songs from *Elephant*, 'You've Got Her In Your Pocket' and a stark reading of Meg's first solo vocal, 'In The Cold, Cold Night'; plus a frantic version of 'Hotel Yorba' to close.

iii The title comes from Jack's childhood mispronunciation of the Sally Army charity shop.

iv The metal muthas have been famously embroiled in an anti-Napster copyright case against many of their own fans.

v As previously covered by Bob Dylan and The Gun Club.

Above: Jack, Hammerstein Ballroom, NYC 19/04/03 (Robert Spencer/Retna)

The hypnotic video saw the pair caught in a triangular frame while the very next frame was engaged in coming towards the camera, and the next frame after that was on its way... and so on. Elephants, skeletons and red and white clips of the couple constantly zoom towards the viewer in a very effectively memorable—if annoying—sequence. The triangle was chosen as being synonymous with the number three, Jack's magical figure. 'Seven Nation Army' reached Number 5 in the UK Charts, while *Elephant* entered the album charts at

Above: The White Stripes with Loretta Lynn, Hammerstein Ballroom, NYC 4/03 (Statia Molewski/Retna)

Number 1, knocking the truly horrendous fake nu metal band Linkin Park off the top spot. Which was nice.

The album has since gone on to sell well over a million copies, worldwide.

The release of 'Seven Nation Army' led to the pair performing with Loretta Lynn. The country singer had been in her kitchen when the video came on TV—she was suitably impressed[vi]. Loretta supported The White Stripes at New York's Hammerstein Ballroom, on April 19. The tickets were sold out in seven minutes. A few days later, Jack and Meg performed four evenings in a row on the Conan O'Brien show—playing a different song each night. On the final night, a skit was run of the pair doing different jobs around the NBC studios: working in the cafeteria, reading the news, and so on. The White Stripes then performed 'Let's Build A Home', which was segued into 'Going Back To Memphis', the old [pre-Soledad Brothers] Henry And June Human Fly 1996 single, which originally had a print run of 300 copies.

"That shows you exactly where Jack's coming from," comments Ben, "that he could perform such an obscure song live on national television. He knows his music."

vi "It sounds like somebody trying to break into a bank," she later told Jack.

Ben Blackwell: "What gets you excited nowadays?"

Jack White: "Tonight..."

Ben: "Loretta opened for The White Stripes the night I conducted this interview. That was definitely out the ordinary. Jack never seems fazed or excited about people he's met or situations he's been in, though. He's really down to earth and super-grounded."

Dan Miller: "Loretta Lynn invited them to her ranch. Her manager was asking, 'What's Detroit like? Don't you ever want to move any place else?' It's not the most cosmopolitan place in the world. But as Jack pointed out, we're not leaving: 'Detroit's home'."

BB: "You play with Loretta Lynn. What do you look forward to?"

JW: "I don't know...some drunken girl asked me that the other night, 'What are your aspirations?' I said, 'I'm doing them right now'. She said, 'Aren't you unhappy? Isn't there something you want to do?' and I said, 'No. This is what I've always wanted to do. To write

ELECTRIC SIX

"Let me be sure to mention The Wildbunch," says Wendy Case. "Those guys were my favourite band besides The Hentchmen, really influenced the scene and were the biggest characters of any of the bands. We were all so excited when we saw their star finally on the rise because nobody deserved it more. And we were all heartbroken when the band split like it did. It truly is the big heartbreak of Detroit."

"The first incarnation of The Wildbunch was in 1995 when I'd just graduated from college," begins vocalist Dick Valentine. "I moved back to Detroit and hooked up with Corey Martin, and we recorded an eight-song demo, including songs like 'Gay Bar' and 'I Lost Control Of My Rock And Roll'."

Both songs turn up on the debut Electric Six album, the soft rock-fest *Fire* (XL, 2003). It was actually the second—maybe third (if you include their *extremely* limited-edition eight-track cassette)—long-player from Valentine's inspired disco-rock outfit, but the previous releases came out under The Wildbunch moniker. Particularly recommended is the lo-fidelity rock feast, *Don't Be Afraid Of The Robot: Live At The Gold Dollar* (Uchu Cult, 1999).

"Corey hung out at Gusoline Alley a lot," continues Valentine, "and he started running into Joe [Surge Joebot] and Anthony [Rock And Roll Indian] there. We asked if they wanted to be in our band. Soon after, Steve Nawara was recruited to play bass. He showed up for the first practice looking like Derek Smalls after consuming another human being. I was excited.

"The way the material has always come in, with the exception of one song, is that I record it or demo it on guitar and it goes out from there. Over the course of the band we experimented with at least 150 or 200 songs, and about 50 or 60 of them ended up being played regularly. If there's a lyric that got discarded it might show up somewhere else. I go through periods of not thinking about songs for four months, then other days I'll drink a lot of coffee and write five. Writing 'Gay Bar', I may well have said I've just written the stupidest song in the world, but I said that about a lot of songs. 'Gay Bar' took two minutes to write. The lyric... was projected. I'd been living in Ann Arbor with a girl who went into her lesbian phrase while we were together.

"We're different from other Detroit bands. Why? I explain it by the fact I didn't come from a musical family at all—my dad orders pizzas and watches football all week and my mom worries about terrorism. I never had an older brother to tell me about some cool band. I happened on to music at a later time—I got into Pere Ubu and Talking Heads through college radio. I never got the sense music had to be taken 100 per cent seriously. It's not sacred to me. It has to be 100 per cent fun, though. I don't want to deal with anything that's going on in reality.

"When we got our record deal with XL, we changed our name because of the pre-existing Wildbunch. Why did the hit happen so fast? Chalk it up to any number of things. It's a catchy song, a catchy video... any number of things. The stars were aligned for us."

In January 2003, Electric Six scored a Number 2 hit in the UK with a song first released two years before by The Wildbunch, as a Flying Bomb seven-inch. The ferociously catchy dance-floor filler, 'Danger! High Voltage', most notably features the incredible high-pitched vocals of Jack White duelling with Dick Valentine's more regular version. (Jack was originally credited as John S O'Leary, his alias for checking into hotels.) It was an overnight smash... albeit one that had taken an incredibly long gestation period.

"That song took so long to evolve," says Valentine, "and even getting to the point to record it was pulling teeth. Some people didn't like it. I think it was Joe [Surge Joebot] who said the way I sung, *'Fire in the Taco Bell'* sounded like Jack, and so we got him in to record that one line. He showed up and said 'I don't want to endorse Taco Bell', but he sang the rest of it and was in and out in 20 minutes. The first mix of the song was more us singing on top of each other but then it got mixed more like a call and response."

At the time Jack White was just another guy in town who'd had a record out on Sympathy.

"It was his voice more than anything," Valentine sighs. "I've seen it written so many times the hit happened because Jack White was willing to do a song with us and we brushed off all the guitars... No, we did it in 2000. It didn't get released for another year. I remember seeing Jack at The Gold Dollar, and he was like, 'When's that song coming out?'"

Following the single's runaway success, Surge Joebot, Steve Nawara (Disco) and the Rock And Roll Indian left the band. Many people—Jim Diamond included—blamed the band's new manager for the split. It has to be said that Electric Six are much the poorer for it. They used to rock like muthas. Now they rock like your mother. Assuming, that is, she can't rock.

Ben Blackwell: I remember you guys doing 'I'm A Demon And I Love Rock And Roll' at the end of 4th Street Fair as an encore in '98, and Wendy Case sang the vocals.

Dick Valentine: It was one of The Go's first shows—I played Nerf Football with Bobby Go. It was just like a bad sound daytime show. I never liked playing outside in the day. I don't remember much of it. I remember having a falafel.

BB: I saw you at The Magic Bag in Ferndale with The Go and They Come In Threes, and you had a big sofa on stage, and all the different T-shirts, and people were throwing water balloons.

DV: We had weight-lifting equipment, a conductor, dancing hula girls and confetti and balloons and a giant robot at the end. I think that one I started in my underwear and built up to a shop. My friend found 10 "Choose Life" T-shirts in his T-shirt shop so I kept putting one on at a time.

BB: Hell's Belles [Ben's first band] might have opened for you at the Bag. It probably wasn't that show, but you started with 'Nuclear War' or 'Gay Bar' and you had homemade flash pods coming in right on time. I was like, 'Holy fuck!' When you're 16, you think of pyrotechnics as being reserved for bands like Kiss.

songs and play them.' It didn't matter if 10 or a million people liked it. I can't complain about anything. I can't aspire to anything else. Once we could quit working and tour, play music and record...that was success. Everything after that was just gravy. I'm amazed and astounded to be able to play with Loretta Lynn, warm up for The Rolling Stones, but it doesn't mean that I'm not happy until we finally record a song with Johnny Cash. I can't live like that."

Ben: "Everyone was kind of nervous that Loretta wasn't going to go over well, that people would boo her or yell, 'Show us your tits!' You expect the worst when people are confronted with something unfamiliar. But it was wonderful, the crowd loved her, I loved her, and The White Stripes played after her and she came out and did an encore with them...to have known them when White Blood Cells *was dedicated to her and only two years later, seeing them perform with her onstage, it gives you hope for the world. It lets you know that anything is really possible."*[vii]

Left: Electric Six. (Courtesy Steve Gullick CTCL Archive)

vii Jack later did some production work on Loretta Lynn's 2003 album at her ranch in Nashville.

viii But not in his red vintage car, as sometimes reported.

ix The two bands had become friends after meeting in Detroit back in 2002, when Jack handed Wayne a fibre optic statue of Jesus. In the grand Lips tradition of unwieldy song titles, Wayne then wrote the fabulous 'Thank You Jack White (For The Fibre Optic Jesus That You Gave Me)'.

GIVEN THE FINGER

After four shows in California, the band returned to Europe in May to play a lengthy tour that took in the Flippaut Rock Festival in Bologna, Italy on June 2, and several other countries including France, Spain, Holland, Germany, Austria and Switzerland.

Another tour of the US followed—Jack now being accompanied to some of these shows by his celebrity girlfriend Renée Zellweger, who he'd met on the set of *Cold Mountain*. The two stars shared a fascination for human skulls, among other things. While filming his role as Georgia for the film, he found one in a Romanian junk shop, which he showed to the *Bridget Jones* actress.

"She told me you can tell if it's a man or a woman by the teeth," he said, visibly impressed. "You think you're going to be surrounded by Hollywood assholes, but she knows a lot about skulls."

After a couple of dates at the Avalon Ballroom in Chicago, and one in St Paul's, Minneapolis, Jack returned to Detroit on July 4th to help celebrate the opening of Young Soul Rebels Records And Tapes, the new venture from old band-mate and label boss, Dave Buick. Guesting with Science Farm, the new band formed by Ben Blackwell and Brian Muldoon (his old upholstery mentor), he sang the old Richard Berry number 'Louie Louie' (most famously released as a Kingsmen single in 1962) with his back to the crowd. Jack later told Ben—who was singing that day—that he should "stick to playing the drums".

Renée was in the audience to witness what nearly turned out to be her boyfriend's final ever show... for, five days later, at one pm on Jack White's 28th birthday, the pair were involved in a car crash in Detroit[viii]. Jack's left index finger was broken, fractured in three places between the knuckle and first joint, requiring three tiny screws to be permanently fixed in place. Initial reports suggested that it was the airbag, not the crash (which happened at a moderate speed) that did the damage.

The accident resulted in the band having to cancel a series of appearances at festivals and shows around the world—including a return engagement at Reading, Scotland's massive T In The Park festival, and Central Park Summer Stage in NYC—as Jack was forced to wear a cast for six weeks that immobilised his wrist. He was philosophical about it, pointing to the fact that 27 seems to have been a bogey year for many stars—Kurt Cobain, Jimi Hendrix and Janis Joplin all died during their 27th year. He figured he'd got off "with a warning". Jack later decided to film the operation and place it on the Internet, by way of an explanation to his fans why he couldn't make the shows.

The White Stripes headline slot at T In The Park was passed along to Oklahoma acidheads (and R.E.M. heirs apparent), The Flaming Lips, well known for their penchant for bunny costumes and drenching themselves with gallons of fake blood on stage. Wayne Coyne and his band performed the show as a tribute White Stripes, dressed in red and white[ix].

JACK'S ASS

Mary Restrepo: Jack has the range of Robert Plant, that's it. (Sings in a high squeaky voice.) That's Jack! When he was younger, he was more, like...man, that dude's voice was so high. I remember him playing one time, and I was like, "Who's that on stage? He's a woman!" His voice has dropped.

He wears tight pants.

Mary: One time this guy was trying to put down Jack, and he goes, "He's got sort of a fat butt". And this one girl goes, "I like that butt", and that was the end of that.

Dave Buick: My gay friend Robert use to call Jack "the ass", because Robert thought he had a nice, hot, little ghetto booty.

Mary: Well, that would make sense because ghetto booties are fat.

Dave: I'm not saying he had a fat ass. I'm saying my friend Robert had a crush on that ass.

Mary: I'm not saying he had a fat ass either! But all of the girls get up and go, "I like that fat ass". We don't like skinny asses. We like asses with something on them!

Dave: Are you guys ass ladies?

Mary: We don't do nothing whoopee-ass, but a nice ass is nice. I don't ever recall saying, "Baby turn around". There is nothing I've ever done with the ass (laughing)... I won't say that, but...(more laughing). Nothing major.

Above: Cover art for 'The Hardest Button' single, and below: artwork for the Frank Sinatra movie *The Man With The Golden Arm* (Ronald Grant Archive)

"I don't know if every band looks for these kind of absurd moments, but they're what I live for," Wayne explained to the *NME* about his band's decision to entirely rewrite their set only a couple of hours before show time. "Luckily, I had the red cape anyway..."

On New Year's Eve 2003, the two bands played together at the Avalon Ballroom—where Wayne led the crowd in a sing along of the self-same number. The Flaming Lips later joined The White Stripes on stage a few minutes before midnight to play apocalyptic joint versions of 'We're Going To Be Friends' and 'Seven Nation Army', Wayne playing the role of demented MC with megaphone.

To add to the general madness during 2003, rumours started appearing on the Internet that Meg was dead and had been replaced by a robot[x]. Evidence? Meg does not move in the video for 'We're Going To Be Friends' because her batteries are flat. In the video for 'Hotel Yorba', Meg plays with a mouse (everyone knows real girls are afraid of mice).

The band thought the stories were hilarious.

BB: "So if Robert Johnson were alive today, would he have a website?"

JW: *(laughs)* "Probably. [John] Baker [White Stripes tour manager] says that to me all the time. Every time he gives me the merch report, he says, 'Robert Johnson never had T-shirts', because I said that once."

Ben: "Jack always kind of said he never wanted to wear band T-shirts, and he didn't want to make band T-shirts—at the same time, if you're going on tour and making no money and you sell two T-shirts, that's next day's gas. That's revenue you can't turn down, especially early on.

"The White Stripes had to borrow money to print their first T-shirts. They'd be carrying them all in a huge garbage bag, and somebody would be like, 'I want a large...'—give me five minutes, I'll find you one. But they sold like crazy. That was my main thing early on, doing merch and roadie-ing. Merch was T-shirts, LPs and singles. Now they sell clocks and slip mats and magnets and record bags and stickers and pins.

"I went out to the West Coast with The White Stripes in September, 2003. That was definitely different. It was surreal. The previous tour I did was approximately two years prior, the same area. They played a show in San Francisco in front of 9,000 people. It was Jack's first show back from busting his finger, and I was getting shivers down my back watching. I still get nervous and tingly watching them, like when I was 15. I hope that never goes away.

"Jack's current guitar tech Jim Vincent was Kurt [Cobain]'s final guitar tech. He's worked with everyone—Helmet, Rage Against The Machine, Sonic Youth...if you can take care of Lee [Renaldo] and Thurston [Moore] and probably Kim [Gordon] as well, with their 28 guitars[xi], then Jack's three guitars and their three different tunings is nothing. We were at the Hard Rock Casino in Las Vegas and there's a big Kurt Cobain display there, and he goes, 'Wrong guitar', because it was a right-handed Fender Mustang. I was playing Devil's Advocate, like I didn't know Kurt played a right-handed guitar strung left-handed, so I started asking questions I knew the answer to...He was like, 'Hey, look, I tech-ed the In Utero tour. I know what I'm

x Very obvious shades of the infamous "Paul is dead" rumours that plagued The Beatles circa *Abbey Road*, partly because Macca's feet were out-of-step with the rest of the Fab Four on that album's cover.

The White Stripes
(Nicky J. Sims/Redferns)

talking about'. I was floored. Being a Nirvana fan, I could probably tell him set lists from that tour he's forgotten about."

xi All three Sonic Youth musicians are known for their fastidiousness when it comes to guitar sound.

Another UK single was released on September 1—the Burt Bacharach cover, 'I Just Don't Know What To Do With Myself' b/w 'Who's To Say' and 'I'm Finding It Harder To Be A Gentleman', recorded live at Peel Villas. For possibly the first time, the B-side of a White Stripes single contained a stronger song than the A-side: the Blanche (and Two Star Tabernacle) cover 'Who's To Say', penned by Jack's old band-mate Dan Miller, is a lovely, lovelorn, country-blues number sung with a real sensitivity and awareness for life's bluer moments.

By now, the A-side felt gimmicky and a little tired—it was the song's *third* release, after all. Jack's high-strung vocals belong to The White Stripes of several years before, and the bombast of the cover begins to grate next to the beautiful melancholy of Dusty Springfield's original. Some of us could have done without the sight of Kate Moss cavorting around a shiny metal pole in the black and white video directed by Sofia Coppola, as well—not quite understanding the link between the music and the exploitative nature of the promotion.

I mean, lovely that you've got a famous fan, Jack, but... Needless to say, MTV and the British tabloids loved it. The single reached the Top 20 in the UK.

The band embarked on another tour of New Zealand, Australia and Japan in October, which included a secret show on October 7 at Freeman's Bay Primary, Auckland.

"Some were really into it," Meg told MTV Asia. "Some in the front row had their hands over their ears. It was kind of loud, you know. *(Laughs)* But they seemed to be into it. It's cool because they had learnt a traditional Maori song that they sung back to us in the end. We did a few songs, 'We're Going To Be Friends', 'Apple Blossom', 'Hotel Yorba'... We were just trying to do all the quieter songs."

During the same interview, the journalist pointed out that the band had previously stated that, in their three trademark colours, red symbolises anger, while white stands for innocence. Yet recently, the band had been sporting red and black. Should fans read that as a subconscious

THE PAYBACKS

Wendy Case

"I'm the guitar-player/singer-songwriter in The Paybacks. When I was 10 years old my mother took me to an old cabin in North Carolina, and the first thing I saw was a snakeskin on the floor, and the second thing I saw was a newspaper clipping tacked to the wall about the Siamese twins Chang and Eng [Bunker]. That was when I first realised I was much more interested in snakeskins and Siamese twins than I should be."

What made you want to get up on stage in the first place?

"I was an attention-starved child."

Where are you from?

"I was born in Ohio, and I was reared in mostly North Carolina, and I came to Michigan around high school, and as soon as I graduated I went to San Francisco. I was an art major and managed to graduate, despite punk rock and drug addiction."

When did you first start getting up on stage?

"I had several failed attempts as a preteen talent show failure. I found that when I started playing in bands, around the time I was 15, I was much more comfortable. This was in 1980. I did open mic nights and had an all-female metal band."

So who inspired you to play guitar?

"Jeff Beck. I was a huge Yardbirds fan. Keith Richards was my all-time biggest hero. I had the opportunity to meet The Rolling Stones, and I was a big fucking chicken and left."

What attracted you to rock'n'roll?

"I was very enamoured of the decadence and the danger. It ignited a passion in me like nothing else could. I was very much involved in the heroin life, and it took many years to get clean, and get sober enough to have a functional life. I came back to Michigan in '88 because I had a high school sweetheart who saw me killing myself in San Francisco. I moved into his closet. Then our house burned down. I camped on couches, and had a boyfriend or two that put me up. So it was this vagabond lifestyle for quite a while.

"I quit doing music, because I was trying to fend off a serious drug habit. I had a major relapse and ended up going to jail here... Then I got to be pretty close with John Krautner from The Go, and he kept telling me to get busy and form a band again. It was his gentle encouragement that made me realise I'm only happy when I'm doing music. So I formed The Paybacks. Originally I had Marco from Rocket 455 on guitar, and Pat Pantano on drums and Marc Watt [The Dirtys] on bass. But Pat wanted to do The Come-Ons and was getting involved in The Dirtbombs... so The Hentchmen guys stepped in."

"We all grew up hearing rock on the radio. It wasn't even garage punk, necessarily—Bob Seger uses the same three chords that I use, and that The Gories used, and that The Hentchmen use. That has never changed. Detroit was never trendy. None of us would ever have believed it six years ago, if you'd told us that this was gonna happen—least of all The White Stripes. I never thought I'd quit my job in 2003 and go on the road. That's living the rock'n'roll dream. And that's unheard of."

i The correct phrase is "conjoined twins". The term "Siamese" actually originated as a result of the worldwide popularity of the Bunker twins.

statement about lost innocence (the reporter asked), a tie-in with "the death of the sweetheart"?

"A little bit, yeah," replied Meg. "I notice that has happened more lately, but that wasn't, you know, thought about too much."

A one-off appearance at the Tim Music Festival in Rio de Janeiro followed the Australasian tour, on October 31, before a slot at the MTV European Music Awards in Edinburgh.

"We did the Tim festival," recalls David Swanson (Whirlwind Heat). "We played first on the main stage, then The Rapture[xii] and all these DJs. The White Stripes headlined. That was a real crazy time, because we'd toured for three months straight without going home. After Brazil, we flew back to America and did it all over again.

"Whirlwind Heat have come up on stage with The White Stripes a couple of times," David adds. "Once in Austin, Texas [June 15, 2003] where we sang the Leadbelly cover, 'Boll Weevil'. Also at the last show we ever did with them in Cleveland, Ohio [November 30, 2003]. Steve [Damstra] played bass with The White Stripes for 'The Big Three Killed My Baby' as part of the encore. That was weird. I thought it sounded good—but we'd just played, so it wasn't like Kim Gordon had come up. By that point, we'd pretty much played everywhere together, except for South Africa, so we said as a joke we'll never play with each other again because we'd conquered the world. We've been touring with The White Stripes ever since *White Blood Cells* in '01. At the Cleveland show, they brought out a big cake and the crew came out during our last song and wrapped us in bubble tape."

Other White Stripes events in November included three dates in Canada, three nights at New York's Roseland Ballroom and a couple towards the end of the month in Detroit at the Masonic Temple—with The Hentchmen in support one night, and The Paybacks on the other. Their old Detroit peers were, as ever, appreciative.

Tom Potter: "Their thing was always a little more interesting in the early days. Meg had these boobs that kind of bounced up and down, and they looked cute..."

Dave Buick: "It was Tom that said that..."

Tom: "Yeah, it was me that said that. It's creepy, because now I think of Meg more like a sister. I see her playing drums and... it's creepy. I'm usually focussing in on Jack's package."

Dave: "That has seemed to rise as much as their star has risen..."

Tom: "Yeah, last Friday at the Masonic I was sitting there with Mary [The Detroit Cobras], and Mary was like, 'You know, I love a pair of tight pants'. I'm like, 'They're tights', and Mary's like, 'Yeah, but check out his package, do you think that's real?' and I'm like, 'Mary! I don't wanna look at it'..."

Dave: "I've seen Jack naked tons of times. *(Laughs)* That's it. That's my statement about The White Stripes. We're scooby guys. Sometimes we just get naked."

November also saw the release of the third UK single to be lifted from *Elephant*, 'The Hardest Button To Button', replete with Frank Sinatra, *Man With The Golden Arm*-style artwork.

Left: The Paybacks. (Chuck Burns)

Above: The White Stripes perform at the 2002 MTV Movie Awards in Los Angeles, June 1, 2002 (Michael Caulfield/WireImage)

It was a storming return to form. A repetitive, almost-house beat drives along a tale of childhood voodoo and worry. The accompanying video—amplifiers and White Stripes drumkits appearing and disappearing by rote is just plain insidious. (The art department was setting up drum sets non-stop throughout the three days.) Once seen, it's difficult to forget—as is Jack's John Waters style moustache. Bruce Brand's sleeve design is full of signifiers: a big, broken finger (symbolising Jack's accident) points down to a button marked with a "3" (the magic number).

On the B-side is a Soledad Brothers cover, the slide guitar-drenched blues of 'St Ides Of March'. It drawls easy splendour and pace.

Elephant cleaned up in the end-of-year polls for 2003, winning best album in *NME*, *Q*, *Mojo*, *Time Out*, *GQ*, *Maxim*, France's *Les Inrockuptibles*, Germany's *Rolling Stone* and *Musik Express*, and the USA's *Entertainment Weekly* and *Spin*… and in dozens of other magazines across the world. 'Seven Nation Army' won Best Single at the *NME* Awards. The White Stripes won a Brit Award for Best International Group.

Clearly, a backlash is long overdue.

xii NYC band who neatly straddle the line between futuristic early Eighties indie dance acts, and 2004.

BB: "You've talked before about how the band has a set life span. I remember you saying that you're not going to be 40-years-old, wearing red and white on stage."

JW: "It's hard to say. It's not that easy. Sometimes I feel I don't want to do this. I've got no free time; it's sapping all my energy. When we play, it's not like other bands where they go out and play the same set list or recreate the album. Every night I'm working without a safety net and throwing so much energy into it, and so much emotion…I'm *trying* to do that and it drains me. I can't do this forever. I don't even know how I'd attack music if I was in another band because I'm so used to the way we've been doing it. It's gonna be odd to be in a band and not have a full-on, full-throttle thing going on. When the band ends, I don't know what else I'm going to do."

BB: "Meg was talking about that. She said it's hard…you're expected to do an amazing show every night. Not just an OK show. Every show, there are 4,000 people there, who pay

BLANCHE

Ben Blackwell: Jack said in the *Metro Times* that he saw Blanche and thought that was what Two Star Tabernacle should have been...

Dan Miller: That's probably true if Jack had been more of a role player. He's more about expressing himself and what's inside. At the time, he wanted to play faster, louder songs, and when he saw Blanche it was more of an eerie, creepy mood, especially early on. With Two Star, it was too up and down and not focused enough. With Blanche everything is in soft focus—slightly consistently out of focus. It felt that Blanche were a garage band because no one was that experienced at their instruments. That awkwardness helped define our sound. Like when we did the cover of The Gun Club's 'Jack On Fire', once we'd figured out how to change the tempo and time signature and put it through the Blanche filter, we knew how it was supposed to sound.

Ben: Without death or sickness what would Blanche songs be about?

Dan: What makes it Blanche dynamically is to have the guts to sing several slow songs in a row and don't feel we have to be rocking out all the time—just a bit of banjo and brush-stroking. You don't have to have that loud feedback coming in. It's about creating uneasiness.

Ben: If you could have someone walk away from a Blanche show with one prevailing thought—what would it be?

Dan: There's something beautifully wrong with those people.

Above: Blanche (Doug Coombe)

their money...and you get people bitching, 'Well, I didn't hear 'Hello Operator'.'"

JW: "When I was in Romania, the drivers and actresses were always listening to Tom Jones. It's easy for him when he does Vegas. A bunch of people come, he plays all his hits and he sings it easy-going. He can go out and it's a nice time. I don't have fun when we play, at all. It's just so much work for me. And because we've set that precedent, if I go up there and phone it in, people are gonna say it's not a very good show because they've seen other things we've done. It's hard to continuously maintain, especially when you play seven shows in a row, and the eighth show you're like, 'I just *don't* feel like playing today'. But we have to. And then we're playing in Norway, and this is the only time they're going to see us this year, so we have to make it a good show. It's really draining."

Ben: *"That was the first time I heard him say that he doesn't have fun. Having just gone out on a month-long playing tour—it was the first time they'd gone out for that long a time. It sounds so evil, what he's saying, because so many people would like to be in that situation. But it is so draining, and it is so taxing, you really have to have the right mindset to get through it—you'll hate your band, every show, each town you're in and your home. Everyone goes through that feeling of being tired.*

"The White Stripes will have certain combinations that usually come together in a set, usually two or three songs—but they've never done the same set twice and I'm sure there's some huge geek who'd say otherwise. You just keep it fresh. Something I dislike about The Dirtbombs is that we do the same entire set for three tours. I've played live with Jack before. One time we played it was just me and him at The Garden Bowl on a Sunday night and we'd rehearsed our songs so we knew what we were going to play, but then we played something new... 'Psycho' by The Sonics or 'Riot In Cell Block 9' by The Coasters. He went into that and I followed him. I live for that spontaneity. It breaks my heart I could play The Dirtbombs' set in my sleep—I want to be surprised.

"You can always tell a lot about a band from equipment failure. The White Stripes always coped with it well. People have told me they used to go see them to see how they'd cope with a missed beat or a wrong chord. I definitely believe that spontaneity is at the heart of rock'n'roll. Jack believes in spontaneity, too. He'll pull out covers I know they've never rehearsed. His knowledge of songs is encyclopaedic—he could probably play you a hundred songs in a row without repeating an artist."

BB: "You have a total backlog of covers you could pull out. Would you ever do just a covers record?"

JW: "I don't think so. It'd probably be a bad move. I don't think I've ever found a good covers record. It'd be too off base. It'd just be going in too many different directions. And really, what does it mean? It's almost like the remake of [Alfred Hitchcock's] *Psycho*. What's the point? When you're doing it once in a while, you're in that tradition of songwriting and minstrels or whatever, you're carrying those songs on. But if that's all we did, it would kind of feel empty."

BB: "Do you ever feel like you have more ideas than you can finish in your lifetime?"

JW: "I don't think so. I do all my ideas." *(Laughs)*

BB: "The *Planned Obsolescence* art attack on Detroit never happened[xii]."

JW: "Oh yeah..."

BB: "The 'Ziggy And Iggy' 45 never happened.[xiii]"

xii At one point, Jack was proposing to mount children's Coup Cars that he'd collected from Detroit garbage piles on freeway overpasses in the town with *Planned Obsolescence* written on them. [Ben: "I kept hoping he would do it. He wanted to post these huge sculptures on overpasses and telephone poles."]

xiii This was a long-talked about single where The White Stripes planned to cover Iggy Pop's 'I'm Bored' and David Bowie's 'Moonage Daydream'. While they stayed in LA with Long Gone John, they took pictures of themselves wearing Iggy's cheetah jacket from the back cover of *Raw Power*.

JW: "Well, some ideas sound good for a moment but you don't get around to them, and you look back and say, 'Eh? Big deal'. You know, it wasn't meant to be. Certain things are supposed to happen whether we like it or not."

BB: "If you had bad stuff out there, it'd be easier for you to put on a great show, but everyone's expecting you to be great—like with those Peel sessions."

JW: "Sometimes, when you set a precedent you have to live with it. But it's funny, with *White Blood Cells* people were saying, 'Oh, it's a great record, but how long is this going to last for a two-piece band?' And now, with *Elephant*, people are saying *again*, 'OK, how long will it last?' You said that two years ago! The next album they're going to say the same thing."

Ben: "It seems that people, even in the wake of The White Stripes, won't take a two-piece band as seriously as a four-piece band. I remember thinking to myself with Nirvana—that's really cool, a power trio. And that was for a three-piece... I wish I could transfer that to being a kid in fourth grade and hearing White Blood Cells *for the first time, and freaking out. I was surprised at how well it always went over on tour. They would win over crowds. They put on a good show. There was a lot for people to grasp on its own: a lot of people really liked the cover of 'Jolene'. A lot of people really liked the slide guitar. It could be anything—people thinking Meg was cute, that they only wore red and white, that Jack only played old guitars—as long as there was something someone could have a reaction to.*

"I don't know if Jack ever took guitar lessons or not. He just listened to a lot of records and practised like crazy. Why did he switch from drums to guitar? It's every drummer's dream. As a drummer, you never have any control of anything. I don't think it was quitting one and doing the other—he probably still considers himself a drummer, but he was focussing more on a guitar. Jack is probably one of the most amazing drummers I've ever heard—it's really discouraging seeing him, sit down at the drums and be just amazing as he is on guitar. He could play anything on the drums."

And still the madness continues...

In January 2004, The White Stripes conducted a large-scale tour of the UK with former Two Star Tabernacle bandmates Blanche[xiv] in support. It included a couple of dates at Blackpool's Empress Ballroom, and two at the ornate Alexandra Palace, way up on a hill in North London[xv]. Walking up the steps towards the cavernous Ally Pally, with its massive Victorian arches, nearly lost in a deluge of merchandise stalls, we were impressed by how *ordinary* (and young) the audience looked. This was clearly an arena band playing to an arena audience: the same audience who would've gone to see Oasis or Bryan Adams a few years before...and presumably will do again.

Indeed, with the reverence Jack pays to the blues—and the extended guitar soloing on songs like 'Ball And Biscuit' (which was particularly fine that night)—it really felt like stepping back into the late Sixties, to the days when Hendrix ruled the earth, and musicians like Keith Richards and Eric Clapton name-checked their sources constantly. This was a far step from the lo-fidelity surrounds of Ghetto Recorders and Toe-Rag, and the International Pop Underground that helped nurture Jack and Meg through their debutante American tours.

Somehow, though, it was reassuring: the minimal stage set-up, the way Meg would lean to one side, aware of Jack's every mood change, the red and the white and the black, the stage-hands standing solemnly at the sides, bedecked in uniform, the crowd bouncing along through 'Hotel Yorba'. Sure there was bombast and Led Zeppelin references a-plenty. But there was also Meg singing all trembling and frail on 'Cold, Cold Night', Jack mischievous and rampant on versions of Bob Dylan's 'Lovesick' and Brendan Benson's 'Folk Singer'. There was humanity, excitement, spontaneity and...*heart*.

And that's more than enough for us.

On February 8, The White Stripes picked up two Grammy's.

The mainstream had come home to roost.

THE FUTURE

BB: "Picture, however many years down the line, and you aren't doing The White Stripes anymore and you've got free time and you don't have to work. What would you want to do? Would you want to do art?"

xiv Their 2004 debut album, *If We Can't Trust The Doctors* (Cass) is a melancholy, morbid beaut—laments and lovers' spats and death and disease dissected sweetly between twin singers Dan and wife Tracee over heart-twangin' pedal steel and banjo. It's the first full-length from Ben Blackwell's Cass label—previously Cass has released several fine seven-inch singles from various garage bands such as The Cyril Lords, Sagger, Tin Knocker and Mooney Suzuki, picking up from where Italy left off.

xv The first place in the world to beam TV signals, if memory serves correct.

JW: "I'm not sure. I have so many interests but I never have any time for them. I haven't worked on a sculpture in years because I've put so much energy into The White Stripes. And my house is in a shambles...it's always been a stop-off office and a drop-off point for equipment. I've been watching television next to fucking amp cases for the last three years. It's ridiculous. It's the same thing like Loretta's said, she's however old, she won't say, but she's still touring, she *does not stop*. She cannot stay home. You get so used to it. I hope that I don't get used to it. I've tried not to love it too much and try to miss home. I hate the feeling of not having a home. It really feels like that. That's why I like to end the set with 'Boll Weevil', *'Looking for a home'*—'cause it really feels like that when you're on tour. You do all this and you come back to Detroit for a couple of days and you're like, 'I might as well be in Cleveland right now because it doesn't even feel like home anymore'. It's ridiculous."

Greg Baise: "Matt wrote this great essay once, it was only like two paragraphs, but I think he used the word boredom, and I can't remember the last time I was bored. Maybe it's because we've got all these great record stores in Detroit, and you can always find great music. We have a backbone, that social background of these people that you can talk to about music—if you know Captain Beefheart or The Silver Apples, you're suddenly part of this not-so-secret society, cos around here everyone knows them too.

"Detroit is different. When bands come here they're blown away by the enthusiasm of the audiences. People do freak out and dance here. That's one thing that's so amazing about The White Stripes—I can't believe that music that's so 'real deal' is so popular. To me that's very, very special. I remember going to see Rocket 455 play to 20 people, and now... A lot has changed.

"Jack had a vision. Ultimately, what's amazing isn't that if no one were paying attention The White Stripes would sound the same, but that everyone is paying attention and they *still* sound the same. He hasn't changed, he hasn't sold out: he isn't making bad music. They have four albums, and it's a very consistent archetype. It seemed for such a long time that 'popular' was the enemy, and that to make good music you had to be obscure and play in front of the same tiny crowds. I remember before any of this happened, my advice was, 'Don't give up your day job, because it won't be worth it to anyone with the compromises you'll have to make'. It's different now.

"Yet even The White Stripes will tell you that success is relative—compared to what Kid Rock sells, they're nothing. When they get played on the alternative rock radio station here, it's like some kind of weird-ass concession, compared to Status Quo."

BB: "The best thing I've ever heard you say is that, 'If anyone knows what's best for The White Stripes, it's us'."

JW: "It's true."

Ben: "Early on, people were like, 'You should play a song with so-and-so or you should play such-and-such a song'. I can only imagine how it is now with so many people around—I've kind of stopped suggesting anything and he's right. If anyone knows what's best for them it's them or God..."

BB: "You deal constantly with people giving suggestions or asking you to do stuff..."

JW: "I'm glad that we're in that position. That's the way it should be. Labels should just do their job: distribute the record and promote. And the artist should create the art. I'm glad we're not in some stupid position where we have to send stuff in for approval or we're forced to use some producer, or always fearful that we might get dropped. I couldn't live like that. I'm glad that never happened to us. Because I don't ever want to live under anybody else's thumb to make the music that I want to make."

MTV Asia: What do you miss most about being a little band from Detroit?

"Well, it's all good," laughs Meg. "When we go back there, it still feels like home. Everyone you know is still there. We miss the little shows we used to perform. But it's fine. We still have fun playing at home."